Second Edition

W9-AGN-710

Proving the
Value of HR

How and Why to Measure ROI

Jack J. Phillips, Ph.D.
and Patricia Pulliam Phillips, Ph.D.

Proving the
Value of HR

How and Why to Measure ROI

Jack J. Phillips, Ph.D.
and Patricia Pulliam Phillips, Ph.D.

Society for Human Resource Management
Alexandria, Virginia
www.shrm.org

Strategic Human Resource Management India
Mumbai, India
www.shrmindia.org

Society for Human Resource Management
Haidian District Beijing, China
www.shrm.org/cn

This publication is designed to provide accurate and authoritative information regarding the subject matter covered. It is sold with the understanding that neither the publisher nor the author is engaged in rendering legal or other professional service. If legal advice or other expert assistance is required, the services of a competent, licensed professional should be sought. The federal and state laws discussed in this book are subject to frequent revision and interpretation by amendments or judicial revisions that may significantly affect employer or employee rights and obligations. Readers are encouraged to seek legal counsel regarding specific policies and practices in their organizations.

This book is published by the Society for Human Resource Management (SHRM®). The interpretations, conclusions, and recommendations in this book are those of the authors and do not necessarily represent those of SHRM.

The Society for Human Resource Management (SHRM) is the world's largest association devoted to human resource management. Representing more than 250,000 members in over 140 countries, the Society serves the needs of HR professionals and advances the interests of the HR profession. Founded in 1948, SHRM has more than 575 affiliated chapters within the United States and subsidiary offices in China and India. Visit SHRM Online at www.shrm.org.

Cover design by: Shirley E.M. Raybuck
Interior design by: Shirley E.M. Raybuck

Library of Congress Cataloguing-in-Publication Data
Phillips, Jack J., 1945-
Proving the value of HR : how and why to measure ROI / Jack J. Phillips and Patricia Pulliam Phillips. —2nd ed.
p. cm.
Includes bibliographical references and index.
ISBN 978-1-58644-231-6
1. Personnel management. 2. Rate of return. I. Phillips, Patricia Pulliam. II. Title. III. Series.
HF5549.P4595 2005
658.3'125—dc22
2004028403
Printed in the United States of America.
10 9 8 7 6 5 4 3 2
11-0141

Contents

Preface:
ROI as an HR Tool

Though your balance-sheet's a model of what a balance-sheet should be,
Typed and ruled with great precision in a type that all can see;
Though the grouping of the assets is commendable and clear,
And the details which are given more than usually appear;
Though investments have been valued at the sale price of the day,
And the auditor's certificate shows everything O.K.;
One asset is omitted — and its worth I want to know,
The asset is the value of the men who run the show.[1]

The date of this poem, 1938, is very telling. For decades, organizations have struggled with placing a value on employees and, more specifically, on HR programs. Although we have made progress, we still have much to do.

Today's HR professionals need a balanced set of measures and processes to show the value of the HR contribution. Measuring the return on investment (ROI) is emerging as a promising tool to provide convincing data about the contribution of specific HR programs and processes. It is now a part of the measurement mix.

The interest in ROI has been phenomenal. The topic appears on almost every HR conference and convention agenda. Articles on ROI appear regularly in HR practitioner and research journals. Several related books have been developed about the topic, and consulting firms have sprung up overnight to tackle this critical issue.

Several issues are driving this increased interest in ROI and in its application to a variety of HR programs. Pressure from clients and senior managers to show the return on their HR investment is probably the most influential driver. Global recessions and competitive economic pressures are causing intense scrutiny of all expenditures, including all HR costs. Total quality management, reengineering, and continuous process improvement have created a renewed interest in measurement and evaluation that also encompasses measuring the effectiveness of human resources. The general trend toward accountability with all staff support groups is causing some HR departments to quantify their contribution. A few progressive HR departments have taken a proactive approach. Without prodding or encouragement, they are using ROI to measure their contributions and have helped generate an unprecedented wave of applications of the ROI process.

Return on investment has become one of the most challenging and intriguing issues facing the HR field. The challenging aspect of the process is the nature and accuracy of its development. The process often seems confusing, inundated with models, formulas, and statistics that often frighten the most capable HR practitioners who joined human resources because they loved working with people, not numbers. Coupled with this concern are misunderstandings about the process and the gross misuse of ROI concepts in some organizations. These issues sometimes leave practitioners with a distaste for ROI. Unfortunately, ROI cannot be ignored. To admit to clients and senior managers that the impact of human resources cannot be measured is to admit that HR programs do not add value or that the HR department should not be held accountable for its impact — positive or negative — on the organization's bottom line. In practice, ROI must be explored, considered, and ultimately implemented in almost every organization — whether it is for profit or nonprofit, public or private.

What is needed is a rational, logical approach that can be simplified and implemented within the constraints imposed by the organization's budget and resource availability. This book presents a proven ROI process based on over 20 years of development and refinement. It is a process that is rich in tradition but sophisticated enough to meet the demands facing HR executives.

Why This Book? Why Now?

When examining current publications related to ROI, we found no book with a practical, concise presentation on ROI for human resources. Most representations of the ROI process ignore or provide little insight into the two key elements essential to developing the ROI: isolating the effects of human resources and converting data to monetary values. Recognizing that many other factors will influence output results, this book provides several strategies to isolate the effects of human resources — far more than any other presentation on the topic. Scant attention has been given elsewhere to the subject of assigning monetary values to the benefits derived from HR programs. This book presents a dozen strategies for converting data to monetary values.

This book was developed at the request of many clients and colleagues who asked for a simplified, concise description of the ROI process, presented in a step-by-step approach. What is needed, according to practitioners, is a book that addresses the ROI process for human resources and presents an approach that is rational, feasible, and understandable to the typical HR practitioner. We designed this book to meet that need.

Who Can Benefit from This Book?

HR professionals in both private and public organizations are the primary audience for this book. With its step-by-step format and case applications, it will also be useful as a self-study guide for this group. Whether an individual is involved in HR consulting, design, implementation, coordination, or evaluation, this book is an indispensable reference. Individuals in all functional aspects of human resources should find the book valuable. These include recruiting and selection, education and learning, compensation and benefits, employee and labor relations, compliance and fair employment practices, safety and health, human capital management systems, and HR consulting services. The ROI process described in the book has been used to measure a variety of HR programs. Individuals in HR leadership positions (managers, supervisors, team leaders, directors, vice presidents) will find this book to be a valuable addition to their professional library.

Another audience is the management group. Because of the tremendous interest in ROI among the management team and clients, this book should be a useful reference for them. In a simple, easy-to-implement process, it shows how the ROI is developed in language that managers, administrators, and executives understand.

Consultants, professionals, researchers, and seminar presenters will find the ROI Methodology to be an effective way to measure the impact of HR programs. The book provides a workable model for consultants to evaluate change initiatives or consulting projects. The book provides researchers with a sound tool for evaluating a variety of HR programs. Its content should stimulate thought and debate about how the ROI is developed and applied. Finally, the book should be a practical textbook or supplemental book for a course on HR evaluation.

How Is This Book Organized?

This book presents the ROI model in a step-by-step process. A chapter is devoted to each major part of the model as the pieces of the ROI puzzle are methodically assembled. At the conclusion, the reader has a clear understanding of the overall ROI process.

Chapter 1, "The Accountability Crisis," explains the issues and concerns about the HR contribution as it traces the key influences for increased accountability. The payoff of increased investment in HR measurement is explored along with an ROI readiness self-test.

Chapter 2, "The ROI Methodology," describes how the ROI process has evolved in recent years and how organizations are confronting the subject. This chapter presents a brief summary of the model for those readers introduced to the process for the first time.

Chapter 3, "Preparing for ROI," shows the initial analysis needed for an effective ROI evaluation process; it also explores when and where to use ROI. The planning for a study is explored in this chapter.

Chapter 4, "Data Collection Issues," presents a variety of approaches to one of the most fundamental issues. Ranging from conducting surveys to monitoring performance data, the most common ways to collect data at all levels are described in this chapter. Useful tips and techniques to help select the appropriate method for a specific situation are presented.

Chapter 5, "Isolating the Effects of the Program," is a principal topic. Several techniques are presented to determine the amount of improvement directly linked to the HR program. This step must always be taken to develop a credible study.

Chapter 6, "Converting Data to Money," is a critical and necessary topic for the ROI calculation. This chapter presents specific techniques and conservative rules to ensure a credible monetary value connected to the project. While having monetary value is essential for ROI, having it in studies to satisfy client needs is also important.

Chapter 7, "HR Costs and ROI," details specifically what types of costs should be included in the ROI formula. Different categories and classifications of costs are explored in this chapter, with the goal of developing a fully loaded cost profile for each ROI calculation. The actual ROI calculation is discussed with several issues surrounding its development and use.

Chapter 8, "Measuring Intangibles," focuses on nonmonetary benefits from the program. Recognizing that not all the outcome measures from human resources can or should be converted to monetary values, this chapter shows how intangible measures should be identified, monitored, and reported. Common intangible measures are examined.

Chapter 9, "Communicating and Using Evaluation Data," provides insight into the most appropriate and effective ways to communicate the results to a variety of target audiences. This chapter shows how to carefully select appropriate messages to meet the unique needs of selected audiences. The strategies for using evaluation data are also presented.

Chapter 10, "Taking a Sensible Approach to ROI," addresses a variety of issues needed to implement the ROI process effectively. By following logical steps, this chapter identifies the challenges that must be overcome for the ROI Methodology to become a useful, long-lasting, and routine process.

Chapter 11. The book concludes with a comprehensive case study showing the ROI on a work-at-home program implemented by an insurance company. The program produced impressive results, and the study is helpful in understanding the applied use of the ROI Methodology. The details are presented, including the conversations, background, and actions taken to have a credible study. The case explores the entire process, from the initial analysis to the data presentation before the senior executive group.

Acknowledgments

No book is a work of the authors alone. We have received much help along the way to make this book a reality. Many of the concepts, issues, and techniques have been developed from research and application. Our previous work on the ROI process provided the basic foundation for this book. In addition, many of our clients around the world have provided helpful suggestions and allowed us to use their organizations to develop new tools and processes. Collectively, they have made this an important and rich new publication. To them we owe a debt of gratitude, particularly for their interest in exploring new frontiers of measurement and evaluation.

One individual stands out as pioneer in the development of HR measurement and evaluation. Jac Fitz-enz blazed new trails in the development of HR measurement and HR benchmarking. Through his work at Saratoga Institute, Jac has made his mark on the HR field, clearly challenging us with the measurement imperative. We are fortunate to count Jac among our colleagues and personal friends and are proud to continue his work through ours.

Jack J. Phillips
Patricia Pulliam Phillips
info@roiinstitute.net

Preface to the Second Edition

The dilemma with the accountability of human resources is perhaps best described in the story from Jack Welch, former CEO of General Electric and the most admired CEO of all time. Welch puts the issue clearly in perspective. In his metaphor, he asks you to imagine you own a sports franchise, like the Boston Red Sox. As the owner, the manager, or the CEO, you would logically want to spend most of your time with the director of player personnel (or its most current title, the vice president of talent.) This is where the capabilities are, as the future of any franchise lies with the talent. You would be interested in who is coming on board, who the outstanding prospects are, and how the team is developing and performing as a whole. Talent is your first and most critical department in the franchise. You probably would not want to spend much time with the chief financial officer (or the accountant). After all, accountants will remind you of issues you do not want to discuss, such as that the revenues are not where they need to be or that costs must be controlled.

Now, relate that example to a business scenario. A top executive rarely spends time with human resources — in fact, a top executive generally avoids human resources because the HR executive often brings bad news, disappointments, or requests for more money. Instead, most of the CEO's time is spent with the CFO, discussing business functions, realized and potential profits, and the challenges that lie ahead. Welch ends this story by suggesting that executives should spend more quality time with human resources. Like the director of player personnel, the HR executive will attract the talent necessary for the future, prepare and develop existing talent, keep the talent motivated and engaged — and when the talent leaves (or gets traded to the Yankees), ensure the departure process is handled appropriately.

Why does the top executive not pay the same attention to the top HR person? Is the reason the lack of appreciation for the function? Is the image the problem? Is it the nature of the work? Is it caused by uncertainty about the value of the largest investment (the people)? The reason may be all of these, but one thing is apparent: If the HR function can show its contributions in a credible way, particularly in terms of major projects or programs, most of the puzzle is solved. The relationship improves; the image is enhanced. The return on investment in people is a little clearer.

For two decades, we have assisted HR teams in improving the accountability of what they do. We show them how to measure and evaluate the success of particular projects or programs, or the entire function overall. The concern is with the major projects. This book will show how to measure the success of HR programs.

We are very pleased to bring you a second edition of this important book. It has been a great seller at SHRM, and we have received much feedback on the book. While the feedback has been positive, the readers have suggested that we include more detail about how to isolate the effects of an HR program from other influences, how to convert data to money, and how to monitor the impact data needed to show the value of human resources. This new edition focuses squarely on these issues, with expanded coverage in all three areas. At the same time, new information, examples, and a few new techniques are included. This edition is capped off with an interesting case study that shows step-by-step how to measure the ROI for a work-at-home program. This type of program can add considerable value to the organization with a high, positive ROI. At the same time, the proposal helps employees by lowering stress, increasing job satisfaction, and enhancing engagement. Perhaps as important, the program can have a huge impact on the environment by reducing carbon emissions created by previously commuting employees now working from home.

We hope you enjoy this second edition. As always, we want your feedback and suggestions. This second edition was enhanced by many previous users of the first edition. We owe much appreciation to our clients, who always provide us with an opportunity to learn as we assist them. They provide us with valuable insight into their issues as we help them improve the accountability. We appreciate their feedback, suggestions, and more importantly, their use of this methodology.

We want to thank Linda Arnall for her meticulous work on this book. Linda juggled many tasks as part of our team but took the time to work specifically on this important second edition. Finally, thanks to Rachel Robinson for her work on the final editing.

Chapter 1.
The Accountability Crisis

John Hamilton, Senior Vice President of the human resources (HR) department at Apex Business Products, was perplexed and a little confused after attending a meeting with the Chief Executive Officer (CEO), Margarita Lopez. She had asked John to develop a plan to show the senior executive team the contributions of the HR function. Although the CEO fully supported the majority of HR programs and services, she questioned the value of a few of them and was concerned about comments from the senior team. As Lopez said, "Our senior execs wonder how much real value is contributed by the human resource function. Some of them think it could be outsourced, or that parts of it could be eliminated altogether. What they want to see," she said, "is a more direct link between your programs and the bottom line."

As John reflected on the meeting, he was aware of the excellent HR programs at Apex. Some had even won awards from professional associations. He knew that the senior team placed value on the employees' annual feedback, which provided an assessment of job satisfaction, motivation, and commitment of the employees. This process had provided valuable information to help plan HR programs. John was also concerned that Lopez had mentioned making a link between HR programs' and the company's bottom line. In other words, Lopez wanted to know about the return on investment (ROI) for HR programs. John was aware of the ROI concept but had not seen it applied to the HR function and wondered if doing so was even feasible.

John felt confused as he began the assignment. At the next senior staff meeting he would have to present his recommended plan for showing the value of the HR function to the senior management team. He knew he must have specific approaches to show the team to obtain buy-in. Otherwise he would have a tough challenge ahead as he entered the budgeting cycle.

John's story raises several questions:

- What possibilities are available for John to show the HR contribution?
- What specific types of measures are appropriate for an overall measurement process?
- Is ROI feasible in this context?
- How does ROI fit into the measurement mix?
- Can ROI become a routine measure?
- How can John win the support of the senior team?
- How can a measurement system be implemented?

Most executives and HR professionals intuitively agree that investing in people and providing appropriate HR solutions and initiatives can pay off significantly for an organization. The problem is that this intuitive knowledge serves only as evidence, not proof, of payoff. Deciding which programs to invest in, how much to invest, and whether a particular HR program provides value is a haphazard process at many organizations.

This cloud of mystery around HR's impact leaves some executives undecided about how much of a commitment to make in terms of time and resources to HR programs. Instead of making a continuous investment in the HR function, executives faced with a lack of tangible bottom-line results tend to resort to sporadic, inconsistent support of certain HR activities that seem to hold some promise in terms of helping the bottom line.

Defining ROI

The ROI Methodology presented in this book can be used to show HR staff and other executives the monetary benefits directly connected to HR programs, particularly major programs that are highly visible, strategic, and expensive. This systematic, comprehensive measurement and evaluation process generates seven types of measures:

- reaction and satisfaction with the HR program
- acquisition of knowledge and skills needed to implement the HR program
- application and implementation of the HR program
- business impact related to the HR program
- costs of the HR program
- return on investment in the HR program
- intangible measures not converted to monetary values

This balanced approach to measurement includes a technique to isolate the effect of the HR program. ROI is measured with the same formula that the finance and accounting staff use to measure the return on investing in building equipment, for example.

About Terminology

Developing a book for the HR field always involves the difficult task of managing the vocabulary used in the field. Table 1.1 defines some key terms found in this book.

Major Influences on HR Accountability

Several developments — positive and negative — in recent years have influenced the need for additional HR accountability. All point toward a need to know more about the connection between investing in human resources and the payoff of the investment.

The Triple Bottom Line

Much attention has focused recently on the concept of the triple bottom line. Not only must an organization be successful financially, as demonstrated by traditional bottom-line measures, but it must also be successful with its employees and the external environment.

The employee "bottom line" is not readily defined, but it typically translates into the organization having favorable work conditions, treating employees fairly and equitably, and compensating them adequately, while

Table 1.1 Some Key Terminology

Term	Definition
Program	A specific entity being evaluated. It may be a recruiting strategy, a new commission plan, a mentoring activity, a diversity initiative, a health-care cost containment measure, or a retention solution. "Program" is a more generic term than activity, solution, plan, initiative, intervention, or process.
Participant	Individuals directly involved in the program. The term "employee," "associate," or "stakeholder" could also be used. In many organizations, the term "participant" appropriately reflects those involved.
Stakeholder	All individuals or entities involved or interested in the program. The list of stakeholders may include the HR manager, participants, the organizer, and the key client, among others.
Client	The individual(s) or entity funding, initiating, requesting, or supporting a particular HR program. Sometimes referred to as the sponsor, it is the key group usually at the senior management level who cares about the program's success and is in a position to discontinue or expand the program.
Immediate Manager	Those in the organization who are one level above the participant(s) involved in the program. For some, the person in this position is the team leader; for others, it is the middle manager, but, most important, this person is the one with supervisory authority over the participant in the program.
Chief Executive Officer (CEO)	The top executive in an organization. The CEO could be a plant manager, division manager, regional executive, administrator, or agency head. The CEO is the top administrator or executive in the operating entity where the HR program is being implemented.

fully recognizing the potential and capabilities of employees in a diverse environment. This measure has stimulated many organizations to search for ways in which to monitor, measure, and even value the employee contribution. Consequently, HR practitioners sometimes feel pressured to address this bottom line, yet they have no clear understanding of what it means. The "external environment" refers to the impact on and interaction with the community, the country, and the environment. Being a good corporate citizen and protecting the environment are two key issues.

Employer-of-Choice Phenomenon

Several publications and organizations recognize employers of choice every year or so. One of the most popular recognitions is *Fortune* magazine's annual list of the "100 Best Companies to Work For." The

Great Place to Work Institute has its list of the "Best Small and Medium Companies to Work for in America." Many organizations strive to be included in the rankings. This status enables them to attract new applicants and to retain valuable employees. Pursuing employer-of-choice status often drives HR programs to improve the work environment and to use this standing to promote the organization to potential candidates. This phenomenon is driven by the employee retention issue that became such a critical topic during the 1990s.

The phenomenon has sometimes caused organizations to create too many programs that offer some fabulous new benefit, perk, or unparalleled opportunity. In some cases, the competition for the awards has placed strains on the HR function. Although improved retention and lower recruiting costs can offer significant value, the programs may not add enough value to overcome their costs. A measurement process is needed to show the payoff of these investments when they are substantial.

HR Investment and Macro-Level Studies

Recent studies attempt to link the investment in human resources to the ultimate payoff for the organization, which is often reflected in productivity or profitability. These macro-level studies, which cut across functions within organizations, attempt to correlate the organization's success with investments in human resources.

Criticism of these studies suggests that they do not show a significant relationship or that they fail to show a cause-and-effect relationship. For example, a profitable and productive firm may have ample funds to invest in a variety of programs to make the organization an attractive place to work. This finding does not, however, mean that the investment in the HR programs has led to the profitability.

Take, for example, QUALCOMM, an innovative, successful research and technology firm that holds the patents for much of the wireless communication technology. QUALCOMM has thousands of highly competent employees, and the company is consistently very profitable. The company invests heavily in building an employer-of-choice workplace. QUALCOMM is a regular on *Fortune's* "100 Best Companies to Work For." But which came first? Did the employer-of-choice workplace generate the profits, or did the profits enable QUALCOMM to afford creating a workplace that merits distinction as an employer of choice? When reviewing macro-level data, such questions abound. Still, putting all criticism aside, these studies represent compelling insights into the power of investing in human capital.

Human Capital Management Focus

The concept of human capital is perhaps overused these days because so much has been written about how to monitor, measure, and value the human aspects of organizations. Nevertheless, much work still needs to be done with this topic. In its early movement, much attention regarding human capital focused in the area of HR accounting — an attempt to account for the value of employees through traditional financial reporting methods. The difficulty lies in the methods for assigning a monetary value on the contribution or capability of human "assets." Although some progress was made, to date very few results and examples have been offered.

The human capital management trend also grew out of early benchmarking work of the 1980s as HR firms began to measure data and compare key indicators. A variety of measures on compliance, compensation, benefits, safety, retention, and absenteeism were developed. Today's human capital measurement mix contains those metrics plus others, such as leadership, innovation, employee engagement, and learning. These new measures are critical to organizational growth and success. The challenge is to identify the appropriate blend of measures that reflects the status of human capital and enables decisions to be made about what to do with them.

Top Executive Demands

Senior executives are asking the HR function to show value. In some cases, human resources is asked to show value or have its budget cut. Sometimes value must be shown before budgets are approved. In a few situations, this concern has led to outsourcing major parts or even all the HR function. For years, human resources escaped this level of scrutiny as employers invested in human capital on faith. They inherently believed that the more they invested in people, the more people would respond to the nature of their work. Today, executives are asking for data.

HR Disasters

Few organizations have the courage to admit to an HR disaster. The consequences of a flawed, ill-advised, or ineffective HR practice, program, or strategy can make excellent reading, particularly in the popular press. Unfortunately, a growing number of these stories are making their way into the HR professional publications. An intriguing example is an exposé of the cost of an unwise HR strategy developed by Rent-A-Center. A decision to eliminate HR contributed to a $47 million payment required to settle litigation. The story is a classic one in which imprudent practices and strategies went astray, not only costing an exorbitant amount in direct payment but ultimately destroying the morale of the organization. Although these types of disasters are reported more frequently in the press now, hundreds of others go unreported but probably represent massive mismanagement of human resources.

From an accountability perspective, HR staff has opportunities to add value. If, however, HR programs are mismanaged, the consequences can be negative. Appropriate data are needed to show how well programs are working and to demonstrate their contribution to the organization. A comprehensive HR measurement system can help prevent some HR disasters, thus minimizing losses and changing the image of the HR function from one of a nice-to-have auxiliary department to one of a critical business function that contributes in a positive way to the organization's bottom line.

HR Technology

Perhaps no development has influenced the HR function as much as the advent of technology. Most HR transactions are now automated, including compensation administration, benefits administration, payroll, employee record keeping, recruiting, training, and orientation. Technology has eliminated the need for some HR staff. In certain cases, human resources has been shifted to other areas (for example, finance or information technology), leaving some HR staff disconnected from where the work is often done. On a positive note, technology has enabled collection of vast amounts of data that were previously unavailable. Employee and performance data can be organized, integrated, and reported in meaningful formats, thereby providing HR staff with the tools to measure the impact of the HR function and major HR initiatives.

HR Outsourcing

Outsourcing of HR services has been a visible trend among organizations during the last decade. Outsourcing means good and bad news. The good news is that many routine HR functions — not central to human resource's primary mission or values — can be outsourced. This trend was initiated primarily in the payroll and employee-processing areas but has now expanded to include almost every part of the HR function. In some cases the entire HR staff and processes have been outsourced to external providers who offer the same services.

The bad news is that outsourcing is sometimes pursued for the wrong reasons. HR practitioners fail to provide appropriate data and results to demonstrate the function's contribution to the organization. Sometimes outsourcing brings a short-term fix of immediate cost savings because fewer people earning lower salaries are doing the work. On a long-term basis, however, the result can be detrimental because satisfaction with the outsourced services can deteriorate.

The Accountability Trend of All Functions

The fact that human resources is not the only function being asked to show accountability is somehow comforting to know. Many other functions are undergoing the same level of scrutiny, paradigm shifts, and changes. To be sure, they are all more accountable for expenditures.

Consider, for example, the information technology (IT) function. A few years ago, technology and IT groups had a blank check. They could implement almost any type of new technology, and it would be accepted because of the prevailing notion that technology was a competitive weapon that no firm could afford to be without. Unfortunately, many technology implementations were dismal failures that added enormous costs but did not improve — or sometimes made worse — the very situations they were supposed to improve. In recent years, IT has been asked to show value even before investments are made and then to carefully track the value to make sure that the projections are realized. This scrutiny has caused those responsible for implementing technology to measure not only the ROI but also a variety of other qualitative and quantitative measures, thereby producing a balanced profile of success — the same process presented in this book.

A Paradigm Shift for HR Accountability

The factors described in the foregoing sections have had a sizable effect on HR functions and their attempt to improve the effectiveness, impact, and the overall accountability of the HR function. Because of these influences, three important shifts have taken place in HR functions, as outlined in the sections that follow.

HR Measurement Trends

Table 1.2 shows some of the major measurement trends developing as a response to major influences on the HR function. These trends are shaping the way that HR functions react to major accountability issues. Not only are they prominent in the United States, but they are also reflective of the trends in major industrialized nations, as reported in surveys of HR practitioners and managers in more than 30 countries. These trends underscore the progress being made to bring accountability to human resources.

Table 1.2. HR Measurement Trends
1.   HR budgets are being justified based on HR measurement and evaluation data.
2.   The strategic focus of many HR programs is requiring measurements before and after the program to predict and judge success.
3.   More HR functions are being outsourced based on credible, balanced analysis of which functions would be best to be outsourced.
4.   The interest in developing HR profit centers continues to progress.
5.   There is increased success in measuring human capital in very difficult and soft areas such as leadership, innovation, and learning.

continued on next page

Table 1.2. HR Measurement Trends (continued)

6.	New HR executives have backgrounds or experience in business, finance, and operations.
7.	Business-minded executives are transforming the way the HR function is being managed.
8.	The HR staff is developing data to understand the relationship between HR measures and the outcomes of the organization.
9.	The HR staff uses a balanced set of measures when evaluating a specific HR program, project, or solution.
10.	Business evaluation is becoming more systematic, methodical, and proactive instead of sporadic and reactive.
11.	Measuring ROI is growing in use as an HR evaluation tool.

Shift from Qualitative to Quantitative Measures

Figure 1.1 shows how measurement approaches have evolved in recent years. In the 1960s and 1970s, most measurement was attitude and compliance oriented. This was the time when attitude surveys, case studies, and HR auditing measured the HR pulse. The concept of management by objectives was introduced. Next, during the 1970s and 1980s, the focus was on benchmarking and tracking key items and costs. Parallel with the advent of major benchmarking efforts, HR executives began to compare processes to others and monitor key indicators over which they had the most control.

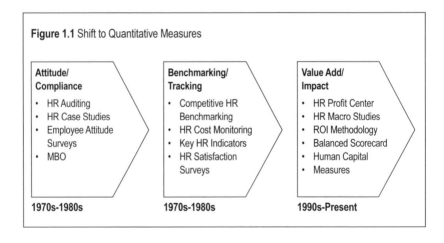

Figure 1.1 Shift to Quantitative Measures

Attitude/ Compliance	Benchmarking/ Tracking	Value Add/ Impact
• HR Auditing • HR Case Studies • Employee Attitude Surveys • MBO	• Competitive HR Benchmarking • HR Cost Monitoring • Key HR Indicators • HR Satisfaction Surveys	• HR Profit Center • HR Macro Studies • ROI Methodology • Balanced Scorecard • Human Capital • Measures
1970s-1980s	**1970s-1980s**	**1990s-Present**

During this time, organizations also focused on understanding the cost of human resources and on trying to control it in any way possible. Now, in the 1990s and continuing into the first two decades of the twenty-first century, the focus is on value-add and impact. Measurement approaches attempt to show value and to include financial measures. The concept of profit centers, scorecards, and ROI dominate the measurement landscape.

This evolution of measurement reveals the current focus on showing the value of human resources in ways that senior executives understand and accept. In some cases this means showing the actual measurement of ROI for specific programs or functions. The ROI relates to the other processes as well. For example, the ROI Methodology is used to show the payoff of an HR program or solution designed to enhance or maintain the current level of a measure taken from the human capital measurement system or balanced scorecard system. The ROI Methodology holds the most promise as a valuable and feasible measurement process that does not drain resources.

Shift to a Results-Based Approach

The approach to organizing, managing, and implementing the HR function has shifted from a traditional activity-based approach to a more results-based approach. Table 1.3 shows the major shifts that have occurred with HR programming. The trend has been away from a focus on generating programs, projects, and inputs to the current focus on results from the beginning of the process to the conclusion of the project.

Though the field of human resources has been moving through this transition for many years, many organizations have shifted completely to a results-based approach for their HR functions.

Moving to Facts

In recent years, the concept of achieving results from various programs has been intensified and adopted. As Figure 1.2 shows, the concept has currently evolved to the more sophisticated idea of value. While the concept starts with a results-based approach to programs, which means that the programs should be connected to results in some way, it has evolved to

Table 1.3. Paradigm Shift for a Results-Based Approach

Traditional Approach	Results-Based Approach
• New programs are initiated by request or at the suggestion of any significant manager of a group.	• New programs are initiated only after a legitimate need is established.
• Human Resources offers a multitude of programs in all areas.	• The emphasis is on having fewer programs that offer great opportunity to make an impact.
• Existing programs are rarely, if ever, eliminated or changed.	• Existing programs are regularly reviewed, revised, or eliminated when necessary.
• HR impact is measured by counting activities, hours of involvement, number of employees involved, and so forth.	• HR impact is measured by determining the bottom-line impact of programs on the organization.
• Management is involved only to a limited extent in the HR process.	• Management is extensively involved and collaborates in the HR process.
• Human Resources is viewed as a cost center.	• Human Resources is viewed as an investment in employees.
• The HR staff is unfamiliar with operations issues.	• The HR staff is very knowledgeable about operations.
• The HR staff lacks knowledge of finance and business concepts.	• The HR staff is versed in basic finance and business concepts.

an evidence-based approach to programs. The evidence is often presented in terms of impact data. The key issue in the evidence-based approach to results is that no attempt is made to isolate the effects of the program on the data, suggesting that isolation is impossible, inappropriate, or unnecessary. This approach is obviously intriguing, but it is still not sufficient for many of the program funders who require proof that the program will work. The next approach, the fact-based approach to results, presents the proof. As many hard-data facts as possible are presented under this approach, and occasionally (but not always) the effects of a program on the data are isolated. This approach verifies that, yes, the program worked and is driving this measure. This proof is obviously more credible for the senior executives who fund programs.

A more sophisticated approach is now emerging, suggesting that all the results should be put into the proper context. This is the truth-based approach. For example, suppose a group of sales representatives is tracked in terms of the success they have achieved from a new sales incentive program, and the results are extremely high. The sales data are compared to that of another group, and the difference represents the amount attributed to the incentive program. These data are impressive, based on the fact that the sales occurred. In addition, a step was taken to isolate the data. But is the data representative of the entire sales force? Can we rest assured that the entire sales team will have the same amount? The truth is . . . no, not necessarily. The pilot group contains the top performers, who are producing results far better than others, and consequently, the pilot group is not comparable to the other group.

The truth-based approach tends to look at all aspects of program evaluation to make sure that the results are credible, believable, and repeatable. The focus of this book is to show how to ascertain the real value and truth of HR programs and to put evaluation results into perspective so that the executives who fund programs will continue to do so, based on the results.

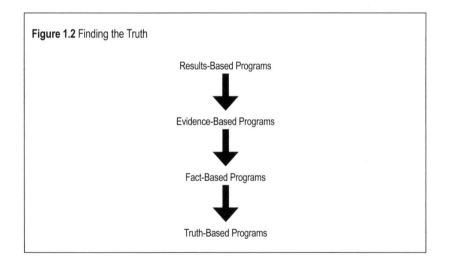

Figure 1.2 Finding the Truth

Results-Based Programs

Evidence-Based Programs

Fact-Based Programs

Truth-Based Programs

Is Human Resources Ready for Additional Measurement and Evaluation?

With all the influences, trends, and progress in measurement, two important questions quickly come to mind: Is human resources ready for *more* measurement and evaluation? Are the influences in place in the organization to drive additional measurement? Figure 1.3 provides a

Figure 1.3 Readiness for Additional HR Measurement and Evaluation

Is Your Organization a Candidate for ROI Implementation?
Read each question and check of the most appropriate level of agreement
(1 = Strongly Disagree; 5 = Strongly Agree)

	Disagree 1	2	3	4	Agree 5
My organization has a wide variety of HR programs and services.	❑	❑	❑	❑	❑
We have a large HR budget that reflects the interest of senior management.	❑	❑	❑	❑	❑
Our organization has a culture of measurement and is focused on establishing a variety of measures including Human Resources.	❑	❑	❑	❑	❑
My organization is undergoing significant change.	❑	❑	❑	❑	❑
There is pressure from senior management to measure results of our HR initiatives.	❑	❑	❑	❑	❑
My HR function currently has a very low investment in measurement and evaluation.	❑	❑	❑	❑	❑
My organization has suffered more than one HR program disaster in the past.	❑	❑	❑	❑	❑
My organization has a new leader for Human Resources.	❑	❑	❑	❑	❑
My management team would like to be the leader in HR processes.	❑	❑	❑	❑	❑
The image of our HR function is less than satisfactory.	❑	❑	❑	❑	❑
My clients are demanding that our HR processes show bottom-line results.	❑	❑	❑	❑	❑
My HR function competes with other functions within our organization for resources.	❑	❑	❑	❑	❑
My organization has increased its focus on aligning processes to the strategic direction of the company.	❑	❑	❑	❑	❑
My HR function is a key player in change initiatives currently taking place in my organization.	❑	❑	❑	❑	❑
We are required to prove the bottom-line value of our HR programs.	❑	❑	❑	❑	❑

checklist of issues that are often drivers for additional measurement. Answering the questions on the checklist now to gain an understanding of how these issues relate to your organization may be helpful for you.

After you have responded to each item, add up your score using the scale at the top of the chart. The scale ranges from strongly disagree (1) to strongly agree (5).

Very high scores indicate a pressing need for increased accountability. For example, a total score in the 60-75 range signifies critical pressures for human resources to measure results and to show value; urgent action is needed. Scores in the 45-60 range indicate that additional HR measurement is needed although not to a point of crisis. Action will be needed in the near future to focus more resources and efforts on HR measurement.

In the 35-45 range, there is little pressure for additional measurement at the current time. Additional measurement may be useful to prevent some of the key issues and problems from surfacing in the future. A score below 30 suggests only slight concern about additional measurement and evaluation unless the HR staff wants to show value and express accountability on a proactive basis. Having a low score is the best time to get started. This brief assessment highlights some of the principal matters about the need to invest in measurement and evaluation. The reality facing most HR executives is that additional investment — in terms of time and money — is needed to show the value of human resources and to heighten accountability for HR programs and solutions.

The Payoff of ROI

The upside of investing in an ROI Methodology can be great. Some of the payoffs, which are outlined in the following sections, can change the role, image, and success of the HR function.

Budgeting for Human Resources

More HR executives have to justify their budgets in terms that managers understand. The recent global recessions have exacerbated this issue. At times HR practitioners must even project the value of specific programs or go back and determine the value of previous programs. Whether budgets are being approved or are being considered for cuts, the pressure exists. Lack of data showing the connection between human resources and its contribution will almost assuredly result in reduced funding. Conversely, showing value is one of the best business cases for justifying or enlarging an HR budget.

Preventing Disasters

An appropriate measurement system can help prevent disasters because the system begins with a thorough analysis of the need for the HR program or initiative. It helps avoid unnecessarily initiating programs. Effective evaluation data provide constant feedback to show how effective (or ineffective) a program is. Evaluation keeps the program on track, allows for making adjustments, or eliminates the program quickly if it cannot add value. A well-known insurance company doubled its HR budget with the use of the ROI Methodology.

Eliminating Unnecessary or Ineffective Programs

The ROI Methodology presented in this book is an excellent tool to determine if a program is adding appropriate value. If changes cannot be made, the course of action may be to end or diminish the program. A sound, credible measurement process can provide data to determine necessary adjustments, even for politically sensitive, controversial programs. Wells Fargo Bank takes this approach. Potentially weak programs are measured. They are improved if they can be; otherwise, they are eliminated. Without this type of measurement, unnecessary and inadvisable programs may continue to flourish, consuming resources and time, thereby tarnishing the image of human resources. Meanwhile, the problems these programs are supposed to solve go unresolved.

Improving HR Processes

A comprehensive measurement process can improve implementation procedures. As data are developed and used, ineffective parts of the program or solution are uncovered so that necessary changes can be made to improve the implementation processes. Barriers to success are always captured, revealing the processes that can be changed to ensure success.

The enablers to success are also identified, revealing the factors that can be adjusted to drive more success.

Expanding or Implementing Successful Programs

Rigorous, bottom-line measures for human resources can be used to justify expansion or application of HR programs. If a similar need exists for an HR program in another division, for example, an ROI evaluation can show that the program can be replicated successfully in another area. Also, when a pilot program is undertaken, the measurement and evaluation process can determine if it should be implemented throughout the organization or in a particular division or area. Wal-Mart uses this approach. A new program is piloted with 25-30 stores, and the results are measured along six types of data. Previously, HR pilot programs were evaluated using subjective and reaction-level data. Now, these programs are being evaluated based on application, impact, and ROI data.

Payoff for investing in measurement and evaluation is realized when a program identified as adding value is then implemented on a broader scale. The impact can be profound, adding value to the entire organization.

Strengthening Relationships with
Key Executives and Administrators

No group is more important to the HR function than the senior executives. They allocate funds, commit resources, and show support for the HR function. They must understand the value and impact of the HR function. Executives need convincing data to accept human resources as a business partner — one that they can include in meetings and decision-making. The ROI Methodology can show the value of human resources and strengthen this relationship with key executives. An HR manager at a major European brewing company reported that the first meaningful business conversation with the CEO occurred during the discussion of an ROI study. In addition, ROI can raise the respect and credibility of the HR staff, thereby shifting from the perception that human resources is an expense to the perception that human resources represents a solid investment.

Building Support from the Management Team

A group often critical of human resources' success is the management team, typically middle managers who often do not support human resources to the extent they should. This group has inherited some of the duties previously performed by the HR staff and need convincing evidence that HR programs are producing results before they will continue to commit time and resources to programs. Having an appropriate mix of data, including ROI, builds the level of commitment and support needed from this crucial group. Without data to document the value added by HR programs, the management team tends to see human resources as a necessary evil; with robust data, they can see human resources as a catalyst to meeting their departments' goals. An HR manager in a retail store chain in Puerto Rico was promoted to general manager after she introduced the ROI Methodology. She attributed much of the credit for her promotion to the use of ROI.

Final Thoughts

This chapter highlighted many of the influences, trends, and issues driving the future direction of the HR function. Collectively, they build a compelling rationale for investing additional time and effort in measurement and evaluation. With the potential payoffs involved, investing more in HR measurement and evaluation makes judicious business sense.

Measurement and evaluation processes come in many varieties. ROI is the tool that satisfies most of the concerns outlined in this chapter. The challenge is to show the value in terms that executives and managers understand and appreciate. All HR stakeholders need to understand the value of this important function in the organization. Without measurement and evaluation, the consequences can be disastrous.

Chapter 2.
The ROI Methodology

The previous chapter set the stage for increased investment in HR measurement and evaluation, and this chapter now makes the business case for using ROI as a part of the measurement process. You will also have the opportunity to learn more about the rationale for the use of ROI Methodology and about ROI's fundamental components. We will also present the ROI standards, which are essential for building the methodology's credibility and respect as a viable tool for the HR department.

The Essential Measurement Mix

The previous chapter described several approaches to HR measurement; pursuing all of them would be impossible and highly undesirable. The challenge is to select the appropriate mix for the organization given its needs, culture, resources, skills, and goals. The selection process usually involves a few measurement strategies that meet various needs of the stakeholders.

The measurement mix shown in Figure 2.1 is recommended as an appropriate mixture of measures that represent both qualitative and quantitative data taken from different sources at different times for different purposes. The first category is **attitudinal data**. In today's organizations, having a finger on the pulse of employees is essential in understanding not only what satisfies them on the job but also what motivates them and builds their commitment. Whether the issue is job satisfaction, organizational commitment, or employee engagement, employee feedback is routinely needed as a source of data.

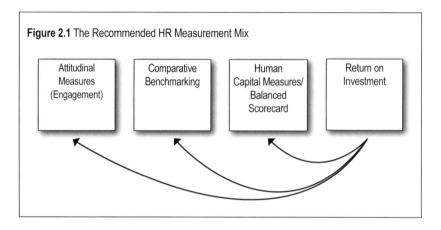

Figure 2.1 The Recommended HR Measurement Mix

The second category in the HR measurement mix is **comparative data**. Many organizations rely on benchmarking as a measurement tool, and it is also important for the HR function to be involved in major benchmarking efforts. These benchmarking studies may include comparing specific output measures (for example, turnover, absenteeism, or accidents) or process steps (for example, time to recruit a new employee), or particular cost items (such as cost per hire or training costs per employee). Although benchmarking shows executives the current level of commitment and progress when compared to other organizations, it does not provide insight into what is needed or the success of current HR strategies. Benchmarking merely compares the current organization with others that may represent best practices.

The third category is **human capital measures**. These are the important people-related indicators, initially tracked in the 1980s as key indicators and enhanced considerably for the twenty-first century. Sometimes these measures are grouped into balanced scorecards that represent both qualitative and quantitative data. Critical to the success of the organization, the measures represent a variety of issues, such as productivity, leadership effectiveness, and innovation. For many high-growth and innovative organizations, human capital measures are significant indicators to monitor.

The fourth category is the **ROI Methodology**, which compares the benefits of HR programs to the costs of those programs. Although other types of analyses show the general relationship between investing in human resources and such outcomes as profits and productivity, most

HR managers need a tool to show the impact of a particular program. The ROI Methodology generates the data needed to convince a senior management team about human resource's contribution. ROI is a new addition to the HR manager's measurement toolkit and is essential for showing managers the connection of human resources to the bottom line and the impact of specific programs. As shown in Figure 2.1, this category links to the others. The ROI Methodology is used to show the impact of a program or solution designed to elevate or maintain a specific human capital measure, a benchmarking statistic, or attitudinal data, such as organizational commitment.

Why ROI?

Several features of the ROI Methodology make it an effectual measure for HR managers:

- *ROI is the ultimate measure.* In the range of measurement possibilities, ROI represents the ultimate: a comparison of the actual cost of an HR program to its monetary benefits by using the same standard ratio accountants have used for years to show the ROI for equipment and buildings.

- *ROI has been the elusive measure.* Many HR managers have long assumed that measuring the return on investments in human resources is impossible. Recognizing that investment is essential and that human potential is an unlimited power, many HR leaders argued that ROI could and should not be applied to human resources. The concept of ROI, therefore, has been surrounded by misconceptions, myths, and mysteries that have prevented many HR executives from pursuing it. Because of the increase in evidence showing otherwise, ROI is no longer an elusive measure.

- *ROI has a rich history of application.* The ROI Methodology is not a fad passing through the organization. It is a measure of accountability that has been in place for centuries. Wherever there is a significant expenditure, there is a need to know the financial impact of the expenditure. ROI will continue to be an economic measure in the future.

- *Operating managers understand and relate to ROI.* Most managers in an organization have special training on how to manage the business.

Some have business or management degrees or even master's degrees in business administration. These managers understand ROI and routinely use it to value other investments. They have a desire to have ROI data for major programs. They know how to use it, appreciate it, and support it.

- *ROI builds excitement among stakeholders.* One of the most visible sources of pride and satisfaction comes when the HR department organizes, implements, or operates an HR program that results in a positive ROI calculation. No other measure can generate the amount of energy, excitement, and enthusiasm as ROI can, particularly when the ROI value exceeds expectations. Most stakeholders involved in HR programs intuitively believe that the programs add value, but ROI, as a measurement tool, confirms this intuition using a credible, validated process.

- *ROI is a top executive requirement.* Thanks in part to the popular press and media attention to ROI as an evaluation tool, executives are suggesting, asking, requiring, and sometimes demanding that ROI be calculated for certain HR programs. Previously, executives assumed that ROI could not be developed, given the logical and persuasive arguments they heard from the HR staff. Now, these executives see many examples in which ROI is becoming a justifiable part of the measurement mix. The global recession has intensified this issue to the point that executives now suggest that ROI should be required for HR expenditures. Human resources is treated the same as other business functions, and the HR department, like other departments, must produce value. Gone are the days of blindly increasing HR investments with no clue as to their financial payoff.

These six factors sway many HR leaders to pursue ROI. It is the ultimate level of evaluation that is not only needed but is being required by some key stakeholders. More important, ROI provides different stakeholder groups with valuable, balanced information about the success of an HR program.

Types of Data for ROI Methodology

At the heart of the ROI Methodology are the varieties of data collected throughout the process and reported at different intervals. Some of the types of data are labeled levels because they reflect a successive effect in which one level affects the next.

The concept of levels has been used for some time. There are very logical steps of succession in any particular project or program. Their use in a sequence can be traced back a few centuries. For example, John Quincy Adams once wrote, "If your actions inspire others to dream more, learn more, do more, and become more, you are a leader." This quote easily breaks into logical steps and levels of outcomes, as shown in Fiure 2.2.

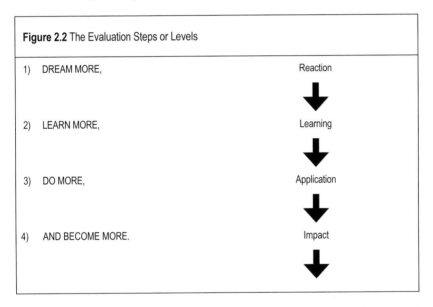

Figure 2.2 The Evaluation Steps or Levels

1)	DREAM MORE,	Reaction
2)	LEARN MORE,	Learning
3)	DO MORE,	Application
4)	AND BECOME MORE.	Impact

The good news is that ROI works extremely well in all types of environments and programs, particularly in HR programs. A human resources program would likely be unsuccessful if an adverse reaction occurred, so the first level is critical. Also, people must understand what they can do to make a project successful; thus, an element of learning is required in new HR programs. Regardless of the type of HR initiative, from a new ethics program to a new recruiting strategy, to a pay-for-performance program, the individuals involved must know their exact roles and activities. Of course, some programs, such as a talent development program, require many skills. However, even the proper learning does not guarantee success. Follow-up is needed to ensure that the people involved are using the program appropriately.

Application and implementation are critical for success; failure in these areas is typically what causes a program to break down. The stakeholders involved simply do not meet expectations.

This is not enough, however, for executives; they characterize application as being busy. The most pertinent data set for those who fund programs is the impact, the consequence of application, often expressed in business terms as output, quality, costs, and time. For a few executives, showing the impact of a program is not enough, though; they want to know the ROI. This demand pushes evaluation to the ultimate level of accountability and return on investment. The ROI is the amount of the improvement at the impact level (attributed to the program), converted to money and compared to the cost of the program.

Table 2.1 lists and describes seven types of data that can be used to measure the overall success of HR programs. As the evaluation moves to the higher levels, the value ascribed to the data by the client increases. However the degree of effort and the cost of capturing the data for the higher levels of evaluation generally increase as well. With proper program planning and design, costs can be minimized. The following sections describe the various qualitative and quantitative measures listed in the table that are basic to the ROI Methodology described in this book.

Table 2.1 Types and Levels of Evaluation Data

Level/Type	Measurement Focus
0. Costs	Measures the fully loaded costs of the HR program
1. Reaction	Measures participant reaction to the HR program and captures planned actions, if appropriate
2. Learning	Measures changes in knowledge, skills, and attitudes related to the HR program
3. Application/Implementation	Measures changes in behavior or actions as the HR program is applied, implemented, or utilized
4. Business Impact	Measures changes in business impact variables
5. Return on Investment	Compares monetary benefits to the costs of the HR program
6. Intangible Data	Impact measures that are not converted to monetary values

HR Program Cost Data

Program cost data reveal the actual cost of the HR solution or program and actually represent a fully loaded cost profile. This data reflect all the direct costs (for example, the cost of photocopying materials for that program) and indirect costs (for example, the support needed from the accounting department to support the program) of the specific HR function, project, solution, or program.

Reaction Data

The first category of outcome data from an HR program is basic reaction data (level 1 evaluation). These data represent an immediate reaction to the program from a variety of key stakeholders, particularly those who are charged with the responsibility to make it work. At this level a variety of basic satisfaction and reaction measures are taken, often representing 5 to 15 separate measures to gain insight into the reception and enthusiasm or disappointment with the HR initiative.

Learning Data

As employees become involved in an HR initiative, they must acquire information, absorb new knowledge, or learn new skills. In some cases as they attempt new skills, employees must gain confidence in using those skills in the workplace setting. This level of measurement (level 2) focuses on the changes in knowledge and skill acquisition and details what employees have learned to make the HR program successful. Some HR solutions have a high learning component, such as those involved in competencies, skill development, compliance, education, and learning. Others may have a low learning component, such as policy changes, reward systems, compensation, and new benefits. In these situations, the learning involves understanding how processes work and what tasks or steps must be taken to make the program successful.

Application and Implementation Data

Application and implementation are key measures that show the extent to which employees have changed their behavior or implemented the HR program (level 3). These data reflect how employees take actions, make adjustments, apply new skills, change habits, implement specific steps, and initiate processes as a result of the HR program.

This is one of the most powerful categories of data because it not only uncovers the extent to which the HR program is implemented but also details the reasons for lack of implementation in some cases. At this level, barriers and enablers to application and implementation are detailed, and a complete profile of success at the various steps of implementation is provided.

Business Impact Data

Every behavior change achieved or action taken in application and implementation has a consequence. This consequence can be described in one or more measures representing an impact on the employee's own work environment, as an impact directly on his or her team or as an impact in other parts of the organization.

This level of data (level 4) reflects the specific business impact and may include measures such as output, quality, costs, time, job satisfaction, and customer satisfaction that have been influenced by the application and implementation of the program. A direct link between business impact and the program must be established for the HR program to drive business value. At this level of analysis, a technique must be used to isolate the effects of the HR program from other influences that may be driving the same measure. Answering the following question is imperative for the HR department: how do you know your HR program caused the improvement and not something else?

Return-on-Investment Data

This level of measure compares the monetary value of the business impact measures to the actual cost of the HR program. Return on investment is the ultimate level of accountability and represents the financial impact directly linked with the program, expressed as a benefit/cost ratio or return-on-investment percentage. HR practitioners often refer to this measure as the "fifth level of evaluation."

Intangible Data

The intangible benefits consist of measures that are intentionally not converted to monetary value. To develop the ROI, you must convert business impact measures to monetary value. In some cases, however, converting certain measures to monetary values simply is not credible. In these situations, the data are listed as an intangible only if linked to the HR program.

Figure 2.3 shows five of the seven types of data arranged as levels in a chain of impact that is necessary if the HR program is to drive business value. Reaction leads to learning, which leads to application, which leads to business impact, and ultimately to ROI. At the business impact level, the effects of the HR program must be isolated from other influences. Also, business impact data must be converted to monetary value and compared to the cost of the HR program to develop the ROI. Intangible benefits are often the business impact data that cannot be credibly converted to monetary value. All stakeholders should understand this chain of impact. It is a novel, yet pragmatic, way to show the consequences of HR programs.

Figure 2.3 Chain of Impact of an HR Program

Participants react favorably to the HR program.

Participants learn new skills and knowledge needed to implement the HR program.

Participants apply new skills or take actions to implement the HR program.

The consequences of application are captured as business impact measures.

A return on investment is calculated as HR program costs are compared to monetary benefits.

An Example

The following example helps explain how the chain of impact works by describing the different type of data and their importance. Table 2.2 shows data collected from an evaluation of an employee suggestion system in a large electric utility. This new HR program represents a typical employee suggestion system design in which employees are rewarded with cash payments if a suggestion is accepted or implemented, resulting in cost savings. The table reflects how the data are developed through the chain of impact. At level 4 (business impact), the results look very promising as $1.52 million in benefits has been achieved in a two-year time frame.

However, the ROI reveals a negative value because the operational costs ($2.1 million) exceed the monetary benefits during the same two-year period. ROI presents the ultimate accountability as the monetary benefits ($1.52 million) are compared to the cost ($2.1 million):

$$\text{ROI} = \frac{\$1.52 \text{ million} - \$2.1 \text{ million}}{\$2.1 \text{ million}} \times 100\% = -28\% \text{ ROI}$$

This evaluation underscores the importance of taking the analysis all the way to ROI for certain programs. If the evaluation had stopped at business impact, level 4, only the business impact of the suggestion system, not the financial value, would be developed.

As shown above, the employee suggestion system results in a negative ROI (-28 percent). Nevertheless, a negative ROI does not always result in an adverse consequence. Some benefit is derived from this program as behavior is changed and the intangibles are linked with the program. The intangible benefits include important measures such as increased cooperation, organizational commitment, pride of ownership, employee satisfaction, and job engagement. In these cases, a negative ROI may be acceptable. However, if a positive ROI was expected, then a negative ROI is unacceptable.

Table 2.2. Example of Types and Levels of Data

Employee Suggestion System				
Type of Data	Data Collection Method	Data Source	Timing	Results
Reaction (Level 1)	Questionnaire	Employees	At the end of the announcement meeting	4.3 out of 5 rating on motivational, satisfaction, and engaging
Learning (Level 2)	Questionnaire	Employees	At the end of the announcement meeting	4.1 out of 5 rating on understanding the procedures, case documentation, award determination, and notification
Application and Implementation (Level 3)	Monitor Records	Employee Suggestion System	Annually	10.4% participation rate
Business Impact (Level 4)	Monitor Business Performance	Employee Suggestion System	Annually	$1.52 million in 2 years
Cost	Monitor Records	Cost Statements	Annually	$2.1 million cost in 2 years
ROI (Level 5)	—	—	—	-28%
Intangibles	Questionnaire	Sample of Employees	Annually	Increased cooperation, commitment to the organization, pride of ownership, and employee satisfaction

The ROI Methodology

The ROI model encompasses the seven types of data in a consistent and systematic way. Figure 2.4 shows the systematic approach for capturing data, processing and analyzing data, and reporting results.

As can be seen in the figure, the activities comprising the ROI Methodology are divided into four basic categories:

- evaluation planning
- data collection
- data analysis
- reporting

Planning for Evaluation

The first step in planning is to develop objectives that reflect all the various types of data. Ideally, for major programs, objectives should be set at each level and linked to baseline data, if available. The challenge is to push the objectives to higher levels beyond reaction and learning objectives to include application, impact, and even ROI. Objectives provide the necessary focus for program designers and the direction needed for program organizers. In addition, objectives show the participants, usually employees, what specifically should be accomplished with the HR program. Higher levels of

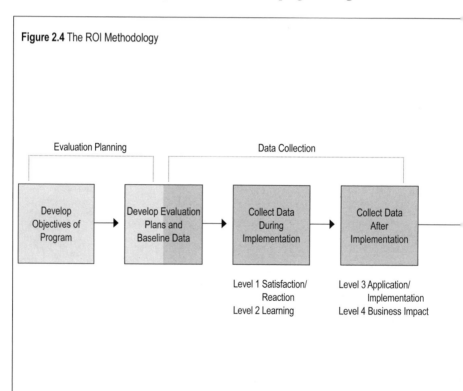

Figure 2.4 The ROI Methodology

Evaluation Planning   Data Collection

Develop Objectives of Program → Develop Evaluation Plans and Baseline Data → Collect Data During Implementation → Collect Data After Implementation →

Level 1 Satisfaction/ Reaction
Level 2 Learning

Level 3 Application/ Implementation
Level 4 Business Impact

objectives also provide program sponsors with meaningful data needed to judge the feasibility and initial effectiveness of the HR program.

The second part of the planning process involves developing the planning documents. Three documents are recommended, although they can be combined into a single plan. The three documents include a data collection plan, ROI analysis plan, and a communication and implementation plan. Additional detail on evaluation planning is presented in Chapter 3.

Data Collection

As Figure 2.4 reveals, data collection involves four different types of data that reflect the first four levels of evaluation (see Table 2.1). Reaction, satisfaction, and learning data are collected during the implementation of the program. After the program is executed, application, implementation, and business impact data are captured on a follow-up basis. Data collection

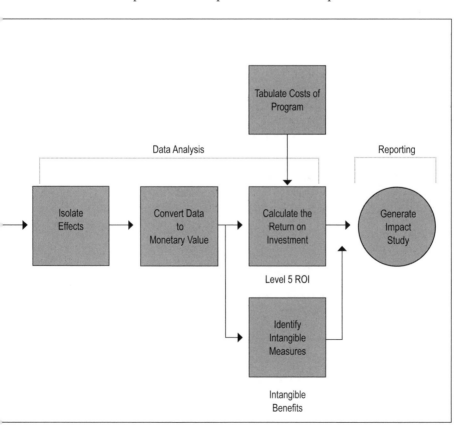

methods used to capture the first four levels of data include questionnaires, observations, interviews, focus groups, and business performance monitoring. These common data collection methods capture a variety of qualitative and quantitative data. Additional information on data collection is presented in Chapter 4.

Data Analysis

Analyzing the collected data requires isolating the effects of the HR program, converting the data to monetary values, integrating HR costs, calculating ROI, and identifying intangible measures. Each step is described briefly here.

Isolating the effects of the HR program. Although difficult, determining the business contribution of the HR program is imperative. Fortunately, the determination can be accomplished in many ways. The typical methods used to isolate the effects of the HR program from other factors include the use of control groups, time series analysis, and expert estimation. Some of these techniques are research focused, whereas others are more subjective but nonetheless valuable. These techniques are described in more detail in Chapter 5.

Converting data to monetary values. Another challenge is converting business data to monetary value. If the actual ROI is needed, either hard or soft data must be converted to monetary value. A variety of techniques are available to make this conversion, including the use of standard values, which are almost always available, as well as the use of records, expert input, external databases, and estimations.

For short-term programs, only the first year's benefits are used to represent one year of improvement. For long-term programs, longer time periods are used. The important challenge is to use the most conservative approach, even one that is more conservative than that used by the chief financial officer. Chapter 6 offers more details.

Representing HR costs. Monitoring the cost of the HR program is essential and must be represented by a fully loaded cost profile. Fully loaded costs should represent both direct and indirect categories, including costs for analysis and development, implementation, the time for employees involved in the program, and overhead. You can access cost data using cost statements, cost guidelines, benchmark data, and estimations. More details on costs are included in Chapter 7.

Calculating ROI. The ROI may be calculated using either the benefit/cost ratio or the ROI formula. The benefit/cost ratio (BCR) is defined as the total monetary benefits for the period of time selected divided by the fully loaded costs of the HR program:

$$\text{Benefit/Cost Ratio (BCR)} = \frac{\text{HR Program Benefits}}{\text{HR Program Costs}}$$

The ROI, although similar to the BCR, uses net benefits divided by costs. (The net benefits are the program benefits minus program costs.) In formula form, the ROI is:

$$\text{ROI (\%)} = \frac{\text{HR Program Benefits - HR Program Costs}}{\text{HR Program Costs}} \times 100$$

or

$$\text{ROI (\%)} = \frac{\text{HR Program Net Benefits}}{\text{HR Program Costs}} \times 100$$

This is the same basic formula used for evaluating capital investments, where the ROI is traditionally reported as earnings divided by investment. In the context of human resources, earnings equate to net HR program benefits (in monetary benefits), and investment equates to the fully loaded HR program costs.

The BCR and the ROI present the same general information but with slightly different perspectives. An example illustrates the use of these formulas. An HR program designed to reduce absenteeism produced benefits of $581,000 at a cost of $229,000. Therefore, the benefit/cost ratio is:

$$\text{BCR} = \frac{\$581,000}{\$229,000} = 2.54 \text{ (or 2.5:1)}$$

As this calculation shows, for every $1.00 invested, $2.54 in benefits is returned. In this example, net benefits are $581,000 - $229,000 = $352,000. Thus, the ROI is calculated as follows:

$$ROI(\%) = \frac{\$352,000}{\$229,000} \times 100\% = 154\%$$

This result means that each $1.00 invested in the HR program returns $1.50 in net benefits after accounting for costs. The benefits are usually expressed as annual benefits for short-term programs, representing the amount saved or gained for a complete year after the HR program has been implemented. Although the benefits may continue after the first year, the impact usually diminishes and is omitted from calculations in short-term situations. For long-term projects, the benefits are spread over several years. This conservative approach is used throughout the application of the ROI Methodology described in this book. Additional information on ROI calculations is presented in Chapter 7.

Identifying intangible measures. Intangibles are measures directly linked to the program and are developed at different timeframes. Although intangible benefits are not converted to monetary value, they represent meaningful data, often having as much perceived value as the tangible ROI calculation. Typical intangible data include job satisfaction, organizational commitment, teamwork, customer service, conflicts, and stress. This list is not meant to imply these measures cannot be converted to monetary value. In most organizations, these items are not converted because the conversion cannot be accomplished credibly. Additional details on intangibles are presented in Chapter 8.

Reporting Results

The final step in the ROI Methodology entails reporting the data to the many stakeholders who need HR success data. The challenge at this step is to determine the appropriate target audience, the information that is needed, the communication media that fit the situation, and the timing of presentation. Collectively, you must address these issues to have a systematic process for reporting data. Chapter 9 presents additional detail on reporting.

ROI Standards

Every process or model must have operating standards to be reproducible, accurate, credible, and sustainable. The operating standards for this process show how data are developed, processed, utilized, and reported using very conservative principles. The conservative approach builds respect, credibility, and buy-in from the management group. The operating standards for the ROI Methodology are labeled guiding principles, which support decision-making and replication of the ROI Methodology. The 12 ROI guiding principles are listed below:

- *When a higher-level evaluation is conducted, data must be collected at lower levels.* A balanced data set is needed that represents all seven types of data and that provides a complete profile of success using both qualitative and quantitative data. Some data represent lower levels of evaluation, and others represent higher levels. Lower-level data are needed to understand the dynamics of the process and to provide insight into problem areas and opportunities. For example, an adverse reaction at the first level can cause the program to fail from the beginning, but this situation will not be discovered unless an adequate amount of reaction data is collected. Also, many HR projects have a tendency to deteriorate during application and implementation. Collecting data at this level exposes the barriers and enablers so that adjustments can be made.

- *When an evaluation is planned for a higher level, the previous level of evaluation does not have to be comprehensive.* This resource-saving principle is designed to keep costs at a minimum. No organization has unlimited resources for funding measurement and evaluation projects. Shortcuts must be used; costs must be controlled; and steps must be taken to keep time commitments to a minimum. When shortcuts are taken, as a general rule, taking them at the lower levels is best. The corollary to this principle is to use the most comprehensive analysis at the highest level of evaluation pursued.

- *When collecting and analyzing data, use only the most credible sources.* Credibility is a substantial concern in HR measurement and evaluation data. When data are presented, credibility will be a primary issue that must be addressed to build respect and support for an impact study. One critical determinant of credibility is the source of the data. Sources must be identified that are the most credible for the particular issue, and this level of credibility can vary with studies and with groups. In some studies the management team is very credible; in others, it is not as suitable for a particular item. The point is to evaluate each data item and determine the most credible source for that particular item.

- *When analyzing data, choose the most conservative method among alternatives.* Some cases present more than one way to conduct a specific analysis. For example, when isolating the effects of an HR program, more than one method may be used. In these cases, the most conservative method (the one that generates the lowest ROI) is recommended. This principle assumes that both processes are equally credible. The net effect of this principle is to eliminate doubt and error by understating rather than overstating results.

- *At least one method must be used to isolate the effects of the HR program.* This principle represents a critical challenge with HR projects. The amount of the improvement in a specific data item related to the project must be isolated from other influences. Although a variety of techniques can measure isolation, at least one technique must always be used. Otherwise, the impact study is not credible because it lacks direct linkage between the program and impact. The default method for isolation is the use of estimates from individuals who know the process best. When all else fails, estimation is used, and it may be the method used in the majority of settings.

- *If no improvement data are available for a particular population or from a specific source, the assumption must be that little or no improvement has occurred.* No data equals no improvement. This guiding principle is perhaps the most conservative. If participants do not respond to questionnaires, surveys, action plans, or other data collection methods, the assumption is that they have achieved no value with the HR program. Also, if the participants are no longer in their job assignments or in the organization, the supposition is that they did not achieve success with the HR program. Realistically, some value may have been developed by the nonrespondents, particularly if they are still on the job, or when employees depart, they may have been successful before leaving the organization. This guiding principle exerts much pressure to obtain as much data as possible from credible sources, a factor that is at the heart of the implementation of the ROI Methodology.

- *Estimates of improvement should be adjusted (discounted) for the potential error of the estimate.* Sometimes estimates will have error. The amount of error is eliminated in the analysis. By using the concept of confidence estimates, an error range is created, and the low side of the error range is used, thus compensating for any doubt or error associated with the estimate. This guiding principle builds credibility because the results are understated instead of overstated.

- *Extreme data items and unsupported claims should not be used in ROI calculations.* Occasionally, extreme data items (sometimes called outliers) appear to be connected to the program or, in some cases, may be directly connected. Because they are extreme, they are omitted from the ROI analysis. Protecting the integrity of the ROI calculation is paramount, and key stakeholders must understand that the payoff is not generated on extreme values. Extreme data items are reported in other parts of an impact study but not in the ROI calculation. Also, unsupported claims are not used in the ROI analysis. For example, if participants do not show the source of data or how they developed monetary value, the claim is omitted from the ROI calculation, although it may be included in the impact study in another section. This guiding principle adds credibility to the analysis.

- *Only the first year of benefits (annual) should be used in the analysis of short-term HR programs and solutions.* The concept of ROI is an annual concept, so one year's worth of benefits is always needed. To be conservative, only the first year is used for HR programs that are short term in their implementation. "Term" is defined as the length of time it takes to implement the program with a particular individual or group. If implementing new sales training takes five days, then it is a short-term program, and the ROI should be developed based on one-year benefits. However, a two-year continuous mentoring and coaching process is a long-term solution, and a longer analysis period is needed. The point is to be conservative by using the number of years that is fair and at the same time as short as possible. This number should be established before the study is initiated and with input from the finance and accounting staff, if possible.

- *Use fully loaded HR program costs for the ROI analysis.* Costs represent the denominator of the ROI calculation. Both direct and indirect costs should be included. Indirect costs are not normally used by some stakeholders. For example, the chief financial officer may argue that the use of meeting room space for meetings connected with an HR program implementation should not be charged because the meeting room is a fixed cost. However, a conservative approach is to account for all expenditures even on an allocated or prorated basis. Including this cost in the analysis may not materially affect the ROI calculation, but it is a significant gesture that may be necessary to gain additional respect for the methodology.

- *Intangible benefits are measures that are purposely not converted to monetary values.* An important issue that can affect the ROI calculation and the credibility of an ROI study is the issue of converting data to monetary values. Some data are considered to be soft (or intangible) and cannot (or should not) be converted to monetary value. If the conversion cannot be made on a credible basis in the specific setting with a reasonable amount of resources, the data item is left as an intangible benefit. The principle issue is the method used to make the conversion. Specific rules are developed to help two different researchers or evaluators decide when a measure should be converted to monetary value or when it should be left as an intangible.

- *Communicate the results of the ROI analysis to all key stakeholders.* Communicating data to the appropriate audience groups is critical. The first step in this process is to identify the stakeholders who need the information and then ensure that these and other groups receive the desired information using the most effective medium at the right time with the appropriate content. You should include four stakeholder groups in your communications: (1) the individual participants who are charged with implementing the HR program, (2) the immediate managers of the participants, (3) the key client or sponsor of the HR program, and (4) other HR team members.

These macro-level guiding principles ensure that the ROI Methodology is consistent, routine, and standardized. At the same time, they keep costs low and credibility high. They are essential to obtain the appropriate buy-in and support needed for the ROI Methodology. The guiding principles are explained in more detail throughout the book.

Final Thoughts

This chapter began with the reasons for implementing ROI Methodology. Next, we explained the different types and levels of data, which provide the framework for the ROI analysis. Step-by-step, the ROI Methodology was explored, showing how the seven types of data are generated, analyzed, and communicated. Finally, the guiding principles of ROI were described, showing how consistency and standardization are used to make the process realistic, replicable, and credible. The next chapter focuses on the planning and preparation needed to conduct an ROI study.

Chapter 3.
Preparing for ROI

Preparing the organization and the HR department for ROI measurement invites a few challenges. One of the early decisions is to choose the appropriate level of evaluation for each program or project. While every program should be evaluated at some level, ROI analysis should be reserved for the most important HR programs in the organization. This chapter explores how to select programs for ROI analysis and describes the preparations necessary to begin each ROI study.

When to Use ROI

Every HR program should be evaluated in some way even if the evaluation involves only reaction data collected from a select group of stakeholders. Including evaluation as a part of every HR program is a fundamental requirement. While reaction data alone are sufficient for evaluating many HR programs, the challenge is to collect additional data at higher levels, when appropriate and feasible.

The appropriate level of evaluation for each HR program is determined when the program is initiated, realizing that the evaluation level may change during the life of the program. For example, a new-employee orientation program can be evaluated with reaction (level 1) and learning (level 2) data. The objective at this point is to ensure that employees learn what they need to know to be successful and that they form accurate impressions about the organization. Later, a follow-up evaluation may be implemented to determine if the new employees are using the information provided in the orientation and if they are progressing acceptably, based on what they have learned during orientation. This follow-up is an application/implementation evaluation (level 3).

If the cost of the new employee orientation rises, some managers may question the value of the process and push the evaluation to higher levels. To carry out level 4 or 5 evaluations, redesigning the new-employee orientation program may be necessary. You can then compare the redesigned version to the previous version to see if a difference exists. The difference may be evaluated with business impact data (level 4) or ROI (level 5) or both. During the life of a particular program or function, the desired level of evaluation may change.

Because of the resources required and the realistic barriers for ROI implementation, ROI analysis is used only for certain programs, using several criteria as outlined in the following sections, when selecting an evaluation level for HR programs.

Recommended Programs for Evaluation at Lower Levels

Reaction evaluation (level 1) can suffice as the only level of evaluation for short programs, such as briefings, policy introductions, or general information distributed to employees. If reaction to the program is critical, ongoing assessment of reaction may be appropriate. For example, a routine analysis of reaction to a telecommuting program is congruous in assessing the extent to which employees continue to perceive the program as fair, responsive, suitable, and helpful.

Learning evaluation (level 2) is appropriate when employees need to acquire specific knowledge or skills presented in an HR program. With training, education, and development programs, learning evaluation is essential. Learning evaluations may also be helpful for certain compliance initiatives in which employees must learn how and why the organization complies with a variety of regulations. These data are also apposite for safety and health programs that safeguard employees' welfare; participants in safety programs must learn correct procedures and practices. Learning evaluation is also important when employees must know certain policies, such as diversity, value systems, and routine guidelines and procedures that are critical to the job and the organization.

Application and implementation evaluation (level 3) is necessary when employees should perform in a particular way on the job as a result of an HR program. For example, if employees are required to deliver a certain level of customer service based on job design, reward systems, or learning and development, monitoring employees may assist in making sure they are delivering the proper service. Periodic audits or observations of employees interacting with customers can often ensure they are displaying correct behavior on the job. If safety and security are issues, evaluating key programs at level 3 is absolutely essential to make certain that employees are doing what they are supposed to do or are reacting properly under particular circumstances.

Deciding which level of evaluation is appropriate is not only a test of the ideal but is also a trade-off with resources available and the amount of disruption allowed in the organization. Because most data collection at this level disrupts the organization in some way, the evaluation must be balanced with the time, effort, and resources that can be committed to the process. Most organizations fall short of the ideal evaluation and settle for a feasible approach within the existing constraints.

Recommended Programs for Impact and ROI Analysis

Programs taken to the levels of business impact and ROI analysis are special ones, and understanding the contributions these programs make to the organization is imperative. Among the criteria you should consider when selecting programs to evaluate with business impact and ROI data are the following:

Expected lifecycle of the program. The first criterion in selecting programs for business impact and ROI analysis is the length of time the program is in existence (its lifecycle). Some HR programs are one-time opportunities designed to react to a particular issue or to address a particular problem in the organization. These programs are intended to be brief, and ROI analysis may not be necessary. For example, an early retirement offer with a short deadline or mandatory ethics training for all employees may be one-shot programs. Conversely, some programs seem to exist forever. For example, a new-employee orientation program will always be needed as long as there are new employees. Consequently, at some point in the lifecycle of a new-employee orientation program, conducting a comprehensive analysis may be helpful. The company DHL pursued an ROI evaluation of its orientation program because it was considered a permanent fixture.

Linkage to strategic initiatives or objectives. Another important issue is the linkage of the program to strategic initiatives or operational goals. A strategic program, designed to address specific strategic objectives, should be subject to a high level of scrutiny.

For example, a major customer service initiative devised to support a strategic goal of improving customer satisfaction may be a candidate for ROI. AT&T evaluated one of its key customer service HR programs because it was linked to several strategic initiatives. Other programs may be operationally focused, adding significant impact to the organization's bottom line. For example, workout programs, similar to those instituted at General Electric in which managers dealt with particular issues and problems in a formal development effort, may be suitable candidates for ROI. These programs are designed to add value and, consequently, should be subjected to ROI analysis to see if they are adding the value as intended. A large metropolitan transit system pursued an ROI study on an absenteeism reduction program for bus drivers because of the resulting operational problems related to excessive absenteeism.

Cost of the program. Expensive programs need a comprehensive level of analysis to ensure that they are adding appropriate value. For example, in a large Canadian commercial bank, an expensive leadership development program costing $100,000 per candidate was subjected to ROI analysis to show the actual value, using a sample of participants. The board of directors wanted this evaluation because of perceived excessive costs. Another example: the Royal New Zealand Navy conducted an ROI study on a retention bonus plan for marine engineers because the plan cost the Navy $4 million. In contrast, however, a tuition reimbursement program for off-the-job education classes, directly related to the work but utilized by only three percent of the employees, may not be a candidate for ROI analysis.

Time commitment. Programs that involve much time are also candidates for business impact and ROI analysis. If employees must take a great deal of time away from their jobs to attend meetings and learning sessions, determining if the process is adding value can be helpful. For example, at Allied

Irish Bank senior executives questioned the value of a 360-degree feedback process because it required so much of the managers' time. The managers complained about filling out the many forms, receiving feedback data, and attending training sessions and meetings to analyze and understand the process. This excessive time caused executives to question the value of the program.

Visibility of the program. Highly visible or controversial programs often generate a need for accountability at higher levels. Because such programs can stimulate concern among their critics, they require a higher level of accountability. For example, a wellness and fitness center built for employees at a major automotive manufacturing complex was selected for ROI analysis because of the center's visibility. In another project, senior executives questioned the value of a work-at-home program that was launched by the CEO to help the environment. Sometimes managers and shareholders question the value of a high-profile project or program, thus elevating the evaluation to the business impact or ROI level.

Management interest. The extent of management interest is often the most critical issue in driving programs for impact and ROI analysis. Senior executives have concerns about some programs but not all of them. Based on feedback they receive or on their own perceptions of the program, they want this level of accountability applied. For example, a National Aeronautics and Space Administration (NASA) executive recently required an impact analysis for one of its education programs, the NASA Faculty Fellowship Program. Senior administrators wanted to know if the program added value to NASA and to the partnering universities.

Client requirement. Particularly since the global recession, funders of HR projects ask for their results. Today, more executives are concerned about every expenditure. For major and significant programs, they may require an ROI calculation. For example, a major oil company required an impact study of an executive leadership program developed by a prestigious university on the west coast. The top executives wanted to see results from this program because it takes a lot of time, commitment, energy, and resources. In another example, the head of sales wanted to see the value of a sales development program, which consisted of a variety of learning and sales-enabling tools. Before the program was implemented, this top executive wanted a proof of concept all the way to the ROI level to be convinced that it would add value. These days, clients are fully in charge of the evaluation requirement and are now specifying evaluation early and often for major programs.

The good news is that only a few programs raise concerns. Even if the other criteria do not apply, elevating the evaluation to these levels to satisfy executive concerns may be beneficial or even necessary. So called soft programs that deal with diversity, motivation, empowerment, and communication are often scrutinized closely by executives who are not clear about the programs' value to the organization.

Table 3.1 lists some programs often taken to higher levels of analysis. The table represents both impact and ROI analysis, but reviewing the distinction between the two levels is useful. Sometimes the business impact of the program is desired without the subsequent ROI analysis. For example, a program designed to improve job satisfaction may be evaluated only at the business impact level. In that case, the direct link between the HR program and job satisfaction is established. The ROI Methodology requires that you develop the monetary benefits of the program and compare them to the costs of the program. Because of the difficulty in converting job satisfaction data to monetary value, you may not wish to pursue ROI analysis in this example.

Table 3.1 Programs Suitable for ROI or Business-Level Analysis

Leadership Development	Recruiting Strategies
Career Development Programs	Talent Retention
Competency Systems	Safety and Health Programs
Diversity Programs	Self-Directed Teams
Recognition and Rewards	Empowerment Programs
Executive Coaching	Flexible Work Systems
Management Development	Skill-Based Compensation
Gain Sharing Programs	Technology and Systems
Employee Relations Program	Process Improvements
Organization Development	Wellness/Fitness Initiatives
Orientation Systems	Green Projects

Programs Unsuitable for ROI Analysis

To determine which programs are not suitable candidates for impact and ROI analysis, the criteria are essentially the opposites of those used to select programs for higher levels of analysis. However, other factors are often helpful in sorting out those that should not be considered for business impact and ROI evaluation.

In some cases, developing an ROI value could send an unintended negative signal. For example, if an ROI evaluation were conducted on a sexual harassment prevention program, a nonsupervisory female employee, who may be a potential victim of sexual harassment herself, would probably not appreciate ROI data. Reporting an ROI in monetary terms may give the impression that the organization is only pursuing this program because of a monetary payoff, ignoring the fact that sexual harassment is illegal and unethical. Therefore, HR leaders must carefully consider the decision of whether to conduct a business impact evaluation or an ROI analysis for each HR program.

Programs required by external regulation or by executive mandate are often not good candidates for ROI analysis. Compliance programs exist for a variety of noneconomic reasons, and the range of options to correct problems or improve programs may be limited. That such programs could be modified significantly is unlikely, making evaluation at this level frustrating or pointless. If change is not an option, evaluation is probably useless. With limited resources available for this level of analysis, compliance programs are typically not subject to ROI evaluation, unless senior executives want to pursue it for some reason.

Programs of short duration are not appropriate for impact and ROI analysis either. For a program to add value, a change in behavior or a significant change in actions must take place. Short-duration programs do not usually drive this type of change.

HR programs that involve only a small group of people are not necessarily good candidates for this analysis. The time and costs for the program may be insignificant to warrant a study.

Job-related programs may not be good candidates for ROI analysis. These programs include entry-level training and job design, such as technical skills necessary for the job or programs covering basic policies, practices, and procedures. These are necessary for on-the-job success, and their value rarely comes into question.

Finally, programs that are important to the value systems of the organization or those designed to make social and political statements are usually not ideal choices for ROI analysis. These programs are in place for a variety of noneconomic reasons, and the actual payoff to the organization in the short term is often not an issue.

Selecting the First Project for ROI Analysis

New to many organizations, ROI analysis can be extremely powerful and requires skills that must be developed through trial and practice.

With these factors in mind, a few requirements for first-time projects are often helpful. The first requirement is simplicity; beginning with a simple project for which the issues are few and the scope is narrow is advised. This focus helps the HR staff achieve early success and undertake ROI analysis for more complicated issues later.

Another issue is perception of the project in terms of current success. Undertaking projects that appear from current feedback to be successful is best. Training programs that are already considered to be successful help ensure that the first ROI study has a positive ROI. Nothing is more discouraging than having the initial study generate a negative ROI, possibly deflating the enthusiasm of the HR team.

Avoiding programs that are controversial, political, or sensitive in nature is prudent. These programs often have hidden agendas and political issues that make success difficult. A study organizer may get caught in the crossfire between feuding executives. Although these programs can be addressed later with the process, excluding them in the early stages is wise.

Finally, HR practitioners should not take on a program that is a pet project of a senior executive. The program may have critics or supporters that can influence the data, conclusions, and recommendations.

Considering these additional criteria can help avert the frustration that may result from the first use of ROI analysis and build confidence in a methodology that can eventually be used to assess any type of program, in any setting, and in any environment.

Initial Analysis — The Beginning
Point of the HR Program

The basis for an HR program adding value rests on the rationale for its existence and the extent to which it relates to a specific business need. This fundamental concept requires much more attention to the initial analysis that leads to the implementation of an HR program or to a continuation of a program. This initial analysis is the beginning point in the ROI Methodology.

The Most Common Reason for Failure

The authors conducted an analysis of almost 1,000 impact studies involving virtually every type of HR program in a variety of settings, including private and public sector organizations. The study revealed that the top reason for lack of success is the failure to align the program with business or organizational needs from the very beginning.

Although most HR managers are confident in the analysis used to decide if the HR program is needed, in many cases the process is not rigorous enough to make a real connection to the business need. And if the initial rationale for the program does not serve a business need, the business impact measures often see little or no improvement, making achieving a positive ROI an impossibility. Thus, for most organizations a more comprehensive approach (described later) is required for the initial analysis leading to HR programs or at least an occasional analysis to see if the program is still necessary. Unfortunately, this initial analysis is often perceived as inessential and inappropriate.

The Analysis Dilemma

The upfront analysis of HR problems or issues leading to specific programs and solutions creates a dilemma for the organization. Analysis is often misplaced, misunderstood, and misrepresented. The process conjures up images of complex problems, confusing models, and a plethora of data involving complicated statistical techniques. Analysis is often not pursued to requisite detail for five reasons:

- *Employee needs and problems appear to point to a solution.* When employee needs and problems are examined, several potential solutions are connected to the needs. The solutions, however, may not be appropriate. If managers are not treating their employees fairly, for example, a training program may not be the answer. Perhaps the managers know how to treat employees fairly and with respect but are not required or encouraged to do so. Consequently, training is not necessarily the appropriate solution.
- *Solutions appear to be obvious.* Some solutions appear obvious when examining certain types of data. If the base pay of a particular group is lower than a competitor's pay for the same group, the obvious solution to an employee turnover problem is to increase the base pay. Nevertheless, pay is not always the principal reason for departure. Low turnover rates can be achieved in organizations that pay lower-than-average salaries. The cause of the problems must be thoroughly analyzed to ensure that funds flow to the right solution, yielding a positive effect on the problem.
- *Everyone has an opinion about the cause of problems.* Almost every HR manager who wrestles with HR problems has an opinion about the actual causes of the problem. Other stakeholders may also have opinions about the cause of the problem. Because there are multiple opinions, accepting the highest-ranking input (usually from the most senior manager) and moving forward with a solution is tempting. Unfortunately, this practice often leads to allocating resources to an inappropriate solution.
- *Analysis takes too much time.* Upfront analysis takes time and consumes resources; however, the consequences of no analysis can be more expensive. If solutions are implemented without determining the cause, time and resources may be wasted, and the results can be more damaging than doing nothing at all. When planned properly and pursued professionally, an analysis can be completed within any organization's budget and time constraints. The key is to focus on the right tools for the situation.
- *Analysis appears confusing.* Determining the causes of problems may appear to be complex and confusing. In reality, analysis need

not be very complicated. Simple, straightforward techniques can uncover the causes of many problems and achieve excellent results.

Steps in the Analysis

For many HR programs, the first step in analysis is to examine the actual business need. Too often programs are initiated because of behavioral issues or perceptions of a problem that may or may not be connected to a business need. Figure 3.1 shows a needs analysis process that begins with feasibility and develops through preference needs. Figure 3.2 shows the links of the levels between needs analysis and evaluation.

Figure 3.1. Levels of Needs Analysis

Levels	Needs Analysis	Key Question
5	Payoff Needs	Is the problem worth solving?
4	Business Needs	What business measures reflect the problem?
3	Performance Needs	What should change in the work environment that will enhance this business measure?
2	Learning Needs	What skills or knowledge must be developed to meet the performance need?
1	Preference Needs	How should the solution be structured and perceived?

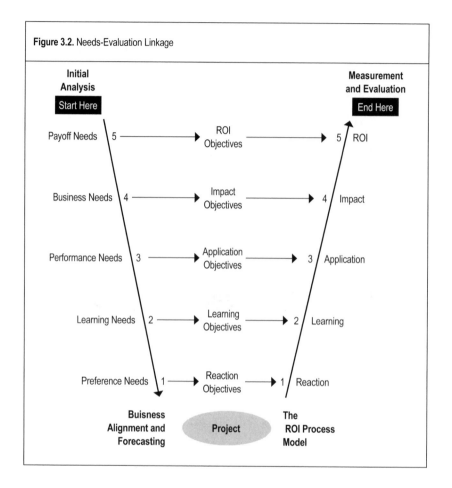

Figure 3.2. Needs-Evaluation Linkage

Payoff Needs

The analysis process begins with initial feasibility issues. The primary question here — whether the problem is worth solving or the opportunity is worth pursuing — addresses the ROI issue. Is a positive ROI in the solution expected? Sometimes a problem cannot be solved, or the monetary value of the measure may not move enough to overcome the potential expense of the solution. This initial analysis is crude but examines the overall viability of confronting the issue. Because limited resources are available, detailed analytical skills (and potential solutions) should be reserved for issues that really make a difference.

Business Needs

The next step of analysis is the connection to the business need. Is an actual business measure not performing as well as it should? The good news is that organizations often have business measures that reflect HR issues that either need to be addressed or that represent opportunities for improvement.

Identifying the business measure(s) is an easy step in the process. Typical business measures include hard data categories of output, quality, costs, and time, as shown in Table 3.2, and soft data categories of work habits, work climate, job attitudes, customer service, advancement development, and initiative, as shown in Table 3.3.

Table 3.2. Examples of Hard Data

OUTPUT	TIME
Units Produced	Downtime
Items Assembled	Overtime
Sales	On Time Shipments
Forms Processed	Time to Project Completion
Loans Approved	Processing Time
Inventory Turnover	Cycle Time
Patients Served	Meeting Schedules
Applications Processed	Repair Time
Productivity	Efficiency
Projects Completed	Work Stoppages
Shipments	Order Response Time
New Accounts Opened	Late Reporting
	Lost Time Days

COSTS	QUALITY
Budget Variances	Scrap
Unit Costs	Rejects
Cost By Account	Error Rates
Variable Costs	Rework
Fixed Costs	Shortages
Overhead Costs	Deviation From Standard
Operating Costs	Product Failures
Number of Cost Reductions	Inventory Adjustments
Accident Costs	Percent of Tasks Completed Properly
Sales Expense	Accidents

Table 3.3. Examples of Soft Data

WORK HABITS	CUSTOMER SATISFACTION
Absenteeism	Churn Rate
Tardiness	Number of Satisfied Customers
Visits to First Aid	Customer Satisfaction Index
Inappropriate Appearance	Customer Loyalty
Violations of Safety Rules	Customer Complaints
Excessive Breaks	Customer Responsiveness
WORK CLIMATE	**DEVELOPMENT/ADVANCEMENT**
Number of Grievances	Promotions
Number of Discrimination Charges	Merit Increases
Employee Complaints	Requests for Transfer
Employee Conflicts	Performance Appraisal Ratings
Litigation	Increases in Job Effectiveness
JOB ATTITUDES	**INITIATIVE**
Job Satisfaction	Implementation of New Ideas
Organizational Commitment	Successful Completion of Projects
Job Engagement	Number of Suggestions Implemented
Employee Loyalty	Creativity
Increased Motivation	Innovation

Performance Needs

One of the most difficult steps in the analysis is establishing performance needs in which the actual cause of the business need improvement is determined. At this level of analysis, the basic issue is to determine what is — or is not — occurring in the job environment that is influencing the business measure in question.

This analysis focuses on the root of the problem or opportunity, detailing what must change to improve the business measure. The upfront linkage to the business measure, this step is often omitted, or the linkage is assumed. This level may involve traditional data collection methods such as questionnaires, surveys, interviews, and focus groups to uncover underlying linkage to business measure improvement. It can also encompass brainstorming sessions, problem-solving sessions, fishbone diagrams, and other techniques to identify the causes of the problem. This level of analysis may unveil non-HR solutions. Many of the problems that may appear to be related to human resources may be associated with other issues, such as technology, environment, systems, and processes, which are beyond the influence and control of the HR group. Sorting out these causes so that the solution is matched to the actual cause is necessary.

Learning Needs

The next level of analysis is the learning gap analysis, which focuses on what individuals need to know to correct the performance gap. Sometimes the learning gap is the actual solution; the principal cause of the performance gap is that the employees do not know how to do something. Even when other solutions prevail, the solution usually calls for a knowledge and learning component. For example, if a reward system is implemented, the learning need involves learning how to use the actual reward system and understanding the processes that make it work successfully. Learning is a minimal part of the actual solution to the performance gap. Too often organizations implement learning solutions even though they did not conduct previous analyses, and they assumed that a deficiency in learning caused the performance gap. This disconnect creates problems when resources are misappropriated and the problem is not addressed; the performance gap remains. In addition, a negative image of learning is created when it is not needed or is misapplied.

Preference Needs

The final level of analysis is the preference for the solution. In this analysis HR managers, participants, and other key stakeholders define their preference for the implementation of a particular solution. Preferences may include the stakeholders' perception of the solution in terms of relevance, importance, necessity, and value. They may also encompass the location, nature of the delivery, the extent of the implementation, and how and who are involved. Because they sometimes shape the actual design and rollout of the solution, preference needs should be addressed after the solutions are clearly defined.

These steps in the analysis are critical but should be applied sparingly. If an HR problem is minor in scope, inexpensive, and not very visible, then it may be better to reduce the analyses to input at the lower levels only. The entire five levels should be reserved for those situations when the projects are strategic or important to operational issues, when the perceived cost of the solution is high, when the expected solution is highly visible, perhaps controversial, and when the accountability of the solution will attract management's interest. These are almost the identical criteria for considering programs for impact and ROI analysis.

Linkage to Evaluation

Figure 3.3 shows the linkage of the needs assessment or front-end analysis with evaluation levels. These links are critical because they often explain salient concepts and reveal many of the problems with dysfunctional processes. The objectives of HR programs represent a transition from the needs to evaluation at that same level. This parallel thinking along the levels is an excellent way to approach HR needs and programs. The analysis at multiple levels leads to the development of objectives at different levels that drives the collection of evaluation data at the different levels.

Figure 3.3. Linking Needs Assessment with Evaluation

	NEEDS ASSESSMENT	PROGRAM OBJECTIVES	EVALUATION	
5	Absenteeism is costly	Achieve 25% ROI	Program achieved 72% ROI	5
4	Absenteeismis 9%. Benchmark is 5%.	Weekly absenteeism rate will reduce to 5% in six months.	Monitor absenteeism data for six months – 4.2%	4
3	Discussions between team leader/ supervisor are not occurring when there is an absence	Counseling discussions conducted in 95% of situations when an unexpected absence occurs	Follow-up questionnaire to participants verified frequency of discussions – 98% in three months	3
2	Deficiency in counseling/ discussion skills	Counseling discussion skills will be acquired/enhanced	Skill practice sessions during program confirmed skills	2
1	Supervisor prefers to attend training one day per week	Program receives favorable rating of 4 out of 5 on the structure of program	Reaction questionnaire at the end of program reported 4.7	1

This example underscores the importance of this linkage. A call center was experiencing unusually high absenteeism, which led to an HR solution. Figure 3.3 shows the analysis that led to the solution. First, the issue of feasibility was addressed. A quick analysis comparing actual absenteeism with benchmarking data, and the perceived cost of absenteeism confirmed that is was a problem worth solving.

The business need, the absenteeism rate, was clearly defined and identified. Unplanned, unexpected absences were the key issue, and the absenteeism rate for this category was growing and was higher than in other call centers in the same area. The manager of the call center expressed concern that it was too high.

The next level was the determination of the cause of absenteeism. Although many reasons for absenteeism related to the work environment and external issues may exist, in this particular case the team leaders failed to confront habitual absentees. In essence, the leaders did not conduct counseling discussions when an employee was unexpectedly absent. These discussions, focusing on concern, care, and consequences, helped change behavior. Therefore, not initiating these discussions was a job performance need with these team leaders. Something that should have occurred on the job did not, and that failure to act influenced absenteeism. In some work environments, discussions about absenteeism would not necessarily be a learning solution if team leaders already knew how to conduct the sessions. However, in this case, team leaders lacked the people skills to conduct these counseling discussions in a productive way. Therefore, a learning solution emerged to equip team leaders with the required counseling skills.

The preference for the solution was defined as two half-day workshops conducted near the job site two weeks apart in which the participants were instructed in using the appropriate counseling skills. Progress was reported in the second session. The team leaders perceived the program to be necessary, practical, and relevant.

With a clear needs assessment up front, the objectives were developed, and the evaluation data were collected. This approach made the evaluation much easier because the data were clearly defined with the objectives.

The Role of Objectives for HR Programs
The previous section presented the linkage between needs assessment and evaluation, with the objectives serving as a transition. At the higher levels,

the objectives provide focus, guidance, and direction. Because the objectives are a critical part of the process, they merit further exploration.

Developing Objectives

Ideally, objectives are developed directly from the initial analysis, which identifies the key issues that must be contained in the objectives. The objectives are arranged in a hierarchy, often showing the chain of impact that should be developed after the program is implemented.

Reaction objectives are defined that identify the issues for acceptance of the HR program. Measures such as usefulness, appropriateness, relevance, importance, and fairness are critical issues that can be examined directly in an objective. The goal is to have an acceptable level of agreement with a particular measure. A typical example of a reaction objective is "participants will perceive the wellness and fitness program to be important to their health."

Learning objectives are classic in their design. They focus on what skills and knowledge should be acquired as the HR solution is launched. A learning objective often has a clearly defined statement with a criterion, possibly even with a condition, for example, "Demonstrate the four steps for closing a sale 70 percent of the time within five minutes."

Application objectives are developed much the same way as learning objectives, but the context is positioned to the job. The application measure may go beyond typical behavior change and include tasks, steps, processes, and procedures that are either implemented or adjusted. Sometimes a specific criterion is used, and the conditions are detailed. An example of an application objective is "employees will use at least three cost-containment features in the new health care plan within 90 days."

Impact objectives are measurable and often cover both hard and soft data categories. Hard data categories include output, quality, cost, and time. Soft data categories include such issues as employee satisfaction and customer satisfaction. The measure may be broad, for example, "Increase sales or improve quality," or specific, "Decrease employee turnover from 38 percent to 25 percent in six months." The specificity depends on the situation.

ROI objectives are developed when the analysis is conducted at that level. The objective is stated as a desired or acceptable ROI percentage or a benefits/cost ratio (BCR). Additional information on establishing ROI objectives is presented in Chapter 7.

Table 3.4 shows typical objectives at the different levels and specific measures of those objectives. Each of these is taken directly from an HR program. The table illustrates the wide variety of possibilities aimed at the different levels. The challenge is to develop objectives for the program that are as detailed as possible at the highest level possible.

Table 3.4. Examples of Objectives for HR Programs

Objective *After completing this program, participants should:*	Evaluation Level
1. Improve work group productivity by 10%.	Impact
2. Initiate at least three cost-reduction projects in one month.	Application
3. Increase the use of counseling discussion skills in 90% of situations where work habits are unacceptable.	Application
4. Achieve a 2:1 benefit-cost ratio one year after the new gainsharing program is implemented.	ROI
5. Be able to identify at least four elements of the employee assistance program.	Learning
6. Increase external customer satisfaction index by 25% in three months.	Impact
7. Handle customer complaints with the 5-step process in 95% of complaint situations.	Application
8. Should perceive the absenteeism control policy to be fair.	Reaction
9. Achieve a leadership simulation score average of 75 out of a possible 100.	Learning
10. Conduct a performance review meeting with direct reports within 30 days to establish performance improvement goals.	Application
11. Achieve a 4 out of 5 rating on appropriateness of new ethics policy.	Reaction
12. Decrease the time to recruit new engineers from 35 days to 20 days.	Impact
13. Reduce turnover rate in call centers to a 20% annual rate.	Impact
14. At least 10% of employees participate in the employee suggestion program.	Application
15. Perceive the flextime work schedule system to be important to work/life balance.	Reaction
16. Involve at least 15% of employees in career enhancement program application.	Application

The Power of Higher-Level Objectives

Ideally objectives are established directly from the upfront analysis. When application and impact objectives are developed, much of the design, development, and implementation of the HR program can be influenced by the objectives. For HR program designers, these objectives provide guidance and direction as they develop various scenarios and support tools that will become part of the HR program implementation. For participants involved in coordinating HR programs, higher-level objectives give them direction so that they can relate their own experience or motivation with the desired outcomes. For individuals struggling to make the HR program work, the higher levels of objectives provide them with the specific goals often needed to be successful. Application and impact objectives take the mystery out of the value the program will deliver. Finally, the individuals who sponsor or support the HR programs often find higher-level objectives helpful and essential in describing the impact because they provide more value than traditional reaction and learning objectives.

When Objectives Are Not Available

In some cases objectives are not clearly defined for an HR program, yet the program must be evaluated at the higher levels — impact and ROI. In these cases, objectives must be developed to reflect the actual or perceived impact of the HR program.

This approach will involve securing input from a variety of experts to clearly define the expected outcome of the program, recognizing all of the consequences, both negative and positive. Table 3.5 shows an example, a contrast between the actual stated objectives from a sexual harassment prevention program and the actual objectives used to capture the value when the program was evaluated. In the initial design, the program was planned to focus on behavior that would ultimately lower the number of complaints. In the revised objectives, some of the outcomes of the program were clearly specified in addition to the sexual harassment complaints. This issue is critical because many impact studies are conducted for programs that were previously developed without defined outcomes. This type of program is not necessarily the best candidate for analysis. Usually, a level 3 (application) evaluation is appropriate to ensure that the inappropriate behavior has been eliminated. However, in this case the HR executive continued to show senior executives that this type of prevention program added value to the bottom line.

Table 3.5. Original and Revised Objectives
Original "Published" Objectives
After participating in this program, participants should be able to: • Understand the company's policy on sexual harassment • Identify inappropriate and illegal behavior related to sexual harassment • Investigate and discuss sexual harassment issues • Ensure that the workplace is free from sexual harassment • Reduce the number of sexual harassment complaints

Revised Objectives	
Level	**Program Objective(s)**
1	Reaction • Perceive the program to be necessary • Perceive the program to be relevant to their work • Perceive the program to be important to their own success • Identify planned actions
2	Learning • Increase knowledge of policy on sexual harassment • Increase knowledge of inappropriate and illegal behavior • Improve skills to investigate and discuss sexual harassment issues
3	Application/Implementation • Properly administer policy on sexual harassment • Within two weeks, conduct meetings with employees to discuss policy and expected behavior • Ensure that workplace is free of sexual harassment
4	Business Impact • Reduce internal complaints • Reduce external complaints • Reduce employee turnover • Reduce absenteeism • Improve employee satisfaction
5	ROI • Target ROI = 25%

Planning for ROI Projects

HR professionals realize the importance of planning for almost any type of undertaking. Most agree that thorough planning can lead to a more effective implementation. ROI analysis is no different. Careful planning for ROI analysis not only saves time and effort but also sometimes affects the success or failure of the entire project. Planning involves three documents described in detail in this section: the data collection plan, the ROI analysis plan, and the communication and implementation plan.

Figure 3.4 Sample Data Collection Plan

Program: Preventing Sexual Harassment

Level	Broad Program Objective(s)	Measures	Data Collection Method/ Instruments
1	**REACTION/SATISFACTION** • Obtain a positive reaction to program and materials • Obtain input for suggestions for improving program • Identify planned actions	• Average rating of at least 4.0 on 5.0 scale on quality, usefulness and achievement of program objectives. • 90% submit planned actions	• Reaction feedback questionnaire
2	**LEARNING** • Knowledge of policy on sexual harassment • Knowledge of inappropriate and illegal behavior • Skills to investigate and discuss sexual harassment	• Ability to identify 10 of 10 policy issues • From a list of actions, and lack of actions, be able to identify 100% of those that constitute sexual harassment or a hostile environment • Demonstrated ability to apply investigative and meditation skills	• Pre and Post Test • Skill Practices
3	**APPLICATION/ IMPLEMENTATION** • Administer policy • Conduct meeting with employees • Ensure that workplace is free of sexual harassment	• Appropriate application of policy • Meeting conducted within 30 days • Actions taken to eliminate hostile work environment	• Self Assessment Questionnaire • Complete and submit meeting record • Employee Survey (25% sample)
4	**BUSINESS IMPACT** • Reduce internal complaints • Reduce external complaints • Reduce employee turnover	• Decrease formal internal and external complaints related to sexual harassment and a hostile work environment • Voluntary turnover	• Performance Monitoring • Self Assessment Questionnaire
5	**ROI** Target ROI: 25%	Comments: *Meet with EEO/AA staff to determine how costs of non-compliance will be identified. Seek management and stakeholder guidance and support to develop a standard monetary value for improvement in employee satisfaction.*	

Data Collection Plan

Figure 3.4 shows a completed data collection plan for a program designed to prevent sexual harassment. This initial planning document

Responsibility: _____ **Date:** _____

Data Sources	Timing	Responsibilities
• Participant	• End of session	• Facilitator
• Participant	• Beginning of session • End of session • During session	• Facilitator
• Participant • Work force	• 6 months after program • 1 month after program • 6 months after program	• Program Evaluator • HRIS Staff • Employee Communications
• Human Resources complaint records • Human Resources exit records	• Monthly for 1 year before and after program • 6 months after program	• Program Evaluator

builds on the revised program objectives and defines key issues for data collection. Defining the objectives through the different levels, including ROI, is vital. The measures are also defined if clarification is needed. This column is particularly relevant for application and impact objectives. For example, a productivity measurement is vague, and therefore, defining it is necessary. The same is true for the many types of sexual harassment complaints; definitions prevent confusion.

The data collection methods detailed here correspond to the different levels of objectives using a range of options described in the next chapter. Next, the data sources are identified. In many cases, data are collected from the records in the organization. In other cases, data are collected by program participants. In some cases, the managers of participants provide data.

Timing is important to determine specifically when the data are collected from the different sources for each level. During implementation, data often come directly from the participants involved in the solution implementation. In other situations the follow-up can be determined based on when the program is operational and successful.

Figure 3.5 ROI Analysis Plan

Program: Preventing Sexual Harassment

Data Items (Usually Level 4)	Methods for Isolating the Effects of the Program/ Process	Methods of Converting Data to Monetary Values	Cost Categories
1. Formal Internal Complaints of Sexual Harassment	1. Trend line Analysis 2. Participant Estimation	1. Historical Costs with Estimation from EEO/ AA Staff	• Needs Assessment • Program Development/ Acquisition • Coordination/ Facilitation Time • Program Materials • Food/ Refreshments • Facilities
2. External Complaints of Sexual Harassment	1. Trend line Analysis 2. Participant Estimation	1. Historical Costs with Estimation from EEO/AA Staff	• Participant Salaries and Benefits • Evaluation
3. Employee Turnover	1. Forecasting Using Percent of Turnover Related to Sexual Harassment	1. External Studies within Industry	

Finally, the responsibilities are detailed, outlining specifically who will be involved in the data collection.

ROI Analysis Plan

Figure 3.5 shows the completed ROI analysis plan for the same program. This plan is connected to the previous plan through business impact data. The first column provides the detailed definition of each impact data measure. The next two columns refer to each specific data item.

The second column defines the method for isolating the effects of the HR program on each data item, using one or more of the specific techniques available. The method of converting data to monetary values is listed in the third column, using one or more available techniques.

The next column defines the cost categories for the specific HR program or solution. Using a fully loaded cost profile, all the categories are detailed here. Completing this action during planning is helpful in determining if specific cost categories need to be monitored during the HR program implementation. The next column defines the intangible benefits that may be derived from this program. When listed here, the

Responsibility: _____ Date: _____

Intangible Benefits	Communication Targets for Final Report	Other Influences/ Issues During Application	Comments
• Job Satisfaction • Absenteeism • Stress Reduction • Image of HR • Recruiting	• All Employees (Condensed Info.) • Senior Executives (Summary of Report with Detailed Backup) • All Supervisors and Managers (Brief Report) • All HR/HRD Staff (Full Report)	• Several initiatives to reduce turnover implemented during this time period • Must not duplicate benefits from both internal and external complaints	• Complaints of sexual harassment is a significant issue with management

intangible benefits are only anticipated; they must be measured in some way to determine if they have been influenced by the program. Finally, the other influences or issues that may affect implementation are specified along with any additional comments.

Communication and Implementation Plan

The communication and implementation plan explains how the results will be communicated to various groups. It also lists the specific schedule of events and activities connected to the other planning documents. The targets for communication identify the specific recipients of the information. The plan should include the communication method, content, and timing as well.

This plan defines the rationale for communicating with the group and anticipated payoffs, along with the individual responsibility for monitoring actions from the evaluation. It clearly delivers the information to the right groups to ensure that action occurs, and in almost every impact study, significant actions can be taken.

Resources and Responsibility for Planning

The person responsible for the impact study, usually someone on the HR staff, is generally the one who completes the planning process. In smaller organizations, the HR manager probably has the responsibility for planning. Planning may take an hour for a simple program evaluation or require a full day for more complex programs. Although a day seems to be a substantial investment in time, it may be the best time spent for the entire project.

Consider planning for ROI early in the process. For programs that are already in operation, planning shows what is involved for collecting, analyzing, and reporting data. For a program that is not yet developed, planning can actually define what would occur in an ideal situation and then drive design and implementation as the program focuses on results.

Final Thoughts

This chapter explored a variety of issues involved in the preparations for ROI. It described in detail when and how ROI should be considered as a process improvement tool. The initial analysis — the beginning point of the ROI Methodology — was explored in terms of what must be accomplished or developed to have a successful ROI evaluation. Objectives, too, are critical to evaluation. This chapter covered how and when objectives are developed and offered several examples of objectives. Finally, the role of planning for an ROI project was presented, detailing the key steps in the process. The data collection plan and the ROI analysis plan are the necessary documents that are developed from this process.

Chapter 4.
Data Collection Issues

Data collection before, during, and after program implementation is the first but most time-consuming and disruptive step of the ROI Methodology. This chapter defines the sources of data and outlines some useful and widely accepted approaches for collecting data.

Sources of Data

An array of possible data sources is available to provide input on the success of an HR program. Six general categories are described in the following sections.

Organizational Performance Records

Perhaps the most useful and credible data source for impact and ROI analysis is the records and reports of the organization. Whether individualized or group-based, these records reflect performance in a work unit, department, division, region, or organization overall. Performance records include all types of measures, which are usually abundant throughout the organization. Collecting data from performance records is preferred for impact and ROI evaluation because these records usually reflect business impact data and are relatively easy to obtain. However, inconsistent and inaccurate recordkeeping may complicate the task of locating performance reports.

HR Program Participants

Perhaps the most widely used data source for an ROI analysis is participants who are usually the employees directly involved in the HR program. Participants are frequently asked about reaction, satisfaction, and extent of learning and how skills, knowledge, and procedures have been applied on the job. Sometimes they are asked to explain the impact or consequence of those actions. Participants are a rich source of data for evaluation data at the first four levels.

HR program participants are credible because they are involved in the program and are expected to make it successful. Also, they are often the most knowledgeable of other factors that may influence results. The challenge is to find an effective, efficient, and consistent way to capture data from this group to minimize the time required to provide input. When program participants are represented by a union, seeking the views of the collective bargaining representative is generally a good idea, or at the very least informing the union that participants will be asked for input.

Participants' Managers

Another important source of data is the individuals who directly supervise or manage program participants. The managers often have a vested interest in the evaluation process because they approve, support, or require the participants to become involved in the program in the first place. In many situations, they observe the participants as they attempt to make the HR program successful by applying their new learning.

Because of this, managers are able to report on the successes linked to the program as well as on the difficulties and problems associated with application. Although manager input is usually best for application (level 3) evaluation, it is also sometimes helpful for impact (level 4) evaluation. The challenge is to make data collection convenient and efficient, not disruptive.

Direct Reports

In situations where supervisors and managers are involved in an HR program, their direct reports can be valuable sources of data. Direct reports can relate perceived changes that have occurred since the program was implemented. Input from direct reports is usually appropriate for application (level 3) data. For example, in a 360-degree feedback program, comments from direct reports are the most credible source of data for changes in manager behavior and leadership.

Team/Peer Group

Individuals who serve as team members or who occupy peer-level positions in the organization are another source of data for some programs. In these situations, peer group members provide input on perceived changes since the program was implemented. This source of data is more appropriate when all team members participate in the program, and consequently, when they report on the collective efforts of the group.

Internal/External Groups

In some situations, internal or external groups, such as the HR staff, program facilitators, expert observers, or external consultants, may provide input on the success of program participants as they learn and apply the skills and knowledge covered in the program. Sometimes expert observers or assessors may be used to measure learning. This source may be useful for on-the-job application (level 3).

Timing for Data Collection

The timing of data collection can vary. When a follow-up is planned after the program, the issue is to determine the best time for a post-program evaluation. The challenge is to analyze the nature and scope of the application and implementation and establish the earliest time that a trend or pattern will evolve. This evolution occurs when the application of skills becomes routine or when the implementation is progressing significantly. When to collect data is a judgment call. Collecting data as early as possible is important so that potential adjustments can still be made. However, evaluations must allow for behavior changes so that the implementation can be observed and measured. In programs spanning a considerable length of time for implementation, measures may be taken at three- to six-month intervals. This approach provides successive input on progress and clearly shows the extent of improve-ment, using effective measures at well-timed intervals.

The timing for impact data collection is based on the delay between application and the consequence, the impact. Subject matter experts familiar with this situation will have to examine the content of the application and implementation, and when considering the context of the work environment, estimate how long it would take for the application to have an impact. In some situations such as the use of software, the impact immediately follows the application; in other processes such as the use of leadership skills, the impact may be delayed for some time. For example, consider managers involved in a leadership program to improve talent retention (essentially keeping employees from leaving). These managers must work more closely with the team, show more caring for the group, and help their employees achieve their individual and professional goals. A change of behavior will not necessarily result in an immediate reduction in turnover. There will be some lag between the new behavior and the corresponding increase in retention; however, the impact will usually occur in the time frame of one to six months in most HR projects. The key is to move as quickly as possible to collect the impact data as soon as it occurs.

Convenience and constraints also influence the timing of data collec-tion. Perhaps the participants are conveniently meeting in a follow-up ses-sion or at a special event. These would be excellent opportunities to collect data. Sometimes, constraints are placed on data collection. For example, sponsors or other executives are eager to have the data to make decisions about the program, so data collection is moved to an earlier-than-ideal time.

Responsibilities

Measuring application, implementation, and impact includes the re-sponsibility and work of others. Because these measures occur after the program has been implemented, a question may surface in terms of who is responsible for this follow-up. Many possibilities exist, from the HR staff to the client staff, as well as the possibility of hiring external, in-dependent consultants. Sometimes in a large organization, the local or division HR team may be responsible for collecting the data. This matter should be addressed in the planning stage, so no misunderstandings about the distribution of responsibilities occur. More importantly, those who are responsible must understand the nature and scope of their roles and what is needed to collect data.

Business Performance Monitoring

One of the more consequential methods of data collection is monitoring the organization's records. Performance data are available in every organization to report on outputs, quality, costs, time, job satisfaction, and customer satisfaction. In most organizations, performance data are available to measure the improvement from an HR program. If not, additional recordkeeping systems must be developed for measurement and analysis. At this point, the question of economics arises. Is developing the recordkeeping system necessary to evaluate the HR program economical? If the cost of gathering or developing the data is greater than the expected value for the entire program, then developing the systems to capture the data is meaningless.

Using Current Measures

The recommended approach is to use existing performance measures if available. Performance measures should be reviewed to identify the items related to the proposed program objectives. Sometimes, an organization has several performance measures related to the same objective. For example, a new sales incentive program may be designed to increase sales and the profits from sales, which could be measured in a variety of ways:

- monthly sales
- average amount of sale
- average sales per customer
- number of sales calls
- close ratio
- average cost of sale
- average sales cycle time
- customer return rate
- customer retention rate

Each of these measures, in its own way, measures the efficiency or effectiveness of the sales team. All related measures should be reviewed to determine those most relevant to the HR program.

Occasionally, existing performance measures are integrated with other data, making isolating them from unrelated data difficult. When this situation occurs, all existing related measures should be extracted and re-tabulated to be compared appropriately in the evaluation. At times, conversion factors may be necessary. For example, the average number of new sales orders per month may be a routine performance measure for the sales department. In addition, the sales cost per sales representative is also reported. However, in the evaluation of an HR program, the average cost per new sale is needed. The two existing performance measures are used when converting sales data to average cost per new sale.

Developing New Measures

In some cases, data are unavailable to measure the effectiveness of an HR program. If economically feasible, the HR staff must work with the participating organization to create systems to develop the measures. Possibly the quality division, the finance department, or information technology section will be instrumental in helping determine if new measures are needed, and if so, how they will be collected. Typical questions to consider when creating new measures include the following:

- Which function will develop the measurement system?
- Who will input the data?
- Where will the data be captured?
- When and how will the data be reported?

In one example, a new employee orientation system was implemented across the organization. Several measures were planned, including early turnover (the percentage of employees who left the company during the first six months of employment), which should be influenced by an improved employee orientation program. At the time of the program's inception, this measure was not available, but when the program was implemented, the organization began to collect early turnover figures for comparison.

Questionnaires and Surveys

The most common method of data collection is the questionnaire. Ranging from short reaction forms to detailed follow-up tools, questionnaires are used to obtain subjective information about participants, as well as objective data to measure business results for ROI analysis. With this versatility and popularity, the questionnaire is the preferred method for capturing the first four levels of data (that is, reaction, learning, application, and business impact). Surveys represent a specific type of questionnaire with several applications for measuring HR program success. Surveys are used in situations where only attitudes, beliefs, and opinions are captured. A questionnaire has more flexibility and captures data ranging from attitude to specific improvement statistics. The principles of survey construction and design are similar to questionnaire design. The development of both types of instruments is covered in this section.

Design Issues

In addition to the types of data sought, the types of questions asked distinguish surveys from questionnaires. Surveys can have yes or no responses if absolute agreement or disagreement is required. Alternatively, a response scale, or Likert scale, allows respondents to select from a range of survey response points, for example, "strongly disagree" to "strongly agree." In contrast, a questionnaire may contain any or all of the following types of questions, including Likert-scale-type questions:

- *An open-ended question* has an unlimited answer. The question is followed by an ample blank space for the response.
- *A checklist* provides a list of items, and the respondent is asked to check those that apply in the situation.
- *A two-way question* has alternate responses (yes/no) or other possibilities.
- *A multiple-choice question* has several choices, and the respondent is asked to select the one most applicable.
- *A ranking scale* requires the respondent to rank a list of items.

Questionnaire design is a straightforward, logical process. Nothing is more confusing, frustrating, and potentially embarrassing than a poorly designed questionnaire. Table 4.1 shows the steps that help develop a valid, reliable, and effective instrument.

Table 4.1 Questionnaire Design Steps

1. Determine the specific information needed for each objective, issue, or level.
2. Involve management in the process, when appropriate and feasible.
3. Select the type(s) of questions. Keeping in mind the time needed for analysis.
4. Develop the questions with clarity and simplicity in mind.
5. Check the reading level and match it to the audience.
6. Test the questions with a small group of individuals knowledgeable about the target audience.
7. Keep responses anonymous or confidential.
8. Design for ease of tabulation and analysis.
9. Develop the completed questionnaire and prepare a data summary.
10. Use an existing user-friendly software tool.

Questionnaire Content

The areas of feedback used on reaction questionnaires depend on the purpose of the evaluation. Some forms are simple, whereas others are detailed and require a considerable amount of time to complete. When a comprehensive evaluation is planned, where impact and ROI are being measured, the reaction questionnaire can be simple, asking only questions that provide pertinent information regarding participant perception. However, when a reaction questionnaire is the only means of gathering evaluation data, then a more comprehensive list of questions is necessary.

Table 4.2 presents a list of the most common types of feedback solicited at this level. Objective questions covering each of the areas in the table can help ensure thorough feedback from participants. This feedback can be useful in making adjustments in a program, assisting in predicting performance after the program, or both.

In most medium to large organizations with significant HR activity, reaction instruments are usually automated for computerized scanning and reporting. Some organizations use direct input into a website to develop not only detailed reports but also databases, allowing feedback data to be compared to other programs.

Table 4.2 Typical Reaction/Satisfaction Questions

- Appropriateness: Was the program appropriate for the target group?
- Implementation: Was the method of implementation appropriate for the objectives?
- Coordinator: Was the program coordinator/administrator effective?
- Motivation: Were you motivated to implement this program?
- Relevance: Was the program relevant to your needs? The organization's needs?
- Importance: How important is this program to your success?
- Logistics: Were the scheduling and organizing efficient?
- Potential barriers: What potential barriers exist for the implementation of the program?
- Planned implementation: Will you implement this program? How?
- Recommendations for others: What is the appropriate target group for this program?
- Overall evaluation: What is your overall rating of this program?

Collecting learning data using a questionnaire is also common. Most types of tests, whether formal or informal, are modeled on questionnaires. However, several questions to measure learning can be developed to use with the reaction questionnaire. For example, in the implementation of a new rewards system, knowing if the employees involved in the system (the participants) fully understand the rules, procedures, and policies of the new system is imperative. Possible areas to explore on a reaction questionnaire, all aimed at measuring learning, are listed below:

- knowledge gain
- skill enhancement
- ability
- capability
- contacts
- competence
- awareness

Questions to gauge learning are developed using a format similar to the reaction part of the questionnaire. They measure the extent to which learning has taken place, usually based on confidence and perception.

Questionnaires are also commonly used to collect post-program application and impact data. Table 4.3 presents a list of questionnaire content possibilities for capturing these follow-up data. Reaction and learning data may also be captured in a follow-up questionnaire to compare with similar data gathered immediately after the introduction of the

HR program. Most follow-up issues, however, involve application and implementation (level 3) and business impact (level 4).

Table 4.3. Typical Content Areas for Post-Program Questionnaires

- Progress with objectives
- Use of program materials, guides, and technology
- Application of knowledge/skills
- Frequency of use
- Success with use
- Change in work or work habits
- Improvements/accomplishments
- Monetary impact of improvements
- Improvements linked to the program
- Confidence level of data supplied
- Perceived value of the investment
- Linkage with output measures
- Barriers to implementation
- Enablers to implementation
- Management support for implementation
- Other benefits
- Other possible solutions
- Target audience recommendations
- Suggestions for improvement

Tests

Testing is important for measuring learning in HR program evaluations. Pre- and post-program comparisons using tests are common. An improvement in test scores shows the change in skill, knowledge, or attitude attributed to the program. You can use performance testing, simulations, role plays, and business games to measure the extent of knowledge or skill increase related to an HR program. Base the design and development of self-assessment questionnaires and surveys on principles similar to those presented in the previous section on questionnaires.

Interviews

Another helpful data collection method is the interview, although it is not used in evaluation as frequently as questionnaires. The HR staff, the participant's immediate manager, or a third party can conduct interviews. Interviews can secure data not available in performance records or data difficult to obtain through written responses or observations. Also, interviews can uncover success stories that can be useful in communicating evaluation results. Participants may be reluctant to describe their results in a questionnaire, although they may be willing to volunteer the information to a skillful interviewer who uses probing techniques. The interview process can reveal reaction, learning, and impact data, but it is primarily used with application data. A major disadvantage of the interview is that it is time-consuming and requires interviewer preparation to ensure that the process is consistent.

Interviews are categorized into two basic types: structured and unstructured. A structured interview is much like a questionnaire. The interviewer asks specific questions that allow the participant little room to deviate from the menu of expected responses. The structured interview offers several advantages over the questionnaire. For example, an interview can ensure that the questionnaire is completed and that the interviewer understands the responses supplied by the participant. The unstructured interview has built-in flexibility to allow the interviewer to probe for additional information. This type of interview uses a few general questions, which can lead to more detailed information as important data are uncovered. The interviewer must be skilled in the probing process. The design issues and steps for interviews are similar to those of the questionnaire. Preparing the interviewer, trying out the interview, providing clear instructions to the participant, and following a plan are all crucial.

Focus Groups

An extension of the interview, focus groups are particularly helpful when in-depth feedback is needed for evaluation application. The focus group involves a small group discussion conducted by an experienced facilitator and is designed to solicit qualitative judgments on a planned topic or issue. Group members are all required to provide their input, as individual input builds on group input.

When compared to questionnaires, surveys, tests, or interviews, the focus group strategy has several advantages. The basic premise of using focus groups is that when quality judgments are subjective, several individual judgments are better than one. The group process, whereby participants stimulate ideas in others, is an effective method for generating qualitative data. Focus groups are inexpensive and can be quickly planned and conducted. They should be small (8 to 12 individuals) and should represent a sample of the target population. Facilitators must have the appropriate expertise. The flexibility of this data collection method makes it possible to explore an HR program's unexpected outcomes or applications.

Focus groups are particularly helpful when qualitative information is needed about the success of an HR program. For example, focus groups can be used in the following ways:

- to gauge the overall effectiveness of program application
- to identify the barriers and enablers to a successful implementation
- to isolate the impact of the HR program from other influences

Essentially, focus groups are appropriate when evaluation information is needed but cannot be collected adequately with questionnaires, interviews, or quantitative methods. The focus group is a convenient way to determine the strengths and weaknesses of HR programs. For a complete evaluation, focus group information should be combined with data from other instruments.

Observations

Another potentially useful data collection method is observation. The observer may be a member of the HR staff, the participant's immediate manager, a member of a peer group, or an external party. The most common observer, and probably the most practical, is a member of the HR staff.

Observation is often misused in or misapplied to evaluation situations, leaving some organizations to abandon the process. Observations should be systematic, minimizing the observer's influence. Observers should be carefully selected, fully prepared, and knowledgeable about how to interpret and report what they observe.

This method is useful for collecting data on job design issues, compensation, reward systems, compliance, employee training, and performance evaluation. For example, observation in the form of mystery shopper is commonplace in retail and service-focused organizations. A mystery shopper observes a customer service employee, for example, to ensure that certain behaviors, processes, and procedures are in place. In another example, observation is used to provide 360-degree feedback for leadership development programs, as the behavior changes are solicited from the direct reports, colleagues, internal customers, immediate managers, and perhaps with self-input. The feedback is taken before a leadership development program and a few weeks or months after the program to observe changes.

For observation to work, it must be either invisible or unnoticeable. "Invisible" means that the person under observation is never aware that the observation is taking place, as in the case of a mystery shopper. "Unnoticeable" means that although the person under observation may know that the observation is taking place, he or she does not notice it because it occurs over a longer period time, as in the case of a 360-degree feedback process.

Five methods of observation can be used, depending on the circumstances surrounding the type of information needed. They are listed in Table 4.4.

Table 4.4 Observation Methods for Data Collection

Observation Method	Description
Behavior Checklist and Coded Behavior Forms	A behavior checklist is used for recording the presence, absence, frequency, or duration of a participant's behavior as it occurs. Codes are used to abbreviate specific behaviors and steps.
Delayed Report Method	The observer does not use any forms or written materials during the observation and subsequently attempts to reconstruct what has been observed during the observation period.
Video Recording	A video camera records behavior in every detail.
Audio Monitoring	Conversations of participants, who are using specific skills as part of the HR program, are monitored.
Computer Monitoring	The computer "observes" participants as they perform job tasks.

The Use of Action Plans

For many projects and programs, business data are readily available. However, at times data will not be easily accessible to the program evaluator. Sometimes, data are maintained at the individual, work unit, or department level and may not be known to anyone outside that area.

Tracking down those data sets may be too expensive and time-consuming. In such cases, other data collection methods may be used to capture data sets and to make them available for the evaluator. Action plans are sometimes used to evaluate leadership development, talent management, and process improvement.

Action plans can capture application and implementation data and can also be a useful tool for gathering business impact data. For business impact data, the action plan is more focused and credible than a questionnaire. The basic design principles involved in developing and administering action plans are the same for business impact data and for application and implementation data. The following steps are recommended when an action plan is developed and implemented to capture business impact data and to convert the data to monetary values.

Set Goals and Targets

As shown in Figure 4.1, an action plan can be developed with a direct focus on business impact data. The plan presented in this figure requires participants to develop an overall objective for the plan, which is usually the primary objective of the program. In some cases, a program may have more than one objective, which requires additional action plans. In addition to the objective, the improvement measure and the current levels of performance are identified. This information requires that the participant anticipate the application of skills and set goals for specific performances that can be realized.

The action plan is completed during the program, often with input and assistance from a facilitator. The facilitator actually approves the plan, indicating that it meets the requirements of being **S**pecific, **M**otivating, **A**chievable, **R**ealistic, and **T**ime-based (SMART). The plan can be developed in a one- to two-hour time frame and often begins with action steps related to the program. These action steps are level 3 activities that detail application and implementation. All these steps build support for, and are linked to, business impact measures.

Figure 4.1 Sample Program Action Plan	
Name_____	
Facilitator Signature_____ Follow-up Date _____	
Objective _____ Evaluation Period _____ to _____	
Improvement Measure_____ Current Performance _____ Target Performance _____	
Action Steps	**Analysis**
1.	A. What is the unit of measure?
2.	B. What is the value (cost) of one unit? $ _____
3.	C. How did you arrive at this value?
4.	D. How much did the measure change during the evaluation period? (monthly value) _____
5.	E. List the other factors that have influenced this change.
6.	F. What percent of this change was actually caused by this program? _____ %
7.	G. What level of confidence do you place on the above information? (100% = Certainty and 0% = No Confidence) _____ %
Intangible Benefits:	
Comments:	

Define the Unit of Measure

The next step is to define the actual unit of measure. In some cases, more than one measure may be used and will subsequently be contained in additional action plans. The unit of measure is necessary to break the process into the simplest steps so that its ultimate value can be determined. The unit may be output data, such as an additional unit manufactured or package delivered, or it may be sales and marketing data, such as additional sales revenue or a 1 percent increase in market share. In terms of quality, the unit can be one reject, one error, or one defect. Time-based units are usually measured in minutes, hours, days, or weeks. Other units are specific to their particular type of data, such as one grievance, one complaint, or one absence. The point is to break down impact data into the simplest terms possible.

Place a Monetary Value on Each Improvement

During the program, participants are asked to locate, calculate, or estimate the monetary value for each improvement outlined in their plans. The unit value is determined using a variety of methods such as standard values, expert input, external databases, or estimates.

The process used in arriving at the value is described in the instructions for the action plan. When the actual improvement occurs, participants will use these values to capture the annual monetary benefits of the plan.

In the worst-case scenario, participants are asked to calculate the value. When participant estimates are necessary, participants must show the basis of their calculations, and space for this information should be provided. The preferred actions are using standard values or having participants contact an expert.

Implement the Action Plan

Participants implement the action plan after the program is conducted. The participants follow action plan steps, and the subsequent business impact results are achieved.

Provide Specific Improvements

At the end of the specified follow-up period — usually three months, six months, nine months, or one year — the participants indicate the improvements made, usually expressed as a daily, weekly, or monthly amount. This reflects the actual amount of change that has been observed, measured, or recorded. Participants must understand the need for accuracy as data are recorded. In most cases, only the changes are recorded, since those amounts are needed to calculate the monetary values of the program. In other cases, before and after data may be recorded, allowing the evaluator to calculate the differences.

Isolate the Effects of the Program

Although the action plan is initiated because of the program, the actual improvements reported on the action plan may be influenced by other factors. Therefore, the program should not be given full credit for all the improvement. For example, an action plan to implement leadership skills could only be given partial credit for a business improvement because other variables may have influenced the impact measures. While several ways are available to isolate the effects of a program, participant estimation is usually most appropriate in the action planning process. Participants are asked to estimate the percentage of the improvement directly related to the program. This question can be asked on the action plan form or in a follow-up questionnaire.

Sometimes, preceding this question with a request to identify all the other factors that may have influenced the results is beneficial. This step allows the participants to think through the relationships before allocating a portion to this program.

Provide a Confidence Level for Estimates

The process to isolate the amount of the improvement directly related to the program is not precise. Participants are asked to indicate their level of confidence in their estimates. Using a scale of 0 to 100 percent — where 0 percent means no confidence and 100 percent means the estimates represent absolute certainty — participants have a way to express their uncertainty with the estimates.

Collect Action Plans at Specified Time Intervals

An excellent response rate is essential, so several steps may be necessary to ensure that the action plans are completed and returned. Usually, participants will see the importance of the process and will develop their plans during the program. Some organizations use follow-up reminders by mail or e-mail. Others call participants to check progress. Still others offer assistance in developing the final plan. These steps may require additional resources, which must be weighed against the importance of having more precise data. Specific ways to improve response rates are discussed later in this chapter.

Summarize the Data and Calculate the ROI

If developed properly, each action plan should have annualized monetary values associated with improvements. Also, each individual should have indicated the percentage of the improvement directly related to the program. Finally, participants should have provided a confidence percentage to reflect their uncertainty with the estimates and the subjective nature of some of the data that they provided.

Because this process involves estimates, it may not appear accurate. Several adjustments during the analysis make the process credible and more accurate. These adjustments reflect guiding principles of the ROI Methodology. The following adjustments are made:

Step 1

For those participants who do not provide data, the assumption is that they had no improvement to report. This approach is very conservative.

Step 2

Each value is checked for realism, usability, and feasibility. Extreme values are discarded and omitted from the analysis.

Step 3

Because the improvement is annualized, the assumption is that the program had no improvement after the first year (for short-term programs). Some add value in years two and three. More on this issue can be found in Chapter 6.

Step 4

The improvement from Step 3 is then adjusted using the confidence level, multiplying it by the confidence percentage. The confidence level is actually an error percentage suggested by the participants. For example, a participant indicating 80 percent confidence with the process provides a 20 percent error possibility. In a $10,000 estimate with an 80 percent confidence factor, the participant suggests that the value can be in the range of $8,000 to $12,000 (20 percent less to 20 percent more). To be conservative, the lower number is used. Then the confidence factor is multiplied by the amount of improvement.

Step 5

The new values are adjusted by the percentage of the improvement related directly to the program using multiplication. This calculation isolates the effects of the program. The monetary values determined in these five steps are totaled to arrive at the final program benefit. Since these values are already annualized, the total of these benefits becomes the annual benefits for the program. This value is placed in the numerator of the ROI formula to calculate the ROI.

Advantages of Action Plans

The action-planning process has several inherent advantages as a useful way to collect business impact data. Most of the data are taken directly from participants and often have the credibility needed for the analysis. Also, much of the responsibility for the analysis and evaluation is shifted to the participants as they address three of the most critical parts of the process. In effect, they collect data to show improvements, isolate the effects of the program, and convert data to monetary values. This method enables the evaluation to be conducted with limited resources and shifts much of the responsibility to those who apply and implement the program.

Improving the Response Rate for Data Collection

One of the greatest challenges in data collection is achieving an acceptable response rate or a certain level of participation. Requiring too much information may result in a suboptimal response rate. The challenge, therefore, is to tackle data collection design and administration so as to achieve maximum response rate. This issue is critical when the primary data collection method hinges on participant input obtained through questionnaires, surveys, interviews, and focus groups.

The following actions may help boost response rates:

- *Provide advance communication.* If appropriate and feasible, participants should receive advance communications about the requirement to provide data. This step minimizes some of the resistance to the process, provides an opportunity to explain in more detail the circumstances surrounding the evaluation, and positions the follow-up evaluation as an integral part of the HR program, not just an add-on activity.

- *Communicate the purpose.* Participants should understand the reason for the data, and they should know who or what initiated a specific evaluation. Participants should know if the evaluation is part of a systematic process or if it is a special request for this program.

- *Explain who will see the data.* Participants should know who will see the data and the results of the data collection. If the input is anonymous, the steps that will be taken to ensure anonymity should be communicated clearly to participants. Participants should know if senior executives will see the combined results of the study.

- *Describe the data integration process.* Participants should understand how the results will be combined with other data, if applicable. Participant input may be only one of the data collection methods used. Participants should know how the data are weighted and integrated in the final report.

- *Keep the data collection as simple as possible.* Although a simple instrument does not always provide the full scope of data necessary for an

ROI analysis, a simplified approach should always be a goal. When questions are developed and the total scope of data collection is finalized, every effort should be made to keep it as simple and brief as possible. Only ask questions if you intend to do something with the results.

- *Simplify the response process.* Make it easy for the participants to respond. If appropriate, include a self-addressed, postage-paid envelope for mailed surveys and questionnaires. E-mail or Internet-based questionnaires are preferable in some settings, especially if the questionnaire is being administered at sites in different countries.
- *Use local manager support.* Management involvement at the local level is critical to response rate success. Managers can help with data collection, make reference to data collection in staff meetings, follow up to see if input is provided, and show support for the process.
- *Let the participants know their input is valued.* If appropriate, participants should know that they are part of a carefully selected sample and that their input will be used to make decisions regarding a much larger target audience. This action often appeals to a sense of responsibility for participants to provide usable, accurate data for the instrument.
- *Consider incentives.* At least three types of incentives can be used to boost response rates:
  - » **Offer an incentive in exchange for input**. For example, if participants return questionnaires or participate in interviews or focus groups, they will receive a small gift, such as a mouse pad or coffee mug. If identity is an issue, a neutral third party can provide the incentive.
  - » **An incentive can be provided to make participants feel guilty if they do not respond**. Examples are coupons attached to the questionnaire or a pen enclosed in the envelope. Participants are asked to "take the coupon, buy a beverage, and fill out the questionnaire" or to "please use this pen to complete the questionnaire."
  - » **Provide a reward for early responses.** This approach stems from the assumption that fast completion rates improve response rates. If an individual puts off completing the instrument, the odds of

completing it diminish considerably. Those who complete and submit their responses first may receive a more expensive gift, or they may be part of a drawing for an incentive. For example, in one study involving 75 participants, the first 25 returned instruments were placed in a drawing for a $500 credit card gift certificate. The next 25 were added to the first 25 for another drawing. After the first 50, there was no incentive. The longer a participant waited, the lower the odds for winning.

- *Have an executive sign the introductory letter.* Participants are always interested in who sent the letter with the request. For maximum effectiveness, a senior executive who is responsible for a major area where the participants work should sign the letter. Employees may be more willing to respond to a senior executive.

- *Use follow-up reminders.* A follow-up reminder should be sent a week after the first request and another reminder one week later. Depending on the instrument and the situation, these times could be adjusted. In some situations, a third follow-up message is recommended. Sometimes the follow-up should be sent via different media. For example, the questionnaire can be sent through regular mail, whereas the first follow-up reminder is from the immediate manager and a second follow-up reminder is sent by e-mail.

- *Send a copy of the results to the participants.* Even in abbreviated form, participants should see the results of the study. More important, participants should understand that they will receive a copy of the study when they are asked to provide the data. This promise often increases the response rate because some individuals want to see the results of others along with their input.

- *Make participants know that action will be taken as a result of their responses.* When participants provide data, they want some assurance that their information will be used in a productive manner. This assurance can be given by providing information about when actions will be taken as a result of their responses. Providing a particular date shows the significance of the data collection, and participants have a sense of knowing that they will make a difference.

- *Review the questions and issues during implementation.* Seeing an advance copy of the actual data collection plan helps participants understand the process. Ideally, the instrument should be distributed and reviewed during the session. Each question should be briefly discussed and any issues or concerns about the questions clarified. Ideally, a commitment to provide data is secured from the participant not only to help the response rate but also to improve the quality and quantity of data.

- *Consider a captive audience.* The best way to have an extremely high response rate is to use a captive audience. In a follow-up session, a routine meeting, or a session designed to collect data, participants meet and provide input, usually during the first few minutes of the meeting. Sometimes a routine meeting (such as a sales, technology, or management meeting) can serve as a favorable setting to collect the data.

- *Communicate the timing of data flow.* Participants should be provided with specific deadlines for providing the data. They also need to know when they will receive results. The best approach is to determine the last date the instruments will be accepted, the date the analysis will be complete, the date participants will receive the results of the study, and the date the sponsor will receive the results. A specific time line builds respect for the entire process.

- *Select appropriate media.* The medium for data collection (whether paper-based, face-to-face, Internet-based, or e-mail) should match the culture of the group and not necessarily be selected for the convenience of the evaluator. Sometimes an optional response medium is allowed. The key is to make the medium fit the audience.

- *Consider collecting anonymous input.* For surveys and questionnaires, anonymous data is often more objective and sometimes more freely given. If participants believe that their input is anonymous, they are more likely to be constructive and candid in their feedback, and their response rates will generally be higher.

- *Keep data confidential.* Confidentiality is an important part of the process. A confidentiality statement should be included, indicating that participants' names will not be revealed to anyone other than the data collectors and those involved in analyzing the data. In some cases, indicating specifically who will actually see the raw data may be appropriate. Detail the specific steps to be taken to respondents to ensure confidentiality, such as that individual results will not be released and that data will be combined for reporting so that no one person's responses can be singled out.

- *Conduct pilot-testing.* Consider using a pilot test on a sample of the target audience. This method is one of the best ways to ensure that data collection is designed properly and that the questions flow logically. Pilot-testing the data collection process can be accomplished quickly and effectively with a small sample size. The findings of a pilot test can be very revealing.

- *Explain how long the data collection will take.* Although a seemingly trivial issue, participants need to have a realistic understanding of how long providing the data will take them. There is nothing more frustrating to a participant than discovering that an instrument takes much longer to complete than what was estimated. The pilot test should be able to indicate how much time should be allocated for the response.

- *Personalize the process if possible.* Participants generally respond to personal messages and requests. If possible, the letter accompanying the data collection instrument should be personalized. Also, a personal phone call is a helpful follow-up reminder. The personal touch brings appropriate sincerity and responsibility to the process.

- *Provide an update.* In some cases providing an update on current response rate and the progress on the entire project may be appropriate. Understanding how others are doing is helpful for individuals, and sometimes this communication creates a subtle pressure and reminder to submit data.

Collectively, these items help boost response rates on follow-up data. Using all of these strategies can yield a 60 percent to 80 percent response rate for surveys and questionnaires and 90 percent to 100 percent response rate for interviews and focus groups, even with lengthy processes that may take 45 to 60 minutes to complete.

Selecting an Appropriate Method

This chapter presented a variety of methods to capture post-program data for an impact analysis. Several issues should be considered when deciding which method is appropriate for a given situation.

Type of Data

The first consideration when selecting the method is the type of data to be collected. Some methods are more appropriate for impact, but others are better for application. Still others are more useful for reaction or learning evaluation.

Table 4.5 shows the most appropriate type of data for a specific method. Questionnaires and surveys are suited for all levels. Tests are useful for level 2 (learning). Questionnaires and surveys are best for level 1 (reaction); although interviews and focus groups can be used for level 1, they often are too costly. Performance monitoring, action plans, and questionnaires can easily capture level 4 (business impact) data.

Table 4.5. Methods of Collecting Data				
	Level 1	Level 2	Level 3	Level 4
Performance Monitoring				✓
Questionnaires/Surveys	✓	✓	✓	✓
Tests		✓		
Interviews			✓	
Focus Groups			✓	
Observations		✓	✓	
Action Plans			✓	✓

Participants' Time for Data Input

Another factor when selecting the data collection method is the amount of time that participants need to provide their input for data collection. Time requirements should be minimized, and the method should be positioned so that it is a value-added activity (that is, the participants perceive the activity as valuable, so they will not resist). This requirement often means that sampling is used to keep the total participant time to a reasonable amount. Some methods, such as business performance monitoring, require no participant time, whereas others, such as focus groups and interviews, require a significant investment in time.

Management's Time for Data Input

The time that a participant's immediate manager must allocate to data collection is another relevant issue when selecting a data collection method. Always strive to keep the managers' time requirements to a minimum. Some methods, such as focus groups, may require involvement from the manager prior to and after the program. Other methods, such as performance monitoring, may not require any manager time.

Cost of the Method

Cost is always a consideration when selecting a method. Some data collection methods are more expensive than others. For example, interviews and observations are expensive. Questionnaires and performance monitoring are usually inexpensive.

Disruption of Normal Work Activities

Another important issue is the amount of disruption the data collection will generate. Routine work processes should be disrupted as little as possible. Some data collection techniques, such as performance monitoring, require little time or distraction from normal activities. Questionnaires generally do not disrupt the work environment and can often be completed in only a few minutes or even after normal work hours. On the other extreme, techniques such as observations and interviews may be too disruptive for the work unit.

Accuracy of Method

Accuracy is a factor to weigh when selecting a data collection method. "Accuracy" refers to the instrument's ability to correctly capture the data desired, with minimum error. Some data collection methods are more accurate than others. For example, performance monitoring usually is highly accurate, whereas a questionnaire is less so. If you need data regarding on-the-job behavior, unobtrusive observation is clearly one of the most accurate processes.

Utility of an Additional Method

Because many different methods for collecting data are available, using multiple data collection methods is tempting but adds time and cost to the evaluation while adding little value. "Utility" refers to the added value of using an additional data collection method. When more than one method is used, the question of utility should always be addressed. Does the value obtained from the additional data warrant the extra time and expense of the method? If the answer is no, the additional method should not be implemented.

Cultural Bias for Data Collection Method

The culture or philosophy of the organization can dictate which data collection methods are used. For example, some organizations are accustomed to using questionnaires and prefer to use them in their culture. Other organizations do not use observation because their culture does not support the potential invasion of privacy associated with it.

Final Thoughts

This chapter has provided an overview of data collection methods that can be used in ROI analysis. Organizations can select from many methods according to their budget or situation. Performance data monitoring and follow-up questionnaires are used to collect data for impact analyses. Other methods can help you develop a complete profile of success of the HR program and its subsequent business impact.

Chapter 5.
Isolating the
Effects of the Program

In almost every program, multiple influences drive the business measures. With multiple influences, measuring the effect of each influence is imperative, at least to the extent that it is attributed to the program. Without this isolation, program success will be in question. The results will be inappropriate and overstated if the suggestion is made that all the change in the business impact measure is attributed to the HR program. When this issue is ignored, the impact study is considered invalid and inconclusive. Evaluators, therefore, face tremendous pressure to show the actual value of their programs when compared to other factors.

To emphasize the significance of isolation of the program effects, a few facts need to be explored.

The Importance of This Issue

1. *Other factors are always present.* In almost every situation, multiple factors create business results. The world does not stand still while HR programs are implemented. Many other functions, processes, or projects attempt to improve the same metrics that are influenced by the HR program in question. A situation where no other factors enter into the process would be almost impossible in dynamic work systems.

2. *Proof of a business linkage requires isolation of the program effects.* Without taking steps to show the contribution, the business measure is the only evidence that the program could have made a difference.

Impact measures have improved, although other factors may have influenced the data. The proof that the program has made a difference on the business comes from this step in the analysis — isolating the effects of the program.

3. *Other factors and influences have protective owners.* The owners of other functions and programs influencing results are convinced that their processes made the difference. Some owners of other factors probably believe that the results are entirely due to their efforts. They present a compelling case to management, stressing their achievements.

4. *Achieving isolation requires discipline.* The challenge of isolating the effects of the program on impact data is critical and can be done, although this step is not always easy for very complex programs, especially when strong-willed owners of other processes are involved. Determination is needed to address this situation every time an impact study is conducted. Fortunately, a variety of approaches are available.

5. *Without isolation, the study is not valid.* Without addressing this issue, a study is not valid because other factors are almost always in the mix, and the direct connection to human resources is often not apparent. These three actions should never occur in a study:

   » Taking all the credit for the improvement without addressing the issue

   » Doing nothing, attempting to ignore the issue altogether

   » Suggesting that this step is impossible

Any of these will decrease the necessity of the results and lower the credibility of the study.

The cause-and-effect relationship between an HR program and performance can be confusing and difficult to prove, but it can be shown with an acceptable degree of accuracy. The challenge is to develop one or more specific techniques to isolate the effects of the process, usually as part of an evaluation plan conducted before the program begins. Upfront attention ensures that appropriate techniques will be met with minimal costs and time commitments.

Chain of Impact: The Initial Evidence

Before presenting the techniques for isolating human resources' impact, examining the chain of impact implied in the various levels of evaluation is helpful. As illustrated in Figure 5.1, the chain of impact must be in place for the HR program to drive business results.

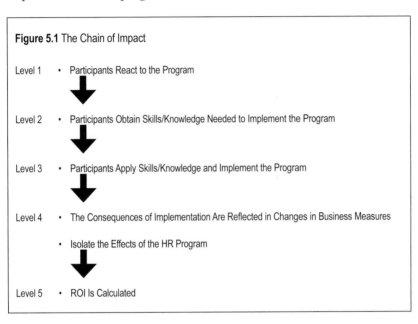

Figure 5.1 The Chain of Impact

Level 1 • Participants React to the Program

Level 2 • Participants Obtain Skills/Knowledge Needed to Implement the Program

Level 3 • Participants Apply Skills/Knowledge and Implement the Program

Level 4 • The Consequences of Implementation Are Reflected in Changes in Business Measures

         • Isolate the Effects of the HR Program

Level 5 • ROI Is Calculated

Measurable business impact achieved through an HR program should be derived from the application of skills or knowledge over a specified period of time after a program has been conducted. Successful application of the HR program should stem from the participants' learning of new skills or acquiring new knowledge in the HR program, so they know what, how, and why to do something differently.

Without the preliminary evidence of the chain of impact, isolating the effects of the HR program is difficult. Without learning or application, HR leaders cannot conclude that the HR program caused any business impact improvements. Furthermore, if the program is not viewed as relevant or important, participants are unlikely to make an effort to learn and apply the knowledge or skills.

Developing this chain of impact requires data collection at four levels for an ROI calculation. If you collect data on business results, you should also collect data for the other levels of evaluation to ensure that the HR program has produced the business results.

Identifying Other Factors: A First Step

As a first step in isolating human resources' impact on business performance, all key factors that may have contributed to the performance improvement should be identified. This step communicates to interested parties that other factors have probably influenced the results, underscoring that the program is not the sole source of improvement. Consequently, the credit for improvement is shared with several possible variables and sources — an approach that is likely to gain the respect of the client. Several potential sources are available to identify influencing factors:

- If the HR program is implemented at the request of a sponsor, the sponsor may be able to identify other initiatives or factors that may influence the impact measure.

- Program participants are usually aware of other influences that may have caused performance improvement. After all, the impact of their collective efforts are being monitored and measured. In many situations, they have witnessed previous movements in the performance measures and can pinpoint reasons for changes.

- The program implementation team is another source for identifying variables that impact results. Although the needs analysis will sometimes uncover these influencing factors, designers, developers, and facilitators may be able to identify the other factors as they implement the program.

- In some situations, the immediate managers of the participants may be able to identify variables that influence the business impact measure. This identification is particularly useful when participants are nonexempt employees (operatives) who may not be fully aware of the other factors that can influence performance.

- Subject-matter experts involved in the program content may identify other factors. They often analyze the need for the program, help design a specific solution, or provide specifications for implementation. They are knowledgeable about these issues, and their expertise may be helpful in identifying the other factors that could affect the program.

- Other process owners may be able to provide input. For most situations, other processes are adding value. Technology, restructuring, job design, new processes, quality initiatives, marketing, reengineering, transformation, or change management are all likely processes inside an organization. The owners of these processes will know whether their processes are in place or have been implemented during this same time period.

- Finally, in the area where the program is implemented, middle and top management may be able to identify other influences. Perhaps they have monitored, examined, and analyzed the variables previously. The authority of these individuals often increases the data's credibility.

Taking time to focus attention on factors and variables that may have influenced performance brings additional accuracy and credibility to the process. This step moves the study beyond presenting results with no mention of other influences — a situation that often destroys credibility. It also provides a foundation for some of the techniques described in this book by identifying the variables that must be isolated to show the effects of a program.

Use of Control Groups

The most accurate approach for isolating the impact of a program is the use of control groups in an experimental design. This approach involves the comparison of an experimental group involved in the program with a control group that is not. The composition of both groups should be as identical as possible, and if feasible participants for each group should be selected randomly. When the desired composition and selection are achieved and when both groups are subjected to the same environmental influences, the difference in the performance of the two groups can be attributed to the program.

As illustrated in Figure 5.2, the control group and experimental group do not necessarily have preprogram measurements. Measurements can be taken during and after the program is implemented, and the difference in the performance of the two groups shows the amount of improvement that is directly related to the HR program.

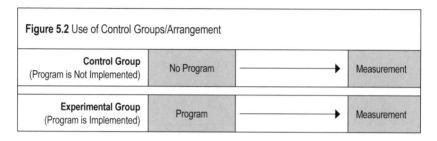

Figure 5.2 Use of Control Groups/Arrangement

Control Group (Program is Not Implemented)	No Program	⟶	Measurement
Experimental Group (Program is Implemented)	Program	⟶	Measurement

Control group arrangements appear in many settings, including both private and public sectors. A turnover reduction program for communication specialists in a government agency used both a control group and an experimental group. The experimental group included individuals in a special program designed to allow participants to achieve a master's degree in information science on agency time and at agency expense. The control group was carefully selected to match up with the experimental group in terms of job title, tenure with the agency, and the college degree obtained. The control/experimental group differences were dramatic, showing the impact of the retention program.

One caution with the use of control groups is that they may create an image of a laboratory setting, which can make executives and administrators uncomfortable. To avoid this stigma, some organizations conduct a pilot program using participants as the experimental group. A similarly matched, nonparticipating comparison group is selected but does not receive any communication about the program. The terms "pilot program" and "comparison group" are a little less threatening than "experimental group" and "control group."

The control group process does have some inherent issues that may make applying them in practice difficult. The most crucial issue is the selection of the groups. From a theoretical perspective, having *identical* control and experimental groups is next to impossible. Dozens of factors can affect performance, some of them individual, others contextual. To address this problem on a practical basis, selecting four to six factors that will have the greatest influence on performance is best, using the concept of the 80/20 rule, or the Pareto principle. With the 80/20 rule, the factors that may account for 80 percent of the difference (the most important factors) are used.

For example, in an HR program for the sales team at the computer company Dell, a control group arrangement was used. The program involved regional sales managers, account managers, account executives, account representatives, and sales representatives. The output measures were profit-margin quota attainment, total revenue attainment, profit margin, and various sales volumes. An experimental group was involved in the program and was carefully matched with a control group that was not involved. The equivalent number of participants for the control group was selected at random using the company database. To ensure that the control group and the program group were equivalent, selections were made on three criteria: job positions, job levels, and experience.

Control groups are inappropriate in some situations. Withholding the program from one group while it is implemented in another may not be suitable, especially when critical solutions are needed immediately. This barrier often keeps many control groups from being implemented. Management is not willing to withhold a solution in one area to see how it works in another. For example, a sexual harassment prevention program was implemented at a hospital chain to correct a problem with excessive complaints. The problem was too serious to withhold it from the majority of hospitals to see if it would work.

In practice, many opportunities arise for the possibility of a natural control group arrangement. For example, if involving everyone in the organization in an HR solution will take several months, there may be enough time for a parallel comparison between the initial group and the last group. In these cases, the groups should be matched as closely as possible so that the first group is similar to the last. These naturally occurring control groups often exist in major enterprise-wide program implementations. The challenge is to address this issue early enough to influence the implementation schedule so that similar groups can be used in the comparison.

Contamination may develop when participants involved in the program group (experimental group) communicate with others who are in the control group. Sometimes, the reverse situation occurs when members of the control group model the behavior of those in the experimental group. In either case, the experiment becomes contaminated as the influence of the experimental HR program is passed to the control group. Contamination can be minimized by ensuring that the two groups are at different locations, have different shifts, or are on different floors in the same building. When separation is not possible, explain to both groups that one group will be involved in the program now and that the other will be involved at a later date. Also, appealing to the sense of responsibility of program participants and asking them not to share the information with others may be helpful.

Time can be an issue. The longer a control group and experimental group comparison operates, the greater the likelihood of factors influencing the impact measures, contaminating the results. However, enough time must be allotted so that a clear pattern can emerge between the two groups. Therefore, the timing for control group comparisons must strike a delicate balance of waiting long enough for their performance differences to show but not so long that the results become seriously contaminated.

Another issue can develop when the different groups function under different environmental influences. Although they may begin the experiment under the same influences, the influences of one group may shift with time. This situation usually occurs when groups are at different locations. Sometimes, the selection of the groups can help with this issue. Another tactic is to use more groups than necessary and discard those with environmental differences.

Because the use of control groups is an effective approach for isolating the impact, it should be considered as a technique when a major ROI impact study is planned. In these situations, isolating the program impact with a high level of accuracy is important, and the primary advantage of the control group process is accuracy.

Using Trend-Line Analysis

Another useful technique for calculating the impact of a program is trend-line analysis. With this approach, a trend line is drawn to project the future, using previous performance as a base. After the program is conducted, actual performance is compared to the trend-line projection. Any improvement in performance over what the trend line predicted can then be reasonably attributed to program implementation. Although this process is not exact, it provides a reasonable estimation of the program's impact.

Figure 5.3 shows an example of a trend-line analysis taken from the claims section of an insurance company. The vertical axis reflects the level of claims examined per week. Data are presented before and after an HR program (telecommuting) implementation. As shown in the figure, a slight upward trend on the data began prior to the program's launch. Although the program apparently had an effect on claims examined, the trend line shows that some improvement would have occurred anyway, given the trend that had previously been established. Program leaders may have been tempted to measure the improvement by comparing the average prior to the program (70 claims) to the amount in week eight (79 claims), yielding a difference of nine. However, a more accurate com-

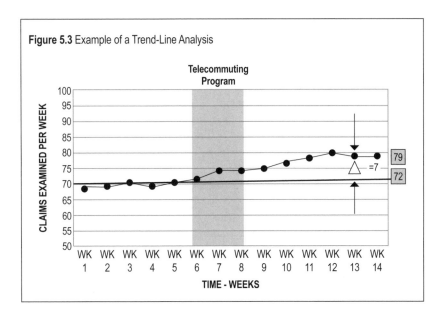

Figure 5.3 Example of a Trend-Line Analysis

parison is the eight-week amount (79) compared to the trend line amount of 72. In this analysis, the difference is seven. Using this more conservative measure increases the accuracy and credibility of the process to isolate the impact of the program.

To use this technique, two conditions must be met:

- The trend developed prior to the program must be expected to continue if the program had not been conducted. Would this trend continue on the same path established before the participants attended the program? The process owners (usually the participants) should be able to provide input to reach this conclusion. If the answer is no, the trend-line analysis will not be used. If the answer is yes, the second condition is considered.
- No new variables or influences entered the process after the evaluation period. The key word is "new," realizing that the trend has been established because of the influences already in place and that no additional influences will enter the process beyond conducting the program. If the answer is yes, another method would have to be used. If the answer is no, the trend-line analysis develops a reasonable estimate of the impact of this program.

Preprogram data must be available before this technique can be used, and the data should have some reasonable degree of stability. The trend line can be projected directly from historical data using a simple routine that is available with many calculators and software packages, such as Microsoft Excel®. If the variance of the data is high, the stability of the trend line becomes a factor. If this issue is extremely critical and the stability cannot be assessed using a direct plot of the data, more detailed statistical analyses can be used to determine whether the data are stable enough to make a projection.

Forecasting Analysis

A more analytical approach to trend-line analysis is the use of forecasting methods that predict a change in impact measures. This technique represents a mathematical interpretation of trend-line analysis when other variables enter a situation during the evaluation period. With this approach, the impact measure targeted by the program is forecast based on the influence of other factors that have changed during the evaluation period. For this method to work, a relationship must exist between the other factors and the impact measure driven by the program. The actual value of the measure is compared to the forecast value. The difference reflects the contribution of the program.

A case study will illustrate this method for isolating program effects. National Computer Company (NCC) sells computers to businesses and consumers. To ensure that customer service and support were sufficient, NCC established customer care centers in six geographic regions. In recent years, NCC care centers had experienced a high employee-turnover rate. To reduce turnover, a new HR program was developed to help managers improve employee engagement, appreciate employee concerns and differences, and communicate with employees effectively.

When considering the impact of the new program on employee turnover, the staff identified an additional factor that was driving improvement: the change in the unemployment rate. In the area of the customer care center where the program was implemented, the unemployment rate increased from 5 percent to 6 percent. Figure 5.4 shows the relationship between the unemployment rate and the voluntary turnover rate. The mathematical relationship is $y = 50 - 3x$, where x is the unemployment rate and y is the voluntary turnover rate. As the unemployment rate increased from 5 percent to 6 percent, the turnover rate went down by 3 percent. The actual turnover rate went from 41 percent to 30 percent, an 11 percent difference. The mathematical relationship between the unemployment rate and the turnover rate is used to estimate how much of the reduced turnover was caused by the increased unemployment rate, not the program. In the absence of other factors, the improvement in turnover rate not allocated to increased unemployment is attributed to the program. In this case, it is 8 percent (11 percent minus 3 percent).

With the forecasting approach, a major disadvantage occurs when several factors enter the process. The complexity multiplies, and the use of sophisticated statistical packages for multiple variable analyses is necessary. Even then, a good fit of the data to the model may not be possible. Unfortunately, some organizations have not developed math-

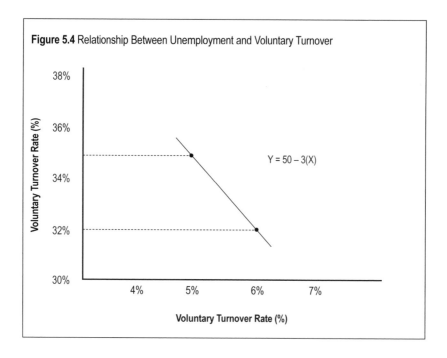

Figure 5.4 Relationship Between Unemployment and Voluntary Turnover

Y = 50 – 3(X)

Voluntary Turnover Rate (%)

Voluntary Turnover Rate (%)

ematical relationships for output variables as a function of one or more inputs, and without them, the forecasting method is difficult to use.

The primary advantage of this process is that it can accurately predict business performance measures without the program if appropriate data and models are available. The presentation of specific methods is beyond the scope of this book.

Using Estimates

The most common method of isolating the effects of a program is the use of estimates from the most credible sources. Estimating the amount of improvement connected to a particular program is the least effective method from an analytical viewpoint, and because it is perceived to be the weakest method, every step should be taken to make it as credible as possible. The good news is that this process can be made very credible if some precautions are taken, and these are described in this section.

The beginning point in using this method is ensuring that the estimation is taken from the most credible source, who is often the participant directly involved in the HR program. Essentially, four categories of individuals provide input. The individual who provides this information must be able to understand how the HR program has influenced the impact measures. The managers of the participants may be credible if they are close to the situation. Customers provide credible estimates in unique situations when they are involved. External experts may also be very helpful. These categories are all described in this section.

Participant's Estimates of HR's Impact

An easily implemented method for isolating the impact of a program is to obtain information directly from participants (users) during program execution. The effectiveness of this approach rests on the assumption that participants are capable of determining or estimating how much of a performance improvement (impact measure) is related to the program implementation. Because their actions have produced the improvement, participants may have highly accurate input on the issue. They should know how much of the change was caused by initiating the program solution. Although an estimate, this value will usually have considerable credibility with managers because they know that participants are at the center of the change or improvement. Begin by asking participants this series of questions:

- What other factors have contributed to this improvement in performance?
- What is the link between these factors and the improvement?
- What percentage of this improvement can be attributed to the implementation of this program?
- What confidence do you have in this estimate, expressed as a percentage? (0 percent = no confidence; 100 percent = complete confidence)
- What other individuals or groups could estimate this percentage to determine the amount attributed to this program?

Table 5.1 illustrates this approach with an example of one participant's estimations. Participants who do not provide information on the questions are excluded from the analysis. Also, erroneous, incomplete, or extreme information should be discarded before analysis. To be conservative, the confidence percentage can be factored into the values. The confidence percentage is a reflection of the error in the estimate. Thus, an 80 percent confidence level equates to a potential error range of plus or minus 20 percent. With this approach, the level of confidence is multiplied by the estimate. In the example, the participant allocates 60 percent of the improvement to the program and is 80 percent confident in the estimate. The confidence percentage is multiplied by the estimate to develop a usable value of 48 percent. This adjusted percentage is then multiplied by the actual amount of the improvement (post-program minus preprogram value) to isolate the portion attributed to the program. The adjusted improvement is now ready for conversion to monetary values and, ultimately, to use in the return on investment calculation.

Table 5.1 Example of a Participant's Estimate

Factor That Influenced Improvement	% of Improvement Caused by	Confidence Expressed as a %	Adjusted % of Improvement Caused by
Safety Program	60%	80%	48%
Process changes	15%	70%	10.5%
Environmental change	5%	60%	3%
System change	20%	80%	16%
Other	__%	__%	__%
Total	**100%**		

Although an estimate, this approach does have considerable accuracy and credibility. Six adjustments are effectively applied to the participant estimate to reflect a conservative approach:

- Participants who do not provide usable data are assumed to have experienced no improvements.
- Incomplete, unrealistic, or unsupported claims are omitted from the analysis.

- Extreme data are omitted from the analysis, although they may be included in the "other" benefits category.
- For short-term programs, it is assumed that no benefits from the program are realized after the first year of full implementation. (For long-term programs, additional years may be used.)
- The improvement amount is adjusted by the amount directly related to the program, expressed as a percentage. This is the allocated improvement value.
- The allocated improvement value is multiplied by the confidence estimate, expressed as a percentage, to reduce the amount of the improvement, adjusting for the potential error.

For the most part, these adjustments follow the Guiding Principles of the ROI Methodology described in Chapter 2.

When presented to senior management, the result of an impact study is usually perceived to be an understatement of the program's success. The data and the process are considered credible and accurate. As an added enhancement to this method, the next level of management may be asked to review and approve the estimates from the participants.

An example will illustrate the process for participant estimates. A restaurant chain initiated a performance management program. The program was designed to improve the operating performance of the restaurant chain using a variety of empowerment strategies with the employees. Store managers established measurable goals for employees, provided performance feedback, measured progress toward goals, and took action to ensure that goals were met. As part of the program, store managers developed action plans for improvement. Their action plans could focus on any improvement area as long as they considered the performance measure significant to their goals and related to store success. Each improvement would have to be converted to either cost savings or restaurant profits. Managers learned how to convert measurable improvements into an economic value for the restaurant. Some of the improvement areas were inventory, food spoilage, cash shortages, employee turnover, absenteeism, and productivity.

As part of the follow-up evaluation, each action plan was thoroughly documented, showing results in quantitative terms, which were converted to monetary values. The annual monetary value for each participant's improvement was calculated from the action plans. The managers were asked to identify the other factors that could have caused part of the improvement. Next, given that other factors could have influenced the improvement, managers were asked to estimate the percent of the improvement that resulted directly from the program (the contribution estimate). Restaurant managers are usually aware of factors that influence costs and profits and know how much of an improvement is traceable to the program. Therefore, each manager was asked to list the other factors that could have influenced the results. Finally, each manager was asked to be conservative and to provide a confidence estimate for the above contribution estimate (100 percent = certainty and 0 percent = no confidence). The results are shown in Table 5.2.

Estimation of the program's impact can be calculated using the conservative approach of adjusting for the contribution of the program and for the error of the contribution estimate. For example, the $5,500 annual value for labor savings is adjusted to consider the program contribution ($5,500 × 60% = $3,300). Next, the value is adjusted for the confidence in this value ($3,300 × 80% = $2,640). The conservative approach yields an overall improvement of $68,386 for this group. Participant 5 did not submit a completed action plan and was discarded from the analysis, although the costs for this participant are still included in the ROI calculation.

Another interesting observation emerges from this type of analysis. When the average of the three largest improvements is compared with the average of the three smallest values, the potential for return on investment could be much larger. If all the participants in the program had focused on high-impact improvements, a substantially higher ROI could have been achieved. This information can be helpful to the management group, whose support is often critical for program success. While an impressive ROI is refreshing, a potentially greater ROI is outstanding.

This example illustrates the power of this methodology when individuals in a particular program focus on different measures. This would be the case for many HR programs, such as reward systems, creativity and

Table 5.2 Estimates of Program Impact from Participants

Participant	Total Annual Improvement (Dollar Value)	Basis	Contribution Estimate from Manager (Participants)	Confidence Estimate from Store Managers (Participants)	Conservative Value Reported
1	$5,500	Labor savings	60%	80%	$2,640
2	15,000	Turnover	50%	80%	6,000
3	9,300	Absenteeism	65%	80%	4,836
4	2,100	Shortages	90%	90%	1,701
5	0	------	------	------	------
6	29,000	Turnover	40%	75%	8,700
7	2,241	Inventory	70%	95%	1,490
8	3,621	Procedures	100%	80%	2,897
9	21,000	Turnover	75%	80%	12,600
10	1,500	Food spoilage	100%	100%	1,500
11	15,000	Labor savings	80%	85%	10,200
12	6,310	Accidents	70%	100%	4,417
13	14,500	Absenteeism	80%	70%	8,120
14	3,650	Productivity	100%	90%	3,285
Total	$128,722				$68,386

innovation, performance management, talent management, leadership development, executive development, teambuilding, management development, competency-based pay, communications, process improvements, problem-solving, and negotiations. In those situations, the specific impact measure may not be known at the beginning of the program.

However, for other programs, the specific measure or measures are known and are often just a small number. For example, a program designed to improve retention, sales, quality, or safety performance will focus on one or a few measures. This isolation technique is effective in all of these situations.

Manager's Estimate of Impact

In lieu of, or in addition to, participant estimates, the participants' immediate managers may be asked to provide input as to the program's influence on improved performance. In some settings, the participants' manager may be more familiar with the other influencing factors. Therefore, he or she may be better equipped to provide impact estimates. The recommended questions to ask managers, after describing the improvement, are similar to those asked of the participants. Manager estimates should also be analyzed in the same manner as participant estimates. To be more conservative, actual estimates may be adjusted by the confidence percentage. When participants' estimates have also been collected, the decision of which estimate to use becomes an issue. If some compelling reason makes one estimate more credible than the other, then the more credible estimate should be used. If they are equally credible, the lowest value should be used with an appropriate explanation.

In some cases, upper management may estimate the percent of improvement attributed to a program. After considering additional factors that could contribute to an improvement, such as technology, procedures, and process changes, management applies a subjective factor to represent the portion of the results that should be attributed to the program. Although subjective, the input is usually accepted by the individuals who provide or approve funding for the program. Their comfort level with the processes used is sometimes the most important consideration.

Customer Estimates of Impact

Another helpful approach in some narrowly focused program situations is to solicit input on the impact of programs directly from customers. In these situations, customers are asked why they chose a particular product or service or to explain how their reaction to the product or service has been influenced by individuals or systems involved in the program. This technique often focuses directly on what the program is designed to improve. For example, after implementing a customer service program involving customer response in an electric utility, market research data showed that the percentage of customers who were dissatisfied with response time was reduced by 5 percent when compared to market survey data before the program. Since response time was reduced by the program and no other factor contributed to the reduction, the 5 percent reduction in the number of dissatisfied customers was directly attributed to the program.

Routine customer surveys provide an excellent opportunity to collect input directly from customers concerning their reactions to an assessment of new or improved products, services, processes, or procedures. Pre- and post-data can pinpoint the changes related to an improvement driven by a new program. When collecting customer input, linking it with the current data collection methods and avoiding the creation of surveys or feedback mechanisms is recommended. This measurement process should not add to the data collection systems. Customer input could perhaps be the most powerful and convincing data if they are complete, accurate, and valid.

Internal or External Expert Estimates

External or internal experts can sometimes estimate the portion of results that can be attributed to a program. When using this technique, experts must be carefully selected based on their knowledge of the process, program, and situation. For example, an expert in quality may be able to provide estimates of how much change in a quality measure can be attributed to a quality training program and how much can be attributed to other factors.

Collecting the Estimates

Whether the estimates come from participants, managers, customers, or experts, they must be collected from those individuals in a non-threatening, unbiased way. Several approaches are available, ranging from a very structured, credible process of using focus groups to interviews, action plans, and questionnaires. These are all effective ways to collect the data. Estimates are often collected in conjunction with other data sets. For example, if a questionnaire is used to collect the data to isolate the effects of the program, that same respondent will provide other data about the program. In essence, the impact is that the results are reported on the questionnaire, and the isolation technique follows with a series of questions. Listed next are the different ways to collect this important data.

Using Focus Groups for Estimates

The focus group works extremely well for this challenge if the group size is relatively small — in the range of 8 to 12 participants. If much larger, groups should be divided into multiple groups. Focus groups provide the opportunity for members to share information equally, avoiding domination by any one individual. The process taps the input, creativity, and reactions of the entire group.

The meeting should take about one hour (slightly more if multiple factors affect the results or if multiple business measures need to be discussed). The facilitator should be neutral to the process (that is, the program leader should not conduct the focus group). Focus group facilitation and input must be objective. The task is to link the results of the program to business performance. The group is presented with the improvement, and group participants provide input to isolate the effects of the program.

The following steps are recommended to obtain the most credible value for program impact:

1. *Explain the task.* The task of the focus group meeting is outlined. Participants should understand that performance has improved. While many factors could have contributed to the improvement, this group must determine how much of the improvement was related to the program.

2. *Discuss the rules.* Each participant should be encouraged to provide input, limiting his or her comments to two minutes (or less) for any specific issue. Comments are confidential and will not be tied to a specific individual.

3. *Explain the importance of the process.* The participants' role in the process is critical. Because their performance has improved, the participants are in the best position to indicate what has caused this improvement; they are the experts in this determination. Without quality input, the contribution of this program (or any other processes) may never be known.

4. *Select the first measure and show the improvement.* Using actual data, the facilitator should show the level of performance prior to and following program implementation; in essence, the change in business results is reported.

5. *Identify the different factors that have contributed to the performance.* Using input from experts — others who are knowledgeable about the improvements — the facilitator should identify the factors that have influenced the improvement (for example, the volume of work has changed, a new system has been implemented, or technology has advanced). If known, these factors are listed as possible contributors to the performance improvement.

6. *Ask the group to identify other factors that have contributed to the performance.* In some situations, only the participants know other influencing factors, and those factors should be identified at this time.

7. *Discuss the link.* Taking each factor one at a time, the participants individually describe the link between that factor and the business results. For example, for the program influence, the participants would describe how the program has driven the actual improvement by providing examples, anecdotes, and other supporting evidence. Participants may require some prompting to elicit comments. If they cannot provide dialogue regarding this issue, chances are good that the factor had no influence. Each person is allocated the same amount of time, usually one or two minutes.

8. *Repeat the process for each factor.* Each factor is explored until all the participants have discussed the link between all the factors and the business performance improvement. After these links have been discussed, the participants should have a much better understanding of the cause-and-effect relationship between the various factors and the business improvement.

9. *Allocate the improvement.* Participants are asked to allocate the percent of improvement to each of the factors discussed. Participants are provided a pie chart, which represents a total amount of improvement for the measure in question, and are asked to carve up the pie, allocating the percentages to different improvements, with a total of 100 percent. Participants could be provided with a table to complete

instead of a pie chart. Some participants may feel uncertain with this process but should be encouraged to complete this step using their best estimates. Uncertainty will be addressed next.

10. *Provide a confidence estimate.* The participants are then asked to review the allocation percentages and, for each one, to estimate their level of confidence in their estimates. Using a scale of 0 to 100 percent, participants express their levels of certainty with their estimates in the previous step. A participant may be more comfortable with some factors than with others, so the confidence estimates may vary. These confidence estimates will adjust the results.

11. *Ask participants to multiply the two percentages.* For example, if an individual has allocated 35 percent of the improvement to the program and is 80 percent confident, he or she would multiply 35% × 80%, which is 28 percent. In essence, the participant is suggesting that at least 28 percent of the business improvement is linked to the program. The confidence estimate serves as a conservative discount factor, adjusting for the possible error of the estimate. The pie charts with the calculations are collected without names, and the calculations are verified. Another option is to collect pie charts and make the calculations for the participants.

12. *Report results.* If possible, the average of the adjusted values for the group is developed and communicated to participants. Also, participants should receive the summary of all the information as soon as possible. Participants who do not provide information are excluded from the analysis.

This approach provides a credible way to isolate the effects of a program when other methods will not work. It is often regarded as the low-cost solution to the problem because it takes only a few focus groups and little time to arrive at a conclusion. In most of these settings, the actual conversion to monetary value is not conducted by the group but is developed in another way. Converting data to monetary values is detailed in Chapter 6. However, if participants must provide input on the value of the data, it can be approached as another phase of the same focus group meeting. To reach an accepted value, the steps are very similar to the steps for isolation.

Using Interviews

Sometimes focus groups are not available or are considered unacceptable for the use of data collection. The participants may not be available for a group meeting, or the focus group process becomes too expensive. In these situations, collecting similar information with an interview may be beneficial. With this approach, participants must address the same elements as those addressed in the focus group but with a series of probing questions in a face-to-face interview. The interview may focus solely on isolating the effects of the program or be a part of collecting other data sets. Telephone and Internet-based interviews (for example, using Skype) are also feasible options.

Action Plans

As described in the previous chapter, the action planning process is an important way for participants in an HR program to drive improvements desired by either them or the organization. The action plan provides a way to indicate the specific steps taken, when they are taken, and the impact the actions are having on the organization. When the planning process is complete and the impact has occurred, the improvement is a fact. This improvement is reported on the action plan itself. With this in mind, three additional questions are needed in the action plan to isolate the effects of the program on that data:

1. What other factors could have caused this improvement?
2. What percent of this improvement is directly related to this HR program?
3. What is your confidence in this allocation, on a scale of 0 to 100 percent, where 0 is no confidence and 100 percent is complete confidence?

These questions, which have been presented before, isolate the effects of the program on the data. Isolation is usually an easy task for these types of programs, because the participants have taken a variety of steps to cause the business impact. Thus, they have a good understanding of how they have influenced this particular project. When these three questions are addressed, the accuracy can be very credible.

Some consultants suggest that if an action plan is developed for a particular program, all the improvement should go to the program with no steps needed for the isolation process. Not so. Some of these projects or actions would be initiated anyway. Also, other factors often cause the measures to change. Take, for example, the sales development process, where sales representatives are focused on very ambitious goals. Part of the HR project involves a variety of tactics, techniques, or processes presented by the sales vice president to achieve success. The target business measure is an increase in sales with existing customers. Action plans are developed by each participating sales representative. When an increase occurs in six months, many underlying factors could have triggered it. The isolation is absolutely critical to make sure that only the amount of increase driven by the action plans is reported.

Using Questionnaires

Sometimes improvement in a particular project or program is collected by questionnaire, in which success with application and impact is detailed in literally dozens of questions. In the follow-up, when improvement has been achieved, the results need to be isolated to the program. Three additional questions as reported above are suggested:

1. What other factors could have caused this improvement?
2. What percent of this improvement is directly related to this HR program?
3. What is your confidence in this allocation, on a scale of 0 to 100 percent, where 0 is no confidence and 100 percent is complete confidence?

This approach can still be very credible because the results reported on the questionnaire have been achieved by the responding participant, who will usually have some understanding of the connection. The error adjustments can often take care of the uncertainties in this process. This approach does have the inherent weaknesses that parallel the use of the questionnaire when compared to other methods. Individuals can ignore it or provide inaccurate or perhaps even biased data. To ensure success, the techniques described in the previous chapter to obtain a favorable response rate must be applied.

Calculating the Impact of Other Factors

Although not appropriate in all cases, sometimes calculating the impact of factors (other than the program) that influence part of the improvement is possible. In this approach, the program takes credit for improvement that cannot be attributed to other factors.

An example will help explain the approach. In a consumer lending training program for a large bank, a significant increase in consumer loan volume was generated after the program was implemented. Part of the increase in volume was attributed to the program, and the remaining was due to the influence of other factors in place during the same time period. Two other factors were identified: an increase in marketing and sales promotion and falling interest rates, which caused an increase in consumer volume.

With regard to the first factor, as marketing and sales promotion increased, so did consumer loan volume. The amount of this factor was estimated using input from several internal experts in the marketing department. For the second factor, industry sources were used to estimate the relationship between increased consumer loan volume and falling interest rates. These two estimates together accounted for a modest percentage of increased consumer loan volume. The remaining improvement was attributed to the program.

This method is appropriate when the other factors are easily identified and the appropriate mechanisms are in place to calculate their impact on the improvement. In some cases, estimating the impact of other factors is just as difficult as estimating the impact of the program, leaving this approach less advantageous. However, this process can be very credible if the method used to isolate the impact of other factors is also credible.

Using the Techniques

With all these techniques available to isolate the impact of a program, selecting the most appropriate techniques for the specific program can be difficult. Some techniques are simple and inexpensive, but others are time-consuming and costly. When attempting to decide, the following factors should be considered:

- feasibility of the technique
- accuracy provided with the technique
- credibility of the technique with the target audience
- specific cost to implement the technique
- amount of disruption in normal work activities as the technique is implemented
- participant, staff, and management time needed for the particular technique

Multiple methods or sources for data input should be considered, since two sources are usually better than one. When multiple sources are used, a conservative method is recommended for combining the inputs. The reason is that a conservative approach builds acceptance. The target audience should always be provided with explanations of the process and of the subjective factors involved. Multiple sources allow an HR team to experiment with different strategies and to build confidence with a particular technique. For example, if management is concerned about the accuracy of participants' estimates, a combination of a control group arrangement and participants' estimates could be attempted to verify the accuracy of the estimates.

Final Thoughts

Taking credit when credit is due is the most critical step in the analysis. This chapter presented a variety of techniques for isolating the effects of a program. The techniques represent the most effective approaches available to address this issue and are used by some of the most progressive organizations. The use of control groups, trend-line analysis, and estimates from credible sources will be the dominant approaches in human resources. Too often, results are reported and linked with the program without any attempt to isolate the exact portion that can be attributed to it. If HR professionals are committed to improving the image of their functions, as well as meeting their responsibilities for obtaining results, this issue must be addressed early in the process for all major programs. The next chapter focuses on converting data to money.

Chapter 6:
Converting Data to Money

To calculate the ROI, calculating monetary benefits by converting data to monetary values is necessary. While results at lower levels are important, converting the positive outcomes into monetary figures is more valuable from an executive viewpoint. This chapter explains how HR professionals are moving beyond simply tabulating business results to developing monetary values. A variety of methods available to convert impact data to money are presented in this chapter.

Why Calculate Monetary Benefits?

The answer to this question is not always clearly understood. An HR program could be labeled a success without converting to monetary values, just by using business impact data showing the amount of change directly attributed to the program. For example, a change in quality, cycle time, market share, or customer satisfaction could represent significant improvements linked directly to a new program. This evidence may be sufficient for some programs. However, many sponsors need the actual monetary value, and more evaluators take this extra step of converting data to monetary values.

Value Equals Money

For some stakeholders, the most significant value is money. As described in Chapter 2, many different types of value exist. However, money is becoming one of the most meaningful values as the economic benefits of programs are desired particularly by executives, sponsors, clients, administrators, and top leaders. They are concerned about the allocation of funds and want to see the contribution of an HR program in monetary values. Anything short of this value for these key stakeholders would be unsatisfactory.

Impact Is More Understandable

For some HR programs, the impact is more understandable when the monetary value is developed. For example, consider the impact of a leadership development program aimed at all the middle managers in an organization. As part of the program, the managers were asked to address at least two measures that matter to them and that have to change or improve for those managers to meet their specific goals. The measures could literally represent dozens, if not hundreds, of different measures. When the program impact is captured, all these measures have changed, leaving a myriad of improvements, difficult to appreciate without a conversion to monetary value. When the first-year monetary value is developed for each of the measures, the results provide the evaluator and sponsors with a sense of the impact of the program. Without converting to monetary values, understanding the contribution is difficult.

Money Is Necessary for ROI

Monetary value is required to develop ROI. As described in Chapter 2, a monetary value is needed to compare to costs in order to develop the benefit/cost ratio, the ROI (as a percent), and the payback period. In fact, the monetary benefits become the other half of the equation and are absolutely essential.

Monetary Value Is Needed to Understand Problems

In all businesses, costs are necessary for understanding the magnitude of any problem. Consider, for example, the cost of employee turnover. The traditional records and even those available through an analysis of cost statements will not show the full value or cost of the problem. A variety of estimates and expert input may be required to supplement cost statements to arrive at a particular value, that is, the monetary value needed in a fully-loaded format to understand the problem. The good news is that many organizations have developed a number of standard cost items representing issues that are undesired.

For example, an insurance company was experiencing a 35 percent annual turnover of financial analysts. When the cost of turnover was calculated using comparable external studies, the total annual cost was over $3 million. This amount shocked the executives and sparked the creation of a retention solution.

Key Steps to Convert Data to Money

Before describing the techniques to convert either hard or soft data to monetary values, five general steps should be completed for each data item:

1. *Focus on a unit of improvement.* First, define a unit of measure. For output data, the unit of measure is the item produced (one item assembled), service provided (one package shipped), or sale completed. Time measures might include the time to complete a program, cycle time, or customer response time, and the unit is usually expressed as minutes, hours, or days. Quality is a common measure, with a unit being defined as one error, reject, defect, or rework item. Soft data measures vary, with a unit of improvement representing such things as an absence, a turnover statistic, or a one-point change in the customer satisfaction index. Table 6.1 provides examples of these units.

Table 6.1 Breaking Down the Units of Measure

UNITS OF MEASURE	
• One Unit Produced	• One Hour of Downtime
• One Student Enrolled	• One Minute of Wait Time
• One Package Delivered	• One Day of Delay
• One Patient Served	• One Hour of Cycle Time
• One Sale Made	• One Hour of Employee Time
• One Loan Approved	• One Hour of Overtime
• One Project Completed	• One Customer Complaint
• One Call Escalated	• One Person Removed from Welfare
• One FTE Employee	• One Less Day of Incarceration (Prison)
• One Reject	• One Unit of Rework
• One Error	• One Lost Time Accident
• One Grievance	• One Unplanned Absence
• One Voluntary Turnover	• One Lost Accident

2. *Determine a value for each unit.* Now the challenge. Place a value (V) on the unit identified in the first step. For measures of production, quality, cost, and time, the process is relatively easy. Most organizations have records or reports that can pinpoint the cost of one unit of production or one defect. Soft data items are more difficult to convert to money. For example, the monetary value of one customer complaint or a one-point change in an employee attitude is often difficult to determine. The techniques described in this chapter provide an array of approaches for making this conversion. When more than one value is available, usually the most credible or the lowest value is used in the calculation.

3. *Calculate the change in performance data.* Calculate the change in output data after the effects of the program have been isolated from other influences. The change (D) is the performance improvement, measured as hard or soft data that is directly attributable to the program. The value may represent the performance improvement for an individual, a team, a group of participants, or several groups of participants.

4. *Determine an annual amount for the change.* Annualize the change value to develop a total change in the performance data for one year (ΔP). Using annual values has become a standard approach for organizations seeking to capture the benefits of a particular program, although the benefits may not remain constant throughout the entire year. First-year benefits are used if the solution is short term. This approach is considered conservative. More about this method will be discussed later.

5. *Calculate the total value of the improvement.* Arrive at the total value of improvement by multiplying the annual performance change (ΔP) by the unit value (V) for the complete group in question. For example, if one group of participants is involved in the program being evaluated, the total value will include total improvement for all participants in the group. This value for annual program benefits is then compared to the cost of the program, usually through the ROI formula presented in this chapter.

Table 6.2 presents an example of a values-based selection process that illustrates the five-step for converting data to money. A hotel chain based in Singapore implemented a values-based selection system to ensure that new employees matched the culture and values systems in the organization. The chain experienced high turnover in the first 60 days of employment (32 percent). An examination of why the employees were leaving revealed that they did not fit the culture of the organization. A new selection process aimed at matching the applicant to the culture of the hotel was implemented, and turnover was dramatically reduced, with a total savings of $326,400.

Table 6.2 Converting Early Turnover Data to Monetary Values	
Step 1	**Define the Unit of Measure.** One early turnover in the first 60 days.
Step 2	**Determine the Value of Each Unit.** Using internal experts and external studies, the cost of an average early turnover was estimated at $3,200, when time and direct costs were considered. (V = $3,200).
Step 3	**Calculate the Change in Performance Data.** Six months after the program was completed, the early turnover in the first 60 days improved from 32 percent to 12 percent, for a change of 20 percent. It was estimated that 68 percent was related to the new selection program (Isolating the Effects of the Program). This provided an improvement of 13.6 percent turnover prevented because of this program.
Step 4	**Determine an Annual Amount for the Change.** An improvement of 13.6 percent represents 17 turnovers every two months, or 17 x 6 = 103 for one year.
Step 5	**Calculate the Annual Value of the Improvement.** Annual Value = ΔP times V $\qquad$ = 102 x $3,200 $\qquad$ = $326,400

Standard Monetary Values

Most hard-data items are converted to monetary values and have standard values. By definition, a standard value is a monetary value on a unit of measurement that is accepted by key stakeholders. These standards have been developed because these are often the measures that matter in the organization. They are critical. They reflect problems, and thus efforts have been made to convert them to monetary values to show their impact on the operational and financial wellbeing of the organization. The best way to understand the magnitude of any problem is to put a monetary value on it.

A variety of quality programs spanning the last two decades have focused only on the cost of quality. Organizations have been obsessed with placing a value on mistakes or on the payoff of avoiding these mistakes. This trend is one of the most prominent outgrowths of quality management systems — the standard cost of items. In addition, a variety of process improvement programs — such as reengineering, reinventing the corporation, transformation, continuous process improvement, and many others — have had a measurement component in which the cost of a particular measure has been developed. Finally, a variety of cost controls, cost containment, and cost management systems have been developed, such as activity-based costing. These have forced organizations, departments, and divisions to place costs on activities and, in some cases, to relate those costs directly to the revenue or profits of the organization.

Standard values are usually available for the hard data categories of output, quality, and time. Figure 6.1 shows how they have been converted to the other hard data category, cost. Output is converted to either profits or cost savings. Output in the form of sales, new customers, market share, and customer loyalty add value through additional profits obtained from additional sales. Outputs in which profits are not connected, such as the output of an individual workgroup, can be converted to savings. For example, if the output of a work group can be increased as a result of a particular program, with no additional resources needed to drive the output, then the corresponding value is in the cost savings. That is, additional output presented or the cost per unit of output actually goes down, resulting in a cost savings. When quality is improved, the result is either cost savings when quality is a problem or cost avoidance if the program is preventive — preventing a mistake or a quality issue.

Time is converted in the same way. If time is reduced, it is converted to a cost savings. If the time does not increase when it normally should, it represents cost avoidance. Therefore, the ultimate payoff of typical hard data items is profits, cost savings, or cost avoidance. This logic also explains why most ROI studies pay off on cost savings or cost avoidance instead

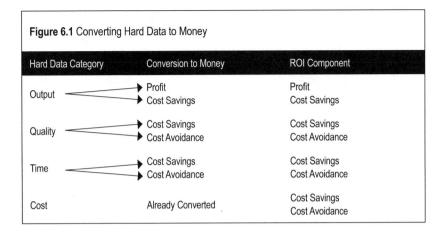

Figure 6.1 Converting Hard Data to Money

Hard Data Category	Conversion to Money	ROI Component
Output	Profit Cost Savings	Profit Cost Savings
Quality	Cost Savings Cost Avoidance	Cost Savings Cost Avoidance
Time	Cost Savings Cost Avoidance	Cost Savings Cost Avoidance
Cost	Already Converted	Cost Savings Cost Avoidance

of on profits. Those programs directly related to customers and sales are normally converted to profits. Others are converted to cost savings or cost avoidance. The additional details on how these conversions are made are presented next. However, almost all hard data items have been converted to monetary values as standard values.

Converting Output Data to Money

When a program produces a change in output, the value of the increased output can usually be determined from the organization's accounting or operating records. For organizations operating on a profit basis, this value is typically the marginal profit contribution of an additional unit of production or service provided. For example, a team within a major appliance manufacturer was able to boost the production of small refrigerators after employing a comprehensive work cell redesign program developed by human resources. The unit of improvement was the profit margin of one refrigerator. For organizations that are performance driven rather than profit driven, this value is usually reflected in the savings accumulated when an additional unit of output is realized for the same input. For example, in the visa section of a government office, an additional visa application was processed at no additional cost. Thus, an increase in output translated into a cost savings equal to the unit cost of processing a visa application.

The formulas and calculations used to measure this contribution depend on the type of organization and the status of its record-keeping. Most organizations have standard values readily available for performance monitoring and setting goals. Managers often use marginal cost statements and sensitivity analyses to identify values associated with changes in output. If the data are not available, the HR team must initiate or coordinate the development of appropriate values.

One of the more substantial outcomes is productivity, particularly productivity in a competitive organization. Today, most organizations competing in a global economy do an excellent job of monitoring productivity and placing value on it. For example, consider Snapper Inc., the lawnmower manufacturer. Productivity has increased threefold in 10 years. Robots do the welding; lasers cut parts; and computers control the steel stamping processes. At Snapper, each factory worker is measured every hour, every day, every month, and every year, and everyone's performance is posted publicly for everyone to see. Production at the Snapper plant is rescheduled every week according to the pace at which stores sell across the nation. A computer juggles work assignments and balances the various parts of the assembly process. Productivity is not only important, it is measured and valued. Snapper knows the value of improving productivity by an infinitesimal amount because the president knows that the factory must be efficient to compete in a global market with low-cost products. This goal requires that every factory worker be measured every hour of every day.

The benefit of converting output data to money with this approach is that these calculations are already completed for the most essential data items and are reported as standard values. Table 6.3 shows a sampling of measures in the sales and marketing area that are routinely calculated and are considered to be standard values.[1] For example, the first two entries go together. The sales cannot be used in an ROI value until they have been converted to profit. Sales are usually affected by the profit percentage to generate the actual value of the improvement. Other profit margins can be developed for a particular unit, a product line, or even a customer. Retention rates and return rates are routinely developed, as is the lifetime value of a customer. Even these days, the market

Table 6.3 Examples of Standard Values from Sales and Marketing

Metric	Definition	Converting Issues
Sales	The sale of the product or service recorded in a variety of different ways: by product, by time period, by customer.	This data must be converted to monetary value by applying the profit margin for a particular sales category.
Profit Margin (%)	(Price – Cost)/Cost for the product, customer, time period.	The most common way factored to convert sales to data.
Unit Margin	Unit Price less the Unit Cost.	This shows the value of incremental sales.
Channel Margin	Channel profits as a percent of channel selling price.	This would be used to show the value of sales through a particular marketing channel.
Retention Rate	The ratio of customers retained to the number of customers at risk of leaving.	The value is the money saved to retain a new replacement customer.
Churn Rate	Churn rate is the complement of the retention rate. It is the percent of customers leaving compared to the number who are at risk of leaving.	The value is the money saved for acquiring a new customer.
Customer Profit	The difference between the revenues earned from and the cost associated with the customer relationship during the specified period.	The monetary value add is the additional profit obtained from customers. It all goes to the bottom line.
Customer Value Lifetime	The present value of the future cash flows attributed to the customer relationship.	This is bottom line as customer value increases, it adds directly to the profits. Also, as a new customer is added, the incremental value is the customer lifetime average.
Cannibalization Rate	The percent of the new product sales taken from existing product lines.	This needs to be minimized because it is an adverse effect on existing product, with the value add being the loss of profits from the sales loss.
Workload	Hours required to service clients and prospects.	The salaries and commissions and benefits from the time the sales staff spends on the workloads.
Inventories	The total amount of product or brand available for sale in a particular channel.	Since the inventories are valued at the cost of carrying the inventory, space, handling, and the time value of money. Insufficient inventories is the cost of expediting the new inventory or loss sales because of the inventory outage.

continued on next page

Table 6.3 Examples of Standard Values from Sales and Marketing (continued)

Metric	Definition	Converting Issues
Market Share	The sales revenue as a percent of total market sales.	The actual sales are converted to money through the profit margins. This is a measure of competitiveness.
Loyalty	This includes the length of time the customer stays with the organization, the willingness to pay a premium, and the willingness to search.	The additional profit from the sale or the profit on the premium.

share and loyalty are developed because they translate directly into additional sales. For the most part — with the exception of workload and inventories — the value is developed through profits. Even market share and customer loyalty are valued based on sales or additional sales obtained from the customer.

Calculating the Cost of Quality

Quality and the cost of quality are prominent issues in most manufacturing and service firms. Because some HR programs are designed to increase quality, the program team may have to place a value on the improvement of certain quality measures. With some quality measures, the task is easy. For example, if quality is measured with the defect rate, the value of the improvement is the cost to repair or replace the product. The most obvious cost of poor quality is the scrap or waste generated by mistakes. Defective products, spoiled raw materials, and discarded paperwork are all the result of poor quality. Scrap and waste translate directly into a monetary value. In a production environment, for example, the cost of a defective product is the total cost incurred up to the point at which the mistake is identified, minus the salvage value. In the service environment, a defective service is the cost incurred up to the point that the deficiency is identified, plus the cost to correct the problem, plus the cost to make the customer happy, plus the loss of customer loyalty.

Employee mistakes and errors can be expensive. The most costly rework occurs when a product or service is delivered to a customer and must be returned for correction. The cost of rework includes both labor and direct costs. In some organizations, rework costs can be as much as 35 percent of operating expenses.

In one example, an HR program focused on customer service provided by dispatchers in an oil company. The dispatchers processed orders and scheduled deliveries of fuel to service stations. A measure of quality was the number of pullouts experienced, which was considered excessive. A pullout occurs when a delivery truck cannot fill an order for fuel at a service station. The truck must then return to the terminal for an adjustment to the order. This event is essentially a rework item. The average cost of a pullout is developed by tabulating the cost from a sampling of actual pullouts. The elements in the tabulation included driver time, the cost of the truck while adjusting the load, the cost of terminal use, and extra administrative expenses. This value was developed and became the accepted standard following completion of the program. Organizations have made great progress in developing standard values for the cost of quality.

Quality costs can be grouped into six major categories:
- Internal failure represents costs associated with problems detected prior to product shipment or service delivery.
- Penalty costs are fines or penalties received as a result of unacceptable quality.
- External failure refers to problems detected after product shipment or service delivery. Costs include product support, complaint investigation, and remedial fixes.
- Appraisal costs are the expenses involved in determining the condition of a particular product or service.
- Prevention costs include efforts undertaken to avoid unacceptable product or service quality. These efforts include quality management, audits, and process improvements.
- Customer dissatisfaction is perhaps the costliest element of inadequate quality. In some cases, serious mistakes result in lost business.

As with output data, the good news is that a high number of quality measures have been converted to standard values. Table 6.4 shows a sampling of the quality measures usually converted to actual monetary value.

The definition of these measures can vary slightly with the organization, and the magnitude and the costs can vary significantly. The most common method for converting cost is to use internal failure, external failure, appraisal, or penalty costs. Table 6.4 shows the variety of quality measures that are monitored and represents only a small sampling from a typical organization. Some larger organizations track literally thousands of quality measures as standard values have been developed for many of them.

Converting Employee Time Using Compensation

Saving employee time is a common objective for HR programs. In a team environment, a self-directed team program may enable the team to complete tasks in less time or with fewer people. A major program could drive a reduction of several hundred employees. On an individual basis, a time management program is implemented to help professional, sales, and managerial employees save time in performing daily tasks. The value of the time saved is an important measure, and determining the monetary value for it is relatively easy.

The most obvious time savings are from reduced labor costs for performing the same amount of work. The monetary savings are found by multiplying the hours saved by the labor cost per hour. For example, after using the time management program in one organization, participants

Table 6.4 Examples of Standard Quality Measures

Standard Quality Measures	
Defects	Failure
Rework	Customer Complaint
Variances	Delay
Waste	Missing Data
Processing Errors	Fines
Date Errors	Penalties
Incidents	Inventory Shortages
Accidents	Unplanned Absenteeism
Grievances	Involuntary Employee Turnover
Down Time – Equipment	Risk
Down Time – System	Days Sales Uncollected
Repair Costs	Queues

estimated that they saved an average of seventy-four minutes per day, worth $31.25 per day, or $7,500 per year. The time savings were based on the average salary plus benefits for the typical participant.

For most calculations the average wage, with a percent added for employee benefits, will suffice. However, employee time may be worth more. For example, additional costs in maintaining an employee (office space, furniture, telephones, utilities, computers, administrative support, and other overhead expenses) could be included in calculating the average labor cost. Thus, the average wage rate may escalate quickly. In a large-scale employee reduction effort, calculating additional employee costs may be more appropriate for showing the value. However, for most programs the conservative approach of using salary plus employee benefits is recommended.

When developing time savings, caution is needed. Savings are only realized when the amount of time saved translates into a cost reduction or a profit contribution. If a team-based program sparks a new process that eliminates several hours of work each day, the actual savings will come from a reduction in staff or overtime pay. Even if a program produces savings in manager time, a monetary value is not realized unless the manager puts the additional time saved to productive use. Having managers estimate the percentage of saved time used on productive work may be helpful if followed by a request for examples of how the time was used. Therefore, a necessary preliminary step in developing time savings is determining whether the expected savings will be genuine, that is, if the time saved is put to productive use.

Finding Standard Values

As this section has illustrated, standard values are available for all types of hard data and are available in all types of functions and departments. Essentially, every major department will develop standard values that are tracked and monitored in that area. Table 6.5 shows the common functions in a major organization where standard values would be tracked. Sometimes, the data set that the departments monitor, collect, and publish need to be understood. Thanks to enterprise-wide systems software, these functions, including the standard values in some cases, are integrated and

Table 6.5 Locating the Standard Values

Standard Values Are Everywhere	
• Finance and Accounting • Production • Operations • Engineering • IT • Administration • Sales and Marketing	• Customer Service and Support • Procurement • Logistics • Compliance • Research and Development • Human Resources • Legal and Risk Management

available for use by a variety of people. Access may be an issue that needs to be addressed or changed to ensure that the data can be obtained.

Some HR team members, using the ROI Methodology, have taken the extra step of collecting the standard values from the various systems and developing a handbook of values. This step involves tapping into the databases or departmental files of these functions and others. The result is an interesting list of what activities are worth. When previously compiled, this list was much-sought-after because others reviewing cross-functional processes also needed the value of the measures. This program would be excellent for wide-scale implementations.

Data Conversion When Standard Values Are Not Available

When standard values are not available, several strategies for converting data to monetary values exist. Some are appropriate for a specific type of data or data category, while others may be used with virtually any type of data. The challenge is to select the strategy that best fits the situation. These strategies are presented next, beginning with the most credible approach.

Using Historical Costs from Records

Sometimes historical records contain the value of a measure and reflect the cost (or value) of a unit of improvement. This strategy relies on identifying the appropriate records and on tabulating the actual cost components for the item in question. For example, a large construction firm initiated an HR program to improve safety. The program improved several safety-related performance measures, ranging from government fines to total workers' compensation costs. By examining the company's records using one year of data, the average cost for each safety measure was developed. This amount involved the direct costs of medical payments, insurance payments, insurance premiums, investigation services, and lost time payments to employees, as well as payments for legal expenses, fines, and other direct services. Also, the amount of time used to investigate, resolve, and correct any of the issues had to be included. This time involved not only the health and safety staff but other staff members as well. In addition, the cost of lost productivity, the disruption of services, morale, and dissatisfaction were estimated to obtain a fully-loaded cost. Corresponding costs for each item were then developed. This brief example shows the difficulty in working to keep systems and databases in operation to find a value for a particular data item. This case raises several concerns about using records and reports.

Sorting through databases, cost statements, financial records, and a variety of activity reports takes an immense amount of time, time that may not be readily available. Keeping the time required for this process in perspective is helpful. This is only one step in the ROI Methodology (converting data to monetary value) and only one measure among others that may need to be converted to monetary value. Resources need to be conserved.

In some cases, data are not available to show all the costs for a particular item. While some direct costs are associated with a measure, often the same numbers of indirect or invisible costs, or costs that cannot be obtained easily, are associated with the program. Calculating the cost of an involuntary turnover is one example.

Figure 6.2 shows the fully-loaded costs of turnover and can be compared to the Iceberg Principle.[2] The visible part of the iceberg is the green money — the visible costs in the records, reports, and cost statements. In contrast, the invisible part of the iceberg — the part of the iceberg that cannot be seen from a surface observation — is the blue money, the invisible costs. Often labeled hidden or indirect, the invisible costs can be significant and make converting data to monetary values a time-consuming process involving estimates and expert input.

Although capturing all the visible costs would be challenging, capturing the invisible costs is even more difficult.

In some cases, the effort just to secure data from databases becomes difficult. With the proliferation of data warehousing and data capturing systems, combined with existing legacy systems that may not talk to each other, finding the values for a particular cost item becomes a sometimes insurmountable task.

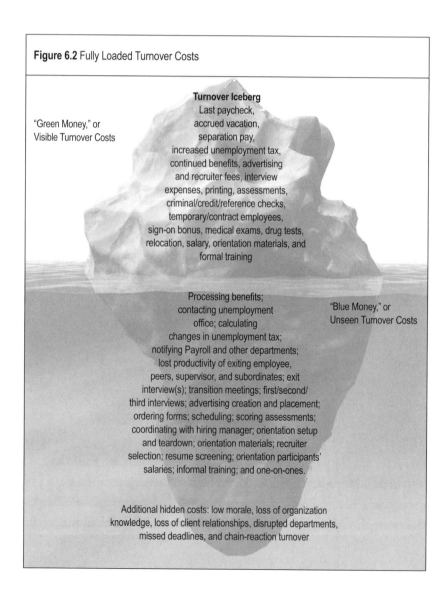

Figure 6.2 Fully Loaded Turnover Costs

Turnover Iceberg

"Green Money," or Visible Turnover Costs

Last paycheck, accrued vacation, separation pay, increased unemployment tax, continued benefits, advertising and recruiter fees, interview expenses, printing, assessments, criminal/credit/reference checks, temporary/contract employees, sign-on bonus, medical exams, drug tests, relocation, salary, orientation materials, and formal training

"Blue Money," or Unseen Turnover Costs

Processing benefits; contacting unemployment office; calculating changes in unemployment tax; notifying Payroll and other departments; lost productivity of exiting employee, peers, supervisor, and subordinates; exit interview(s); transition meetings; first/second/third interviews; advertising creation and placement; ordering forms; scheduling; scoring assessments; coordinating with hiring manager; orientation setup and teardown; orientation materials; recruiter selection; resume screening; orientation participants' salaries; informal training; and one-on-ones.

Additional hidden costs: low morale, loss of organization knowledge, loss of client relationships, disrupted departments, missed deadlines, and chain-reaction turnover

Compounding the problem of time and availability is access. Sometimes, monetary values may be needed from a system or record set that is under someone else's control. In a typical program implementation, the HR team may not have full access to cost data. Cost data are more sensitive than other types of data and are often protected for many reasons, including the competitive advantage. Therefore, easy access becomes difficult and sometimes is even prohibited unless an absolute need to know exists.

Finally, an acceptable level of accuracy is needed in this analysis. While a measure calculated in the current records may give the impression that it is founded on accurate data, this may be an illusion. When data are calculated, estimations are involved, access to certain systems is denied, and different assumptions are necessary (which can be compounded by different definitions of systems, data, and measures). Because of these limitations, the calculated values may be suspect unless care is taken to ensure that they are accurate.

Calculating the monetary value of data using records should be done with caution and only when these two conditions exist:

- The sponsor approves spending additional time, effort, and money to develop a monetary value from the current records and reports.
- The measure is simple and available in a few records.

Otherwise, moving to another method is preferred. Other methods may be more accurate and certainly less time-intensive than this particular approach.

Using Input from Experts

When faced with converting data items for which historical cost data are not available, using input from experts may be an option. Internal experts provide the cost (or value) of one unit of improvement. The individuals with knowledge of the situation and the respect of management must be willing to provide estimates — as well as the assumptions made in arriving at the estimates. Most experts have their own methodology for developing these values. So when requesting their input, explaining the full scope of what is needed and providing as many specifics as possible is critical.

Internally, experts are not difficult to find. Sometimes, they reside in the obvious department, where the data originated or where it was collected. For example, the quality department generates quality measures; the payroll department generates payroll measures; the IT department generates IT data; the sales department generates sales data; and so forth.

In some cases, the expert(s) is the individual or individuals who send the report. The report is sent either electronically or entered into a database, and the origins are usually known. If it is sent on a routine basis, the person sending the report may be the expert, or at least someone who can lead program leaders to the expert. Sometimes, an individual's job title can indicate whether he or she is a possible expert. For example, in an insurance firm, when a claim was turned down, the customer could appeal the process. An HR program was implemented to lower the number of customer appeals, and the ROI of the program had to be developed based on the reduction of appeals. The cost of an appeal was needed. To find the cost, the HR program leader contacted the individuals whose title was customer appeals coordinator and in a focus group developed the data directly from their input.

When identifying the expert is not as obvious as looking in the directory, asking may be helpful. A few questions may lead to the person who knows. Internally, for almost every data item generated, someone is considered an expert about that data.

Externally, the experts — consultants, professionals, or suppliers in a particular area — can be found in some obvious places. For example, the costs of accidents could be estimated by the workers' compensation insurance carrier, or the cost of a grievance could be estimated by the labor attorney providing legal services to defend the company in grievance transactions.

The credibility of the expert is the central issue when using this method. Foremost among credibility measures is the individual's experience with the process or the measure. This individual must be knowledgeable of the processes for this measure and, ideally, work with it routinely. This person must also be unbiased. Experts must be neutral in terms of determining the measure's value, and should not have a personal or professional interest in this value. Such an interest can be subtle to detect. For example, labor relations internal experts (the individuals who coordinate grievances for the company) may exaggerate the cost of a grievance to show the impact of their particular jobs. However, , they may have the most knowledge since they work with this needed data, and the bias may have to be filtered in some way. In a case like this, going to an external expert who is not connected with the issue may be more appropriate. Externally, part of the expertise may be based on the credentials of the person, such as degrees or certifications in a related area. Publications, degrees, and other honors or awards are desirable for validating and supporting their expertise. For professionals who routinely provide information, their track records of estimating are important. If the value they estimate has been validated in more detailed studies and found to be consistent, this track record could be the most credible confirmation of their expertise to provide this data.

External experts must be selected based on their experience with the unit of measure. Fortunately, many experts are available who work directly with relevant measures, such as employee attitudes, customer satisfaction, turnover, absenteeism, and grievances. They are often willing to provide estimates of the cost (or value) of these intangibles. Because the accuracy and credibility of the estimates are directly related to the expert's reputation, his or her reputation is critical.

Using Values from External Databases

For some soft data, using cost (or value) estimates based on the work and research of others may be appropriate. This technique taps external databases that contain studies and research projects focusing on the cost of data items. Fortunately, many databases include cost studies of data items related to programs, and most are accessible through the Internet. Data are available on the cost of turnover, absenteeism, grievances, accidents, and even customer satisfaction. The difficulty is in finding a database with studies or research appropriate to the current program. Ideally, the data should come from a similar setting in the same industry, but that goal is not always attainable. Sometimes, data on all industries or organizations are sufficient, perhaps with some adjustments to suit the program at hand.

For some, the Internet holds the most promise for finding monetary values for data not readily available from standard values and experts. Remarkable progress has been made — and continues to be made — in online searches to develop monetary values. Here are a few guidelines. General Internet directories and portals may be very helpful and have quite a bit in common with search engines. Even though the databases may include less than 1 percent of what search engine databases cover, general Internet directories still serve unique research purposes and in many cases may be the best starting point.

A specialized directory is more appropriate for accessing immediate expertise in online resources on a specific topic. A specialized database such as ERIC (www.eric.ed.gov) may be useful. These sites assemble well-organized collections of internet resources on specific topics and provide a first step.

An example in Table 6.6 shows selected turnover cost data captured from dozens of impact studies. The data are arranged by job category, ranging from entry-level, non-skilled jobs to middle managers. The ranges represent the cost of turnover as a percentage of base pay of the job group. The ranges are rounded off for ease of presentation. The costs included in these studies are fully loaded to include exit costs of departing employees, recruiting, selection, orientation, initial training, wages and salaries while in training, lost productivity, quality problems, customer dissatisfaction, loss of expertise/knowledge, supervisor's time for turnover, and temporary replacement costs. The sources for these studies follow these general categories:

- Industry and trade magazines in which the costs have been reported for a specific job within the industry
- Practitioner publications in general management, HR management, HR development, and performance improvement
- Academic and research journals where professors, consultants, and researchers publish the results of their work on retention
- Independent studies conducted by organizations and not reported in the literature but that are often available on a website or through membership arrangements; these organizations are research-based groups supported by professional and management associations
- Reports on cost impact studies developed by consulting firms

Table 6.6 Turnover Costs Summary

Job Type/Category	Turnover Cost Ranges as a Percent of Annual Wage/Salary
Entry Level – Hourly, Non-Skilled (e.g. Fast Food Worker)	30 – 50%
Service/Production workers – Hourly (e.g. Courier)	40 – 70%
Skilled Hourly (e.g. Machinist)	75 – 100%
Clerical/Administrative (e.g. Scheduler)	50 – 80%
Professional (e.g. Sales Representative, Nurse, Accountant)	75 – 125%
Technical (e.g. Computer Technician)	100 – 150%
Engineers (e.g. Chemical Engineer)	200 – 300%
Specialists (e.g. computer Software Designer)	200 – 400%
Supervisors/Team Leaders (e.g. Section supervisor)	100 – 150%
Middle Managers (e.g. Department Manager)	125 – 200%

Percents are rounded to reflect the general range of costs from studies. Costs are fully loaded to include all of the costs of replacing an employee and bringing him/her to the level of productivity and efficiency of the former employee.

This list, though not intended to be all-inclusive, illustrates the availability of special databases.

The search engines hold promise for searches because of their vast coverage. General internet search engines such as Google stand in contrast to an online directory in three primary ways:

- They are much larger, containing over a billion instead of a few million records.
- Virtually no human selectivity is involved in determining which websites are included in the search engine's database.
- They are designed for searching (responding to a user's specific query), rather than for browsing and, therefore provide much more substantial searching capabilities than directories.

A range of news resources are also available on the Internet, including news services, news wires, newspapers, news consolidation services, and more. Because some studies around particular values are newsworthy, these may be excellent sources for capturing the values of data. Overall, internet searches are an important tool for the HR team in collecting data.

A typical concern about online searches is the quality of the content. Some think that the internet has low-quality content, although in reality it is no different from other sources. As an example, high-quality newsstand publications are often available alongside those with low-quality content. Here are a few guidelines:

- Consider the source. From what organization does the content originate? Look for the organization to be identified both on the website itself and in the URL. Is the content identified as coming from known sources, such as a news organization, the government, an academic journal, a professional association, or a major investment firm? The URL will identify the owner, and the owner may be revealing in terms of the quality.

- Consider the motivation. What is the purpose of this site — academic, consumer protection, sales, entertainment, or political? The motivation can be helpful in assessing the degree of objectivity.

- Look for the quality of the writing. If the content contains spelling and grammatical errors, then the source may also contain content quality problems.

- Look at the quality of the source documentation. First, remember that even in academic circles, the number of footnotes is not a true measure of the quality of the work. On the other hand, if facts are cited, does the page identify the origin of the facts? Check out some of the cited sources to see if the facts were actually quoted.

- Are the site and its content as current as they should be? If the site is reporting on current events, the need for currency and the answer to the question of currency will be apparent.

- Verify the facts used in the data conversion using multiple sources, or choose the most authoritative source. Unfortunately, many facts given on websites are simply inaccurate due to carelessness, exaggeration, guessing, or for other reasons. They are often wrong because the person creating the page content did not check the facts.

These are helpful ways to help focus only on the quality content, which is critical when determining the monetary value of a particular measure.

Linking with Other Measures

When standard values, records, experts, and external studies are not available, a feasible approach might be to find a relationship between the measure in question and some other measure that may be easily converted to a monetary value. This process involves identifying existing relationships, if possible, that show a strong correlation between one measure and another with a standard value.

For example, a classical relationship, depicted in Figure 6.3, shows a correlation between increasing job satisfaction and employee turnover. In a program designed to improve job satisfaction, a value is needed for changes in the job satisfaction index. A predetermined relationship showing the correlation between improvements in job satisfaction and reductions in turnover can link the changes directly to turnover. Using standard data or external studies, the cost of turnover can easily be developed, as described earlier. Therefore, a change in job satisfaction is converted to a monetary value or, at least, to an approximate value. The estimate is not always exact because of the potential for error and other factors, but it is sufficient for converting the data to monetary values.

Sometimes, finding a correlation between a customer satisfaction measure and another measure that can easily be converted to a monetary value is possible. Usually, a significant correlation exists between

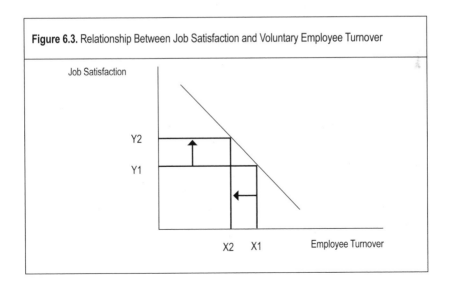

Figure 6.3. Relationship Between Job Satisfaction and Voluntary Employee Turnover

customer satisfaction and revenue. Many organizations are able to show a connection between these two measures. By connecting these two variables, estimating the actual value of customer satisfaction is possible by linking it to other measures. Furthermore, a correlation often exists between customer loyalty — which may be defined in terms of customer retention or defection — and the actual profit per customer.

In some situations, a chain of relationships may establish a connection between two or more variables. In this approach, a measure that may be difficult to convert to a monetary value is linked to other measures that in turn are linked to measures upon which a value can be placed. Ultimately, these measures are traced to a monetary value often based on profits. A model used by Sears, one of the world's largest retail chains, connects job attitudes (collected directly from the employees) to customer service, which is directly related to revenue growth.[3]

A 5-point improvement in employee attitudes will drive a 1.3-point improvement in customer satisfaction. This, in turn, drives a 0.5 percent increase in revenue growth. Thus, if employee attitudes at a local store improved by five points and previous revenue growth was 5 percent, the new revenue growth would be 5.5 percent.

These links between measures, often called the service-profit chain, create a promising way to place monetary values on hard-to-quantify measures. This research practice is significant, and the opportunity for customized work is immense.

Using Estimates from Participants

In some cases, participants in the HR program should estimate the value of improvement. This technique is appropriate when the participants are capable of providing estimates of the cost (or value) of the unit of measure improved with the program. When using this approach, participants should be provided with clear instructions, along with examples of the type of information needed. The advantage of this approach is that the individuals closest to the improvement are often capable of providing the most reliable estimates of its value.

Using Estimates from the Management Team

Sometimes, participants in a program may be incapable of placing a value on the improvement. Their work may be so far removed from the value of the process that they cannot reliably provide estimates. In these cases, the team leaders, supervisors, or managers of participants may be capable of providing estimates. Therefore, they may be asked to provide a value for a unit of improvement linked to the program.

In other situations, managers are asked to review and approve participants' estimates and to confirm, adjust, or discard the values. For example, an HR program involving customer service representatives was designed to reduce customer complaints. While the program resulted in a reduction of complaints, the value of a single customer complaint was still needed to determine the value of the improvement. Although customer service representatives had knowledge of some issues surrounding customer complaints, they could not gauge the full impact, so their managers were asked to provide a value. These managers had a broader perspective of the full impact of a customer complaint.

In some cases, senior management provides estimates of the value of data. With this approach, senior managers interested in the program are asked to place a value on the improvement using their perception of its worth. This method is used when calculating the value is difficult or when other sources of estimation are unavailable or unreliable.

Using HR Staff Estimates

The final strategy for converting data to monetary values is using internal HR staff estimates. Using all the available information and experience, the staff members most familiar with the situation provide estimates of the value. For example, a program for an international oil company was designed to reduce dispatcher absenteeism and to improve other performance problems. Unable to identify a value using other strategies, the HR staff estimated the cost of an absence to be $200. This value was then used in calculating the savings for the reduction in absenteeism that followed the training. Although the HR staff may be capable of providing accurate estimates, this approach is sometimes perceived as being biased.

It should therefore be used only when other approaches are unavailable or inappropriate.

Technique Selection and Finalizing the Values

With so many techniques available, the challenge is to select one or more strategies appropriate for the situation and the resources available. The guidelines that follow may help determine the proper selection and finalize the values.

Use the Technique Appropriate for the Type of Data

Some strategies are designed specifically for hard data, while others are more appropriate for soft data. The type of data often dictates the strategy. Standard values are developed for most hard data items. Company records and cost statements are used with hard data. Soft data are often involved in external databases, linking with other measures, and using estimates. Experts are used to convert both types of data to monetary values.

Move from Most Accurate to the Least Accurate

Table 6.7 shows the techniques presented in order of accuracy, beginning with the most accurate. Working down the list, each technique

Table 6.7 Accuracy of the Techniques to Convert to Money		
Accuracy	**Technique Using:**	**Comment**
Most Accurate	Standard Values	80% of measures that matter have standard values, monetary values that are accepted by stakeholders.
	Organizational Records and Cost Statements	Use only if complete and fully loaded. Unfortunately, it takes much time to complete.
	Experts	Most have a comprehensive knowledge of the issue and can be unbiased and neutral.
	External Databases of Other Studies	The Internet has opened many opportunities. The studies must have similar settings.
	Linking with Other Measures	More relationships are being developed.
Least Accurate	Estimates	Use most credible source.

should be considered for its suitability in the situation. The technique with the most accuracy is always recommended if it is feasible for the situation.

Consider the Resources

Sometimes, the availability of a particular source of data will drive the selection. For example, experts may be readily available. Some standard values are easy to find; others are more challenging. In other situations, the convenience of a technique may be a principal selection factor. The internet is making external database searches more convenient.

As with other processes, keeping the time invested in this phase to a minimum is key so that the total effort for the ROI study does not become excessive. Some techniques can be implemented in much less time than others. Too much time spent on this step may dampen otherwise enthusiastic attitudes about the use of the methodology.

When Estimates Are Sought, Use the Source with the Broadest Perspective on the Issue

According to the third ROI Guiding Principle, the most credible data source must be used. The individual providing estimates must be knowledgeable of the processes and the issues surrounding the value of the data. For example, consider estimating the cost of a grievance in a manufacturing plant. Although a supervisor may have insight into what has caused a particular grievance, he or she may be limited in terms of a broad perspective. A high-level manager may be able to understand the total impact of the grievances and how the impact will affect other areas. Thus, a high-level manager would be a more credible source because of his or her broader perspective.

Use Multiple Techniques When Feasible

Sometimes, having more than one technique for obtaining values for the data is beneficial. When multiple sources are available, they should be used to serve as comparisons or to provide additional perspectives. The data must be integrated using a convenient decision rule, such as the lowest value. A conservative approach of using the lowest value is recommended in the fourth ROI Guiding Principle, but only if the sources have equal or similar credibility.

Converting data to monetary value does have its challenges. As the particular method is selected and used, several adjustments or issues need to be considered to make it the most credible and applicable value with the least amount of resources.

Apply the Credibility Test

The techniques presented in this chapter assume that each data item collected and linked to a program can be converted to a monetary value. Although estimates can be developed using one or more strategies, the process of converting data to monetary values may lose credibility with the target audience, which may question its use in analysis. Highly subjective data, such as changes in employee attitudes or a reduction in the number of employee conflicts, are difficult to convert. The key question in making this determination is: Could these results be presented to senior management with confidence? If the process does not meet this credibility test, the data should not be converted to monetary values but listed as intangibles. Other data, particularly hard data items, would normally be used in the ROI calculation, leaving the highly subjective data expressed in intangible terms.

This issue of credibility when combined with resources is illustrated quite clearly in Figure 6.4. This figure represents a logical way either to convert data to a monetary value or to leave it as an intangible, and it addresses both the minimum resources. Essentially, if no standard value exists, many other ways are available to capture or convert the data to monetary value. However, there is a question of resources: Can the method be used with minimum resources? Some of the techniques mentioned in this chapter — such as searching records, maybe even searching the Internet — cannot be used with minimum resources. However, an estimate obtained from a group or a few individuals would use minimum resources. Then we move to the next challenge, credibility. Our standard credibility test is simple — if an executive who is interested in the program will buy into the monetary value for the measure in two minutes, then it is credible enough to be included in the analysis — if not, then move it to the intangibles. Incidentally, the intangibles are very important and are covered in much more detail in the next chapter.

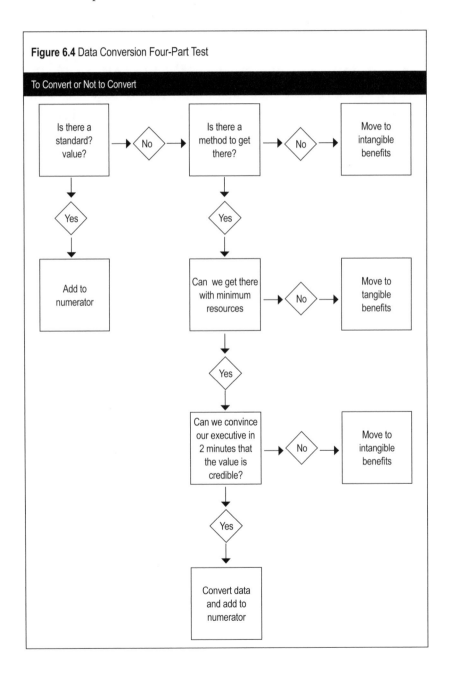

Figure 6.4 Data Conversion Four-Part Test

Review the Client's Needs

The accuracy of data and the credibility of the conversion process are concerns. Program managers sometimes avoid converting data because of these issues. They are more comfortable reporting that a program reduced youth unemployment from 26 to 18 percent, without attempting to place a value on the improvement. They may assume that the sponsor will place a value on the reduction. Unfortunately, the target audience for the program may know little about the cost of unemployment and will usually underestimate the actual value of the improvement. Consequently, some attempt should be made to include this conversion in the ROI analysis.

Is This Another Project?

Because the efforts involved in developing a credible monetary value may be extensive and yet desired by the sponsor, an appropriate response to this question is: Yes, developing the value can be done; no, it cannot be done using minimum resources; and yes, it will be another program.

Essentially, bringing up the issue of converting data to monetary value in terms of the resources required is appropriate. Although it is part of the planning for a study, the resources required can be discussed. If the sponsor is interested in converting data to money when it has not been done before, then this program should realistically be considered separate. This approach keeps the data conversion to money from hindering the ROI study and places the proper emphasis and resources on the process to do a credible job on the conversion.

Consider a Potential Management Adjustment

In organizations in which soft data are used and values are derived with imprecise methods, senior managers and administrators are sometimes offered the opportunity to review and approve the data. Because of the subjective nature of this process, management may factor (reduce) the data so that the final results are more credible. In one example, senior managers at Litton Industries adjusted the value for the benefits derived from implementing self-directed teams.[4]

Consider the Short-Term/Long-Term Issue

When data are converted to monetary values, usually one year of data is included in the analysis. This recommendation is the ninth ROI Guiding Principle, which states that only the first-year benefits are used for short-term solutions. The benefits would be considered long-term for some programs, and the issue of short-term or long-term is defined in the context of the time it takes to complete or implement the program. If one individual participating in the program and working through the process takes months to complete it, then the program is probably not short term. Some programs literally take years to implement with even one particular group. Considering a program short term is generally appropriate when the time is a month or less, with one individual learning what needs to be done to make the program successful. When the lag between implementing the program and the subsequent consequences is relatively short, a short-term solution is appropriate. No set time is used when a program is long term, but the time value should be set before the program evaluation. Input should be secured from all stakeholders, including the sponsor, champion, implementer, designer, and evaluator. After some discussion, the estimates of the time factor should be very conservative and should perhaps be reviewed by finance and accounting. When the solution is long term, the concept of forecasting will need to be used to estimate multiple years of value. No sponsor will wait several years to see how a program turns out. Some assumptions have to be made, and forecasting must be used.

Consider an Adjustment for the Time Value of Money

Since a program investment is made in one time period and the return is realized at a later time, some organizations adjust program benefits to reflect the time value of money using discounted cash-flow techniques. The actual monetary benefits of the program are adjusted for this time period. The amount of adjustment, however, is usually small when compared with the typical benefits of programs.

Although an adjustment for time may not be an issue for every program, it should at least be considered for each program, and some type of standard discount rate should be used. Consider an example of how the adjustment is calculated. Assume that a program cost $100,000, and a two-year period will be used before the full value of the estimate will be covered. In other words, this is a long-term solution spanning two years. Using a discount rate of 6 percent, the amount of cost for the program for the first year would be $100,000 x 106 percent = $106,000. For the second year it is $106,000 x 106 percent, or $112,360. Thus, the program cost has been adjusted for a two-year value with a 6 percent discount rate. This amount assumes that the program sponsor could have invested the money in some other program and obtained at least a 6 percent return on that investment; hence, another cost is added.

Final Thoughts

With some programs, money is a meaningful value. Evaluators strive to be more aggressive in defining the monetary benefits of an HR program. HR managers are no longer satisfied to simply report the business performance results. Instead, they take additional steps to convert impact data to monetary values and to weigh them against the program costs. In doing so, they achieve the ultimate level of evaluation: the return on investment. This chapter presented several strategies used to convert business results to monetary values, offering an array of techniques to fit any situation or program. The costs are presented in the next chapter.

Chapter 7.
HR Costs and ROI

The cost of providing HR programs is on the rise, increasing the pressure for HR managers to know how and why money is spent. Managers need to know the total cost of an HR program, meaning that the cost profile must go beyond direct costs to include all indirect costs as well. When using HR program costs in the ROI formula, it is important to understand that cost accumulation and tabulation steps are required, as is knowing which costs are necessary in the calculations and economical ways to develop cost data.

Cost Issues

Tabulating HR program costs is an essential step in developing the ROI calculation. Fully loaded cost information is needed to manage resources, develop standards, measure efficiencies, and examine alternative delivery processes. Here is a recap of why measuring program costs is necessary and of some important issues around cost data.

Why Measure HR Costs?

Several influences have increased the need to monitor HR costs accurately and thoroughly. Every manager should know how much money is spent on human resources. Some HR executives calculate this expenditure and compare it to similar expenditures at other organizations, although such comparisons are often unreliable because of the different bases for cost calculations. HR costs as a percentage of operating costs is a standard calculation.

HR staff should know the relative cost of programs and their components. Monitoring costs by program allows the staff to determine how costs are changing. If a program's cost rises, reevaluating the program's impact and overall success may be appropriate. HR staff may also compare specific components of costs with those of other programs or organizations. Significant differences may signal a problem. Also, costs associated with analysis, design, development, implementation, or operation can be compared with those of other programs within the organization and used to develop cost standards.

Accurate costs are necessary to predict future costs. Historical costs for a program serve as a basis for predicting future costs of a similar program or for budgeting for a program. Sophisticated cost models make estimating or predicting costs with reasonable accuracy possible.

When an ROI or benefit/cost analysis is needed for a specific program, it is necessary to develop cost data. For these analyses, cost data are just as relevant as the program's economic benefits. Although establishing direct costs is easy, determining indirect costs related to a program is more difficult. To develop a realistic ROI, costs must be accurate and credible. Otherwise, the painstaking attention given to the monetary benefits is wasted because of inadequate or inaccurate costs.

Fully Loaded Costs

The conservative approach to calculating ROI has a direct connection to cost accumulation. HR program costs should be fully loaded for ROI analysis. With this approach, all costs that can be identified and linked to a particular program are included. A fully loaded cost profile includes items such as those in Table 7.1 below. When ROI is calculated and reported to target audiences, the methodology should withstand even the closest scrutiny in terms of its accuracy and credibility. The only way to meet this test is to ensure that *all* costs are included. Of course, from a realistic viewpoint, if the controller or CFO insists on not using certain costs, then leaving them out is best.

The Danger of Costs without Benefits

Communicating the costs of an HR program without presenting

benefits is risky. Unfortunately, many HR managers have fallen into this trap for years. They present costs to management in all types of ingenious ways (for example, cost of the program or cost per employee). Although these costs may be helpful for efficiency comparisons, they can be troublesome without benefits. When most executives see the costs of an HR program, a logical question follows: What benefit was received from the program? This is a typical management reaction, particularly when costs are perceived to be high. To avoid this situation, some organizations have developed a policy of not communicating cost data for a specific HR program unless the monetary benefits can be demonstrated or a strategy is in place to develop the monetary benefits. This approach helps maintain a balance between the two issues.

Cost Guidelines

Some organizations may want to detail the philosophy and policy on costs in guidelines for the HR staff or others who monitor and report costs. Cost guidelines specify what costs are included with an HR program and how cost data are collected, analyzed, and reported. Cost guidelines can range from a one-page job aid to a 50-page document in a large, complex organization. The simpler approach is better. When developed, the guidelines should be reviewed by the finance and accounting staff. When an ROI is calculated and reported, costs are included in summary form, and the cost guidelines are referenced in a footnote or attached as an appendix.

Cost Monitoring Issues

Several issues will surface when costs associated with HR programs are monitored. Listed below are four issues.

Prorated versus Direct Costs

Usually all cost data related to an HR program are collected and expensed to that program. However, some cost categories should be prorated. For example, initial analysis, design and development, and acquisition are significant costs that should be prorated over the life of the program. Using a conservative approach, the life of the program is usually considered to be short-term. Some organizations consider one year of operation for the program; others may consider two or three years. For major HR technology investments, the life could be up to five years. If the specific time period to be used in the prorating formula is disputed, the shorter period should be used. If possible, finance and accounting staff should be consulted to help calculate the prorated costs.

Consider, for example, the cost of developing an online knowledge exchange program for a large consulting organization. In this website, consultants are encouraged to enter and retrieve data about knowledge, capability, and experience. The system was designed to save time and costs with proposals and consulting projects as consultants used the website. The cost of the software and programming was prorated over the expected life of the project, which was estimated to be five years. An ROI evaluation was undertaken based on benefits for one year. Therefore, to arrive at an annual ROI, the HR staff used one-fifth of the development costs in the analysis.

Employee Benefits Factor

The ROI analysis should include salaries for the time spent by stakeholders and HR staff associated with HR programs, as well as the cost of their benefits over that time. Employee benefits are expressed as a percentage of payroll (salaries). Organizations usually have this figure readily available for use in a variety of cost applications. It represents the cost of all employee benefits expressed as a percent of base salaries. In some organizations this value is as high as 50 percent or 60 percent. In others, it may be as low as 25 percent or 30 percent. The U.S. Chamber of Commerce estimates the average in the United States is approximately 38 percent.

Estimates Are OK

Although the direct costs are easily retrieved from the cost-tracking system, the indirect costs are not always readily available. Estimates are appropriate. For example, if an evaluation is made of an HR program initiated two years ago that produced initial analysis, design, and development costs, an estimation of the total costs would be appropriate. These costs are then prorated across the life cycle of the program. When conference or meeting rooms are used to discuss and announce the program, the cost of those facilities would be allocated to the program if a significant amount of time is involved (usually more than a couple of hours). The estimated cost of renting a facility on a daily basis, for example, would be plugged in and prorated to the length of the meeting. Tracking down the detail on these types of costs is unnecessary. Just remember: The indirect costs are probably debatable. We are including them to be conservative, so a high level of precision is not required.

Be Sensible

A reasonable amount of caution must be exercised to avoid too much precision when estimating or including costs. The tenth ROI Guiding Principle will serve you well, as it suggests that all costs categories should be included. While all costs should be represented when they are significant, they can be omitted when they are not. For example, a new gainsharing program is implemented to encourage a work team to meet certain performance goals aimed at lowering the costs in a particular organization. The total costs of the program would include all the categories listed in Table 7.1. An issue surfaces in terms of including participants' time for meetings. The team leader holds a monthly team meeting to review the previous month's status and to discuss ways in which costs can be monitored, lowered, and controlled. This meeting lasts about thirty minutes and probably substitutes for a normal meeting that would be conducted anyway. Including this 30-minute meeting may not be appropriate, since it may be too conservative. Obviously, if the meeting lasted a full day and was not part of the normal work processes, the costs of that time and the facility should be used; otherwise, it should not.

Major Cost Categories

One way to consider HR program costs is within the framework of how the HR program unfolds. Figure 7.1 shows the HR program implementation cycle, beginning with initial analysis and progressing to evaluation and reporting of the results. These functional process steps represent the typical flow of work.

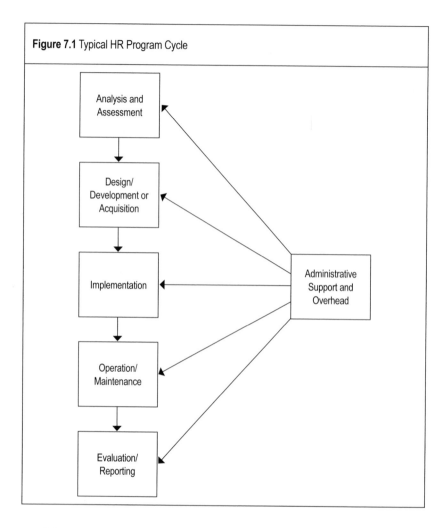

Figure 7.1 Typical HR Program Cycle

To address an HR need, the organization develops or acquires a solution and then implements it. The HR staff routinely reports to the client or sponsor throughout the process and then undertakes an evaluation to show the project's success. A group of costs also supports the process, for example, administrative support and overhead costs. To fully understand costs, the project should be analyzed in these different categories.

The chief task is to define which specific costs are included in a tabulation of HR program costs. This step involves decisions that will be made by the HR staff and in most cases approved by management. If appropriate, finance and accounting staff may need to approve the list. Table 7.1

shows the recommended cost categories for a fully loaded, conservative approach to estimating costs. Each category is described below.

Initial Assessment and Analysis

One of the most overlooked cost items is the cost of conducting the initial assessment of the need for the HR program. In some programs this cost is zero because the program is implemented without an initial assessment of need. However, as organizations focus increased attention on needs assessment, this item will become a more significant cost in the future.

You should attempt to collect data on all costs associated with the assessment and analysis to the fullest extent possible without taking too much time. These costs include the time of staff members conducting the assessment, direct fees, and expenses for external consultants who conduct

Table 7.1 HR Program Cost Categories

Cost Item	Prorated	Expensed
Initial Assessment and Analysis	✓	
Design and Development	✓	
Acquisition	✓	
Implementation		
• Salaries/Benefits—Coordination Time		✓
• Materials and Supplies		✓
• Travel		✓
• Facilities		✓
• Participants' Salaries/Benefits for the time involved in program		✓
Operation and Maintenance		✓
Evaluation		✓
Overhead/Human Resources	✓	

the needs assessment, as well as internal services and supplies used in the analysis. The total costs are usually prorated over the life of the program. Depending on the type and nature of the program, the life cycle should be kept to a reasonable number in the one- to two-year time frame. The exception would be expensive programs for which the needs are not expected to change significantly for several years.

Design and Development Costs

One of the most significant items is the cost of designing and developing the HR program. This cost item includes internal staff and consultant time for both design and development of software, CD-ROMs, job aids, and other support material directly related to the program. As with needs assessment costs, design and development costs are usually prorated, perhaps by using the same time frame. One to two years is recommended unless the program is expected to remain unchanged for many years, and the design/development costs are considerable.

Acquisition Costs

In lieu of development costs, many organizations purchase HR programs to use off the shelf or in a modified format. The acquisition costs for these programs include the purchase price and other costs associated with the rights to implement the program. These acquisition costs should be prorated usually over one or two years using the same rationale described above. If the organization needs to modify or further develop the program, these costs should be included as development costs. In practice, many programs have both acquisition costs and development costs.

Implementation Costs

An important segment of HR program costs is the implementation costs. Five major categories are included:

- *Salaries of coordinators and organizers.* The salaries of all individuals involved in coordination should be included. If a coordinator is involved in more than one program, the time should be allocated to the specific program under review. The point is to account for all the direct time of internal employees or external consultants who work with the program. Include the employee benefits factor each time direct labor costs are involved.

- *Materials and supplies.* Specific program materials such as brochures, guides, job aids, and iPods should be included in the delivery costs, along with license fees, user fees, and royalty payments.
- *Travel expenses.* Include direct costs of travel, if required, for stakeholders, facilitators, or coordinators. Lodging, meals, and other expenses also fall under this category.
- *Facilities for meetings.* Take into account the direct cost of the meeting facilities. When external meetings are held, this item represents the direct charge from the conference center or hotel. If meetings are held internally, use of the meeting room represents a cost to the organization and should be included even if it is not the practice to include facility costs in other reports.
- *Stakeholders' salaries and benefits.* The salaries plus employee benefits of stakeholders for their time away from work represent an expense that should be included. Estimates are appropriate in the analysis.

Operation and Maintenance

Under this item, you should include all costs related to routine operation of the program. This category encompasses all costs in the same categories listed under implementation, plus equipment and services.

Evaluation

The total evaluation cost is included in the program costs to compute the fully loaded cost. For ROI evaluation, you should incorporate the costs of developing the evaluation strategy and plans, designing instruments, collecting data, analyzing data, and preparing and distributing reports. Cost categories include time, purchased services, materials, purchased instruments, and surveys.

Overhead/Human Resources

A final charge is the cost of overhead — the additional costs in the HR function not directly related to a particular HR program. The overhead category represents any HR department cost not considered in the above calculations. Typical items include the cost of administrative support, administrative expenses, salaries of HR managers, and other fixed costs. A rough estimate developed through some type of allocation plan is usually sufficient.

Cost Reporting

Here is an actual case study that demonstrates how to present total costs. Table 7.2 shows the cost for a major executive leadership program. This extensive leadership program involved four off-site, weeklong training sessions with personal coaches and learning coaches assigned to the participants. Working in teams, participants undertook a project important to top executives. Each team reported the results to management. The project teams could hire consultants as well. These costs are listed as project costs. The costs for the first group of 22 participants are detailed in Table 7.2.

Prorating costs was a principal consideration. In this case, organizers were relatively certain that a second group would be conducted. The analysis, design, and development expenses of $580,657 could therefore be prorated over two sessions. Consequently, in the actual ROI calculation, half of this number was used to arrive at the total value ($290,328). This left a total program cost of $2,019,598 to include in the analysis ($2,309,926 - $290,328). On a participant basis, this amount totaled $91,800, or $22,950 for each week of formal sessions. Although this program was expensive, it was still close to benchmark data of weekly costs for several senior executive leadership programs involving the same time commitments.

ROI: Basic Issues

Now, you will have an opportunity to develop a sound base for performing ROI analyses. The following sections cover some fundamental terminology, use of annualized values, and methods for calculating BCRs and ROI.

Table 7.2 Leadership Development Program Costs

PROGRAM COSTS	
Analysis/Design/Development	
External Consultants	$525,330
Leadership Center	28,785
Management Committee	26,542
Implementation and Operation	
Conference Facilities (Hotel)	142,554
Consultants/External	812,110
Leadership Center Salaries and Benefits (for direct work with the program)	15,283
Leadership Center Travel Expenses	37,500
Management Committee (time)	75,470
Project Costs ($25,000 x 4)	100,000
Participant Salaries and Benefits (class sessions) (Average daily salary x benefits factor x number of program days)	84,564
Participant Salaries and Benefits (project work)	117,353
Travel & Lodging for Participants	100,938
Cost of Materials (handouts, purchased materials)	6,872
Research and Evaluation	
Research	110,750
Evaluation	125,875
Total Costs	**$2,309,926**

Definition

The term "return on investment" is often misused. Sometimes it is used in a broad sense to include any benefit from the HR program, a vague concept in which even subjective data linked to a program are included in the concept of the return. In this book, "return on investment" has a precise meaning: It represents a value developed by comparing program benefits to costs. The two most common measures are the BCR and the ROI formulas. Both are presented along with other approaches that calculate the return.

Annualized Values

The formulas presented in this chapter use annualized values so that the first-year impact of the program investment is developed. Using annual values is a generally accepted practice for developing the ROI. This approach is a conservative way to develop the ROI because many short-term HR programs have added value in the second or third year of operation. For long-term HR programs, longer time frames are used. For example, in an ROI analysis of a masters' degree program offered for high-potential employees in the National Security Agency, a four-year time frame was used. However, for many HR programs, first-year values are appropriate.

Benefit/Cost Ratio

One of the first methods used for evaluating HR investments is the benefit/cost ratio (BCR). As you may recall from Chapter 2, this method compares the benefits of the program to the costs in a ratio. In formula form, the ratio is the following:

$$\text{Benefit/Cost Ratio (BCR)} = \frac{\text{HR Program Benefits}}{\text{HR Program Costs}}$$

In simple terms, the BCR compares the annual economic benefits of the program to the cost of the program. A BCR of 1 means that the benefits equal the costs. A BCR of 2, usually written as 2:1, indicates that for $1.00 spent on the program, $2.00 was returned as benefits. Some HR executives prefer to use the BCR instead of ROI.

ROI Formula

Perhaps the most appropriate formula for evaluating HR investments is *net* program benefits divided by costs. The ratio is usually expressed as a percentage. In formula form, the ROI becomes the following:

$$\text{ROI (\%)} = \frac{\text{HR Program Benefits - HR Program Costs}}{\text{HR Program Costs}} \times 100$$

or

$$ROI\ (\%) = \frac{\text{HR Program Net Benefits}}{\text{HR Program Costs}} \times 100$$

You can derive the ROI value from the BCR subtracting 1.0 and then multiplying by 100. For example, a BCR of 2.45 is the same as an ROI value of 145%:

$$2.45 - 1.0 = 1.45$$
$$1.45 \times 100 = 145\%\ ROI.$$

This formula is essentially the same as ROI in other types of investments. For example, when a firm builds a new plant, the ROI is calculated by dividing annual earnings by the investment. The annual earnings figure is comparable to net benefits (annual benefits minus the cost). The investment is comparable to program costs, which represent the investment in the program.

Using the ROI formula places HR investments on a level playing field with other investments by using the same formula and similar concepts. The ROI calculation is easily understood by key management and financial executives who regularly use ROI with other investments.

The following example illustrates the use of the BCR and ROI. A large metropolitan bus system introduced a new program to reduce unscheduled absences. The increase in absences left the system facing many delays, forcing the system to create a large pool of drivers to fill in for the absent drivers. The pool had become substantial, representing a significant expenditure. The program involved a change in policy and a change in the selection process, coupled with meetings and communication.

The result of the HR programs was some marked improvements, as demonstrated when the program's benefits were compared to its costs in a one-year follow-up. The first year's payoff was $662,000, based on the two major interventions: a no-fault policy and modifications to the screening process. The total, fully-loaded implementation cost was $67,400. Therefore, the BCR can be calculated as follows:

$$BCR = \frac{\$662,000}{\$67,400} = 9.82$$

Thus, for every dollar invested in this program, almost $10.00 in benefits was returned. The ROI can be determined as follows:

$$\text{ROI} = \frac{\$662{,}000 - 67{,}400}{\$67{,}400} \times 100 = 882\%$$

For every $1.00 invested in the program, the costs (investment) were recovered, and an additional $8.82 dollars was "returned" as earnings.

ROI Interpretation

The concept of ROI for human resources is intriguing. Of all of the six data sets collected or generated in the ROI Methodology, only the ROI generates a range of reactions among program sponsors. HR managers may be concerned that executives will respond unfavorably to an ROI calculation unless it is very low and reasonable. If it is too high, executives may not believe the data; if it is negative, they may want to end the program. Because of these concerns, the concept of ROI must be clearly understood, and it should be developed very credibly following the processes and guidelines in this book. This section focuses on those issues that are critical to the use, understanding, and interpretation of ROI.

Choosing the Right Formula

Which quantitative measure best represents top management goals? Many managers are preoccupied with the measures of sales, profits (net income), and profit percentages (the ratio of profits to dollar sales). However, the ultimate test of profitability is not the absolute amount of profit or the relationship of profit to sales. The critical test is the relationship of profit to invested capital, and the most popular way of expressing this relationship is by means of ROI.

The concept of profit for HR programs is usually replaced with monetary benefits. Profits are only generated when HR programs directly affect the sales scenario with their designs to reward the sales team for outstanding performance (commissions and incentives), to build skills to develop high performance (sales training), or to motivate individuals to high levels of achievement (job design, job engagement).

When these programs work and sales are increased, the profit of the sales is used in the ROI calculation.

For most HR programs the monetary benefits will not derive from profits but from cost reductions, cost savings, or avoidance. In practice, more opportunities for cost savings exist than for profit. Cost savings can be generated when improvement in productivity, quality, efficiency, cycle time, or actual cost reduction occurs. A review of almost 1,000 studies in which the authors have been involved showed that cost savings was the basis for profits in the vast majority. Approximately 85 percent of the studies had payoffs based on output, quality, efficiency, time, or cost reduction. The others had payoffs based on sales increases, in which the earnings derived from the profit margin. This issue is relevant for nonprofit and public sector organizations where the profit opportunity is often unavailable. Because most HR initiatives are connected directly to cost savings or to cost avoidance, ROI calculations can still be developed in those settings.

The finance and accounting literature define ROI as net income (earnings) divided by investment. In the context of HR programs, net income is equivalent to net monetary benefits (program benefits minus program costs). Investment is equivalent to program costs. The term "investment" is used in three different senses in financial analysis, thus giving three different ROI ratios: return on assets (ROA), return on owners' equity (ROE), and return on capital employed (ROCE).

Financial executives have used the ROI approach for centuries. Still, this technique did not become widespread in industry for evaluating operating performance until the early twentieth century. Conceptually, ROI has innate appeal because it blends all the major ingredients of profitability into one number; the ROI statistic by itself can be compared with opportunities elsewhere (both inside and outside). Practically, however, ROI is an imperfect measurement that should be used in conjunction with other performance measurements.[1]

The formula for ROI defined above should be used. Deviations from the formula can create confusion not only among users but also among the finance and accounting staff. The CFO and the finance and accounting staff should be partners in the implementation of the ROI

Methodology. Without their support, involvement, and commitment, using ROI on a wide-scale basis is difficult. HR staff should use the same financial terms and in the same way as the CFO and finance and accounting staff do.

Table 7.3 shows how some have misused financial terms in the literature. Terms such as "return on intelligence" (or information) abbreviated as ROI confuse the CFO who is thinking that ROI is the actual return on investment. Sometimes "return on expectations" (ROE), "return on anticipation" (ROA), or "return on client expectations" (ROCE) are used, confusing the CFO who is thinking of return on equity, return on assets, and return on capital employed, respectively. Using such terms in the calculation of a payoff of HR investment does nothing except perhaps to confuse and diminish the support of the finance and accounting staff.

Other terms, such as "return on people," "return on resources," "human capital value," and "return on web," are used with almost no consistent financial calculations. The bottom line: Do not confuse the CFO. Consider him or her to be your ally, and use the same terminology, processes, and concepts when applying financial returns for programs.

Table 7.3 Misuse of Financial Terms

TERM	MISUSE	CFO DEFINITION
ROI	Return of Information or Return on Intelligence	Return on Investment
ROE	Return on Expectation	Return on Equity
ROA	Return on Anticipation	Return on Assets
ROCE	Return on Client Expectation	Return on Capital Employed
ROP	Return on People	?
ROR	Return on Resources	?
ROV	Return on Value	?
HCV	Human Capital Value	?
ROO	Return on Objectives	?

ROI Objectives: The Ultimate Challenge

When reviewing the specific ROI calculation and formula, position the ROI calculation in the context of all the data. The ROI calculation is only one measure generated with the ROI Methodology. Six types of data are developed, five of which are the five levels of evaluation. A specific objective drives the data collection for each level of evaluation, as described earlier. In terms of ROI, specific objectives are often set, creating the expectations of an acceptable ROI calculation. Table 7.4 shows the benefits of a sexual harassment prevention program and links the results at the different levels to the specific objectives of the program.

Table 7.4 The Chain of Impact Drives ROI	
Levels	**Objective**
1. Reaction	• Participants will perceive this program to be necessary. • At least 75 percent of managers (participants) provide an action plan.
2. Learning	• Improve knowledge of policy on sexual harassment/knowledge of inappropriate and illegal behavior. • Learn skills to investigate and discuss informal sexual harassment comments.
3. Application/Implementation	• Conduct meeting with employees. • Administer policy to ensure that workplace is free from sexual harassment. • Complete action items.
4. Business Impact	• Reduce the number of formal internal sexual harassment complaints by 50 percent in one year. • Reduce turnover related to sexual harassment activity. • Reduce absenteeism related to sexual harassment.
5. ROI	• Obtain at least a 25 percent ROI.

As you establish objectives, collect data to indicate the extent to which that particular objective was met. This framework is ideal in clearly showing the powerful connection between objectives and measurement and evaluation data. The table also illustrates the chain of impact as reaction leads to learning, which leads to application, which leads to business impact and to ROI. The intangible data listed in the business impact category are items that are purposely not converted to monetary value.

Intangible measures could have been anticipated in the project before it was implemented. Other measures may not have been anticipated but were described as a benefit by those involved in the program.

This particular example had an expectation of 25 percent for ROI (the ROI objective). This organization uses 25 percent as a standard for all its ROI projects. In this example, the ROI objective was not the motivation to pursue the project. The goal was to remove the potential illegal or unethical behavior. Nevertheless, the HR executive wanted to show the senior executives that the preventive programs could add value beyond the cost of the program. Because of the sensitivity of the ROI data in this example, the HR executive did not distribute the information to a general audience. Rather, implementation and impact data were presented.

ROI Objectives

Specific expectations for ROI should be developed before undertaking an evaluation study. Although no generally accepted standards exist, four strategies have been used to establish a minimum expected requirement, or target, for ROI in an HR program. The first approach is to **set the ROI using the same values used to invest in capital expenditures**, such as equipment, facilities, and new companies. For North America, Western Europe, and most of the Asian Pacific area, including Australia and New Zealand, the cost of capital has been reasonable, and this internal target for ROI is usually in the range of 15 percent to 20 percent. By using this strategy, HR executives would set the ROI target the same as the value expected from other investments.

A second strategy is to **use an ROI target that represents a higher standard than the value required for other investments**. This target value is above the percentage required for other types of investments. The rationale: ROI application in human resources is still relatively new and often involves subjective input, including estimates. Thus, applying a higher standard is appropriate. For most organizations in North America, Western Europe, and the Asian Pacific area, this value is usually set at 25 percent.

A third strategy is to **set the ROI target at the break-even point** (0 percent ROI), which is equivalent to a BCR of 1.0. The rationale for this approach is an eagerness to recapture the cost of the HR program only. Many public sector organizations have this ROI objective. If the funds expended for programs can be captured, there is still value and benefit from the program through the intangible measures, which are not converted to monetary values. Also, there is behavior change that is evident in the application and implementation data.

Finally, a fourth and sometimes recommended strategy is to **let the client or program sponsor set the ROI target**. In this scenario, the individual who initiates, approves, sponsors, or supports the program establishes the ROI objective. Almost every program has a major sponsor, and that person may be willing to offer the acceptable value. If so, this input links the expectations of financial return directly to the expectations of the individual sponsoring the HR program.

ROI Can Be Very High

As the examples in this book have demonstrated, the actual ROI value can be quite high — far exceeding what might be expected from other types of investments in plant, equipment, and other companies. Programs involved in leadership, innovation, retention improvement, productivity improvement, cost reduction, and reward systems may generate ROIs in the 100 percent to 700 percent range. Not all ROI studies are positive, however; many are, in fact, negative. Nevertheless, the impact of some HR programs can be quite impressive when a specific need has been identified, when a performance gap exists, when the HR program is implemented at the right time at a reasonable cost, when the program is implemented and supported in the work setting, and when the program is linked to one or more business measures. When these conditions are met, achieving such high ROI values is possible.

Remembering what drives the ROI value is beneficial. Consider, for example, the investment in team leaders to reduce turnover. If a leader's behavior changes as he or she works directly with the team, a chain of impact can produce a measurable change in performance from the team. This measure now represents the team's measure of turnover. That behavior change, translated into a measured improvement for the entire year, can be quite significant. When the monetary value of the team's turnover improvement is considered for an entire year and is compared to the relatively small amount of investment in one team leader, it is easy to see why this number can be quite large.

What Happens When the ROI Is Negative?

Perhaps one of the greatest fears of the program sponsor or owner and of those who are involved in the design, development, and implementation of the program is the possibility of having a negative ROI value. Few individuals want to be involved in a process that exposes a failure, especially their own. They may be concerned that the failure reflects unfavorably on them.

Ironically, a negative ROI study provides the best opportunity to learn and improve processes. The ROI Methodology reveals problems and barriers. As data are collected through the chain of impact, the reasons for failure become clear. Data on barriers and enablers generated during application and implementation usually reveal why the program was not successful. Although a negative ROI study is the ultimate learning opportunity, no one wants to invite the opportunity to his or her back door. The preference would be to learn from others.

Sometimes the damage created by a negative ROI stems from expectations that are not managed properly up front and from the fear of the consequences of a negative ROI. You can apply the following strategies to help minimize the unfavorable and sometimes disastrous perceptions of a negative ROI:

- *Raise questions about the feasibility of the impact study.* Is using the ROI Methodology appropriate for this particular program? Sometimes, a program by its very nature may appear to be a failure, at least in terms of ROI, but it succeeds in some other important way.
- *Make sure there is a clear understanding of the consequences of a negative ROI.* This issue should be addressed early and often. The ROI Methodology is a process improvement tool and not a performance evaluation tool for the HR staff. The individuals involved should not necessarily be penalized or have their performance evaluated unfavorably because of the negative ROI.

- *Look for warning signs early in the process.* Warning signs are usually everywhere. Reaction data can often send strong signals that an evaluation may result in a negative ROI. Perhaps the participants see no relevance of the program or decline the opportunity to implement it.
- *Manage expectations.* Lowering expectations around ROI is advised. Anticipating a high ROI value and communicating it to the client or other stakeholders can create an expectation that will not materialize. Keep the expectations low and the delivery high.
- *Reposition the story using the negative data.* Instead of communicating that great results have been achieved with this effective program, the story now becomes, "We have excellent information that tells how to change the program to improve results." This is more than a play on words; it underscores the importance of understanding what went wrong and what can be done in the future.
- *Use the information to drive change.* Sometimes the negative ROI can be transformed into a positive ROI with some minor alterations of the program. You may need to address implementation issues in terms of support, responsibility, and involvement. In other situations, a complete redesign of the program may be necessary. In a few isolated cases, discontinuing the program may be the only option. Whatever the option, use the data to drive action so that maximum value of conducting the study can been realized.

Consequences of Not Implementing an HR Program

For some organizations, the consequences of not providing an HR program can be quite serious. An organization's inability to perform adequately might mean that it is unable to take on additional projects or that it may lose existing projects because of major problems. Human resources can also help avoid serious operational problems (absenteeism), noncompliance issues (EEO violations), or retention problems (employee turnover rate). In such situations, the method of calculating the ROI is the same and involves these steps:

- Recognize that a potential problem, loss, or negative consequence will result if the status quo is maintained.

- Isolate the potential problem linked to lack of performance, such as noncompliance issues, a poor safety record, or the inability to take on additional projects.
- Identify the specific measure that reflects the potential problem.
- Pinpoint the anticipated "problem" level of the measure if no program is implemented (for example, industry average or benchmarking data).
- Calculate the difference in the measure from current levels desired and the potential "problem" level of the measure. This amount becomes the change that could occur if the program is not implemented.
- Develop the unit value of the measure using standard values, expert input, or external databases.
- Develop an estimate of the total potential value. This estimate becomes the total expected value of benefits derived from implementing the program.
- Estimate the total cost of the proposed HR program using the techniques outlined earlier in this chapter.
- Compare projected benefits with costs.

An example shows how this process can be used. An organization has an excellent record of avoiding discrimination lawsuits, and HR executives want to maintain it. The industry average shows that discrimination charges occur at a rate of two complaints per 1,000 employees per year. This company has a record average of only 0.25 complaints per 1,000 employees — far below the industry average. The organization would like to implement a diversity program to continue to focus attention on this critical issue and to ensure that the current, acceptable rate does not deteriorate.

The first challenge is to define the specific measure based on charges filed with the U.S. Equal Employment Opportunity Commission (EEOC). The cost of a discrimination charge averages $35,000, according to government and legal databases. Using this as a measure, the payoff for the program is the funds lost if the organization's current average migrated to the industry average. For the company's 4,000-employee workforce, the movement would be from one complaint (the company's average) to eight complaints (the industry average). Thus, the value of seven complaints is 7 x $35,000, or $245,000. This figure represents the potential savings of maintaining the current level of charges, assuming that the company's rate of complaints would rise to the industry level if no program were implemented.

The cost of the program can easily be compared with this monetary value to arrive at the potential payoff. In reality, the rate of charges may never reach the industry average because of present company practices. If this situation arises, a discounted value could be developed. For example, 75 percent of the industry average could be used as the potential value achieved if no program were implemented. This approach has some disadvantages. The potential loss of value (income or cost savings) can be highly subjective and difficult to measure. Because of these concerns, this approach to evaluating the return on HR investments is limited to certain types of situations.

This approach also has some advantages, particularly with the focus on a variety of preventive programs. It provides a vehicle to use the ROI Methodology in situations where the status quo is acceptable and represents best practices. The approach can show the value of investing in new programs to maintain a current favorable position. Essentially, the steps are the same. The challenge is to determine where the measure would be positioned if no program were implemented.

Cautions When Using ROI

Because of the sensitivity of the ROI Methodology, caution is needed when developing, calculating, and communicating ROI. The implementation of ROI is a goal of many HR departments, and a few issues should be addressed to keep the process from going astray:

- *Remember to take a conservative approach when developing both benefits and costs.* Conservatism in ROI analysis builds accuracy and credibility. What matters most is how the target audience perceives the value of the data. A conservative approach is always recommended for both the numerator of the ROI formula (net benefits) and the denominator (program costs). The conservative approach is the basis for the guiding principles.

- *Be careful when comparing the ROI in human resources with other financial returns.* Several methods can calculate the return on funds invested or assets employed. ROI is just one of them. Although the calculation for ROI in human resources uses the same basic formula as in other investment evaluations, it may not be fully understood by the audience. Its calculation method and its meaning should be clearly communicated. More important, it should be an item accepted by management as an appropriate measure for HR program evaluation.

- *Involve management in developing the return.* Management ultimately makes the decision if an ROI value is acceptable. To the extent possible, management should be involved in setting the parameters for calculations and in establishing targets by which programs are considered acceptable within the organization.

- *Fully disclose assumptions and methodology.* When discussing the ROI Methodology and communicating data, it is important to be straightforward about the process, steps, and assumptions used in the process. Communicate clearly the strengths, weaknesses, confidence levels, and shortcomings of the ROI evaluation.

- *Approach sensitive and controversial issues with caution.* Occasionally, sensitive and controversial issues will be generated when discussing an ROI value. Avoiding debates over what is measurable and what is not measurable during a presentation of a study is best. Debates should occur early in the process. Some programs may involve politically sensitive issues that must be considered early and often in the analysis and reporting. Also, some programs are so fundamental to the survival of the organization that any attempt to measure them is unnecessary. For example, a program designed to improve customer service in a customer-focused company may escape the scrutiny of an ROI evaluation on the assumption that if the program is well designed, it will improve customer service.

- *Teach others the methods for calculating ROI.* Each time an ROI is calculated, the HR manager should use the opportunity to educate other managers, colleagues, and the HR staff. Although measurement may not be in their area of responsibility, these individuals will be able to see the value of this approach to HR evaluation. Also, when possible, each project should serve as a case study to educate the HR staff on specific techniques and methods.

- *Recognize, however, that not everyone will buy into ROI.* Not every audience member will understand, appreciate, or accept the ROI calculation. For a variety of reasons, one or more individuals may not agree with the input values. These individuals may be sensitive to the concept of showing accountability for human resources. Attempts to persuade them may be beyond the scope of the task at hand.

- *Do not boast about a high return.* Generating what appears to be a very high ROI for an HR program is not unusual. Several examples in this book have illustrated the possibilities. An HR manager who boasts about a high rate of return is open to potential criticism from others unless the calculation is grounded in indisputable facts. In addition, future programs may not generate the same high ROIs, possibly leaving the manager with a sense of failure and the target audience with feelings of unmet expectations.

- *Choose the time and place for the debates.* The time to debate the ROI Methodology is not during a presentation unless it cannot be avoided. Constructive times to debate the ROI process include during a special forum, among the HR staff, in an educational session, in professional literature, on panel discussions, or even during the development of an ROI impact study. Select the setting and timing for debates with care so as not to detract from the quality and quantity of information presented.

- *Do not attempt to use ROI on all HR programs.* As discussed earlier, the value of some programs is difficult to quantify, and an ROI calculation may not be feasible. Other methods of presenting the benefits may be more appropriate.

Final Thoughts

Costs are important for a variety of uses and applications. They help the HR staff manage the resources carefully, consistently, and efficiently. They also allow for comparisons between different elements and cost categories. Cost categorization can take several different forms; the most common are presented in this chapter. Costs should be fully loaded for ROI calculations. From a practical standpoint, including certain cost items may be optional, given the organization's guidelines and philosophy. Nevertheless, because of the scrutiny involved in ROI calculations, including all costs is recommended, even if they go beyond the requirements of the company policy.

After you collect data on program benefits, convert them to monetary values, and develop a fully loaded cost profile, the ROI calculation becomes an easy next step. It is just a matter of plugging the values into the formula. This chapter has presented the two basic approaches for calculating the return — BCR and the ROI formulas. You also had an opportunity to read about some case studies that utilized the ROI Methodology. Finally, the chapter highlighted some issues and cautions you must keep in mind when performing ROI calculations. The next chapter focuses on intangibles.

Chapter 8.
Measuring Intangibles

Intangible measures are the nonmonetary benefits or detriments directly linked to human resources that cannot or should not be converted to monetary values. These measures are often monitored after an HR program has been implemented, and although not converted to monetary values, they are still relevant to the evaluation process. The range of intangible measures is almost limitless; this chapter describes a few common measures often linked with human resources (see Table 8.1).

Table 8.1. Typical Intangible Variables Linked with HR Programs

• Accountability	• Employee Engagement
• Alliances	• Employee Satisfaction
• Attention	• Employee Tardiness
• Awards	• Employee Transfers
• Branding	• Ethics
• Cooperation	• Human Life
• Conflict	• Image
• Culture	• Innovation and Creativity
• Climate	• Leadership
• Communication	• Networking
• Competencies	• Organizational Commitment
• Corporate Social Responsibility	• Reputation
• Customer Satisfaction	• Stress
• Customer Complaints	• Sustainability
• Customer Loyalty	• Teamwork
• Decisiveness	• Timeliness
• Diversity	• Wellness/Fitness
• Employee Complaints	• Work/Life Balance

Key Concepts about Intangibles

By design, some measures are captured and reported as intangible measures. Although they may not be perceived to be as valuable as the measures converted to monetary values, intangible measures are critical to the overall success of the organization.

In such programs as diversity enhancement, retention improvement, innovation and creativity, leadership development, and customer service, intangible (nonmonetary) benefits can be more important than tangible (monetary) measures. Consequently, intangible measures should be monitored and reported as part of the overall evaluation. In practice, every project or program, regardless of its nature, scope, and content, has intangible measures associated with it; the challenge is to identify and report them efficiently.

Tangibles and Intangibles: What Is the Difference?

Perhaps the first step to understanding intangibles is to clearly define the difference between tangible and intangible assets in a business organization. As shown in Table 8.2, tangible assets are required for business operations; they are readily visible, rigorously quantified, and routinely represented as line items on balance sheets.[1] The intangible assets are the key to competitive advantage. They are invisible, difficult to quantify, and not tracked through traditional accounting practices. With this distinction, understanding why intangible measures are difficult to convert to monetary values is easy.

Table 8.2 Comparison of Tangible and Intangible Assets

Tangible Assets — Required for Business Operations	Intangible Assets — Key to Competitive Advantage in the Knowledge Area
• Readily visible	• Invisible
• Rigorously quantified	• Difficult to quantify
• Part of the balance sheet	• Not tracked through accounting practices
• Investment produces known returns	• Assessment based on assumptions
• Can be easily duplicated	• Cannot be bought or imitated
• Depreciates with use	• Appreciates with purposeful use
• Has finite application	• Multi-application without reducing value
• Best managed with "scarcity" mentality	• Best managed with "abundance" mentality
• Best leveraged through control	• Best leveraged through alignment
• Can be accumulated	• Dynamic: short shelf life when not in use

Another basis for the distinction between tangible and intangible assets is the concept of hard data versus soft data. This concept, discussed earlier, is perhaps more familiar to HR practitioners. Table 8.3 shows the difference between hard and soft data. The most significant part of the definition of soft data lies in the *difficulty in converting* the data to monetary value. Intangible measures are defined as measures that are *purposely not converted* to monetary values. Using this simple definition avoids confusion of whether a data item should be classified as hard data or soft data. Data are considered soft if a credible, economically feasible process is unavailable for conversion. The ROI Methodology discussed throughout this book uses this definition of intangibles.

Table 8.3 Characteristics of Data

Hard Data	Soft Data
• Objectively based • Easy to measure and quantify • Relatively easy to assign monetary values • Common measures of organizational performance • Very credible with management	• Subjectively based in many cases • Difficult to measure and quantify, directly • Difficult to assign monetary values • Less credible as a performance measure • Usually behaviorally oriented

Identification of Measures

Data on intangible measures are available from different sources representing different time frames, as illustrated in Figure 8.1. First, you can uncover them early in the process, during the needs assessment and initial analysis. Once you have identified the sources, you can plan to collect intangible data as part of the overall data collection strategy. For example, a new reward systems program may have several hard data measures, such as productivity and quality, linked to the program. Employee satisfaction is an intangible measure that you can identify and monitor without any intention of or plan for converting it to a monetary value. Therefore, from the very beginning, this measure is destined to be a nonmonetary benefit reported along with the ROI results. This measure is labeled T1 in Figure 8.1.

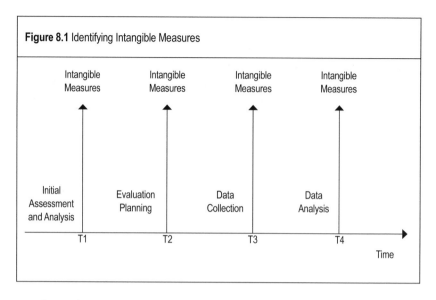

Figure 8.1 Identifying Intangible Measures

Second, you can identify intangible measures during discussions with clients or sponsors about the impact of an HR program. Clients can usually identify intangible measures expected to be influenced by the program. For example, a large multinational company implemented a wellness and fitness program and then planned for an ROI analysis. During the ROI planning session, program designers, the contractor, and a senior executive identified potential intangible measures that were perceived to be influenced by the program. These measures were included on the ROI analysis planning document and are labeled T2 in Figure 8.1.

Third, you can identify intangible measures during a follow-up evaluation. Perhaps a measure is not expected or anticipated in the initial program design, but it surfaces later in a questionnaire, in an interview, or during a focus group. These data collection methods often include questions about other improvements linked to the HR program. Participant responses often provide several intangible measures, and placing a value on the actual measure should not be attempted. This step is labeled T3 in Figure 8.1.

For example, in an innovation and creativity program, participants were asked specifically what had improved in their work as a result of the program. The participants provided several intangible measures, which managers perceived to be linked to the program.

Fourth, you can identify intangible measures during an attempt to convert the data to monetary values. If the conversion process loses credibility, the measure should be reported as an intangible benefit. For example, in a customer relationship management program, customer satisfaction is identified early in the process as one of the measures of program success. A conversion of the data to monetary values was attempted. However, the process of assigning a value to the data diminished the credibility of the analysis; therefore, customer satisfaction was reported as an intangible benefit. This step is labeled T4 in Figure 8.1.

Is the Data Measurable?

Sometimes a debate erupts over whether a particular item perceived as intangible (soft) can actually be measured. In reality, any item that represents the outcome of an HR program can be measured. The measure may have to be a perception of the issue taken from a stakeholder involved in the process, but it is still a measure. The ROI Methodology rests on the assumption that anything, even intangibles, can be measured — some precisely, others not very precisely. For example, the number of team conflicts is a measure that can be assessed and categorized. HR staff can record all conflicts observed and place them into categories. However, to place a value on a conflict may cause the data item to be labeled intangible if no credible, economically feasible way is available to convert it to monetary value.

Can the Data Be Converted?

Chapter 6 focused on various ways to convert data to monetary values. The philosophy is simple: Any data item can be converted to monetary value; a monetary value can be assigned to any measure. The key issue is credibility of the converted value. Is it a believable value? Is a credible process used to convert data to monetary values? Does converting the data to monetary values cost too much? Is that value stable over time? Senior executives weigh these critical issues as they examine the conversion of data to monetary value. For tangible data conversion, the issue is of little concern. Tangible data items, such as increased output, reduction in rejects, and time savings, are easily converted. Soft measures (stress, complaints, attitudes, and so forth), however, tend to lose credibility in the conversion process.

Table 8.4 shows a four-part test for converting intangibles to monetary values, presented in Chapter 6. This test often leads to the classification of data as intangible. The ultimate question is posted in step four, which is a practical issue that protects the credibility of the impact study and also allows for consistency from one study to another. The ROI Methodology would be unreliable if one evaluator converted a particular data item to monetary value whereas another evaluator did not. Maintaining this consistency is a significant part of building the standards necessary for the ROI Methodology.

Table 8.4 Test for Converting Intangibles to Monetary Value
1. Does an acceptable, standard monetary value exist for the measure? If yes, use it; if not, go to step 2.
2. Is there a method you can use to convert the measure to money? If not, list it as an intangible; if yes, go to step 3.
3. Can you accomplish the conversion with minimum resources? If not, list it as an intangible; if yes, go to step 4.
4. Can you describe the conversion process to an executive audience and secure buy-in in two minutes? If yes, use it in the ROI calculation; if not, list it as an intangible.

Analysis

For most intangible data, no specific analysis is planned for intangibles. Any previous attempts to convert intangible data to monetary units would have been unsuccessful. In some cases, you may attempt to isolate the effects of the HR program using one or more of the methods outlined in Chapter 5. This step is necessary when there is a need to know the specific amount of change in the intangible measure linked to the program. In many cases, however, the intangible data reflect evidence of improvement. The precise amount of the improvement or the amount of improvement related directly to the HR program is not needed. Because the value of the intangible data is not plugged into the ROI calculation, intangible measures normally are not used to justify the addition of programs or the continuation of existing programs. Consequently, a detailed analysis is unnecessary. Intangible benefits provide supporting evidence of the program success and can be presented as qualitative data.

Typical Intangible Measures

Most of the remainder of the chapter focuses on a few typical intangible measures. These measures are often presented as intangibles in impact studies. In some cases, organizations do convert intangible data to monetary values. Here are a few examples.

Employee Satisfaction

Employee satisfaction is perhaps one of the most important intangible measures. Improving job satisfaction is the goal of a variety of HR programs. Organizations carry out attitude surveys to measure the extent to which employees are satisfied with the organization, their jobs, their supervisor, co-workers, and a host of other job-related factors. For example, in a vision and values program implemented for all employees at one organization, the annual attitude survey contained five questions tied directly to perceptions and attitudes influenced by the program.

Because attitude surveys are usually taken annually, survey results may not be in sync with the timing of a specific HR program. When employee satisfaction is one of the program objectives and is a critical outcome, some organizations conduct surveys at a prescribed time frame after the HR program is implemented and design the survey instrument around issues related to the program. This approach, however, is expensive.

Although employee satisfaction has always been a topic in employee relations, it has become more significant in recent years because of the correlation between job satisfaction and other key measures. A classic relationship with employee satisfaction is in the area of employee recruitment and retention. Firms with excellent employee satisfaction ratings are often attractive to potential employees. The high ratings become a subtle but effective recruiting tool. "Employers of Choice" and "Best Places to Work," for example, often have high levels of employee satisfaction ratings, which attract employees.

The significance of the relationship between employee satisfaction and employee turnover has grown as turnover and retention have become critical matters in the last decade and are likely to remain so in the future. The relationship is easily developed with current HR information systems, which have modules to calculate the correlation between the turnover rates and the employee satisfaction scores for the various job groups, divisions, departments, and so forth.

Employee satisfaction has a prominent connection to customer service. Hundreds of applied research projects are beginning to show a very high correlation between employee satisfaction scores and customer satisfaction scores. These links, often referred to as service-profit chain, create a promising way to identify important relationships between attitudes and profits in an organization.

Even with these developments, most organizations do not or cannot place credible values on employee satisfaction data. The trend is moving in the right direction, but for now job satisfaction is usually listed as an intangible benefit in impact studies.

Organizational Commitment/Employee Engagement

In recent years, organizational commitment (OC) measures have complemented or replaced job satisfaction measures. OC measures go beyond employee satisfaction and include the extent to which employees identify with organizational goals, mission, philosophy, value, policies, and practices. In recent years, the concept of involvement and engagement with the organization is the key issue. Employee engagement (EE) is now the preferred measure. EE measures the extent to which employees are actively engaged in decisions and issues on the job. OC and EE measures closely correlate with productivity and other performance improvement measures, in contrast to employee satisfaction, which does not always correlate with improvements in productivity. As OC/EE scores improve (according to a standard index), a corresponding improvement in productivity should develop. The OC/EE is often measured the same way as attitude surveys, using a five- or seven-point scale taken directly from employees or groups of employees. Productivity is usually measured by revenue per employee.

OC/EE scores are rarely converted to monetary value. Although some relationships have been developed to link OC/EE to more tangible data, this research is still in development. For most studies, OC/EE scores would be listed as intangibles.

Culture/Climate

In recent years, much attention has been focused on the culture of the organization. Culture is a function of the organization's practices, beliefs, opinions, behaviors, policies, vision, and values. Various HR-driven culture-change projects attempt to strengthen, solidify, or adjust the culture. The culture in some organizations is distinct and defined, but it is always difficult to measure precisely.

Some organizations use culture instruments to collect data on this measure before and after an HR program to gauge improvement. The scores on these instruments represent data that may connect directly to the HR program. In practice, converting culture data to monetary value in a credible way is difficult. Therefore, culture change is usually listed as an intangible measure.

Some organizations conduct climate surveys, which reflect work climate changes such as communication, openness, trust, and quality of feedback. Closely related to organizational commitment and culture, climate surveys are more general and often focus on a range of workplace issues and environmental enablers and inhibitors. Climate surveys conducted before and after an HR program is implemented may reflect the extent to which the program has changed these intangible measures.

Diversity

Diversity continues to be significant as organizations strive to develop and nurture a diverse workforce. HR-initiated programs influence the diversity mix of the organization, and a variety of data is available to measure the impact of focusing on diversity. The diversity mix is a measure showing employee categories along diversity definitions such as race, creed, color, national origin, age, religion, and sex. This diversity mix shows the makeup of the team at any given time and is not a measure that can be converted to monetary value credibly.

Having a diverse group influences several other measures, including absenteeism, turnover, discrimination complaints, morale, and sometimes productivity and quality. Also, many diversity perception instruments are available to measure the attitudes of employees toward diversity issues; they are often administered before and after diversity projects. In addition, some organizations collect input on diversity issues in an annual feedback survey. All of these measures are worthwhile and reveal progress on a meaningful subject, but they are difficult to convert directly to monetary value and are usually listed as intangibles.

Employee Complaints

Some organizations record and report specific employee complaints. These feedback mechanisms are usually highly visible and have catchy names such as "Speak Out," "Talk Back," or "Hey, Mike" (in an organization where the CEO's first name is Mike). A reduction in the number of employee complaints is sometimes directly related to an HR program, such as a team-building program. Consequently, the level of complaints is used as a measure of the program's success and is usually reported as an intangible measure. Because of the challenge in converting complaints to monetary values, this measure is almost always listed as an intangible benefit.

Stress Reduction

HR programs such as work/life balance, personal productivity, or conflict resolution can reduce work-related stress by preparing employees to identify and confront stress factors to improve job performance, accomplish more in a workday, and relieve tension and anxiety. The subsequent reduction in stress may be directly linked to the program. Although excessive stress may be directly linked to other, easy-to-convert data, such as productivity, absenteeism, and medical claims, it is usually listed as an intangible benefit.

Employee Tardiness

Some organizations monitor tardiness, especially in highly-focused work and tightly contained work environments, such as call centers. Tardiness is an irritating work habit that can cause inefficiencies and delays. Organizations can use electronic and computerized time reporting to identify problem areas. A few HR programs are designed to reduce or prevent tardiness. Converting tardiness to a monetary value is difficult because of the many aspects of the impact of the unacceptable work habit. Consequently, when tardiness is presented as an improvement from an HR program, it is usually listed as an intangible benefit.

Employee Transfers

Sometimes employees request a transfer to another section, department, or division of the organization. Requests for transfers often reflect dissatisfaction with a variety of issues, including management, policies, and practices in the organization. Transfers are essentially internal turnover. Some HR programs aim to reduce or remove these unpleasant environmental influences. In such situations, requests for transfer are monitored and reported as an intangible benefit of the HR program. Although placing a value on this internal turnover is possible, usually no attempt is made to assign monetary values to transfers.

Innovation and Creativity

For many progressive organizations, innovation is vital to success. A variety of innovation and creativity programs are implemented to improve this critical area. Innovation is a paradox in that it is both easy and difficult to measure. Measuring outcomes is easy in areas such as copyrights, patents, inventions, new projects, and employee suggestions. Measuring the creative spirit and behavior of employees is more difficult.

An employee suggestion system, a longtime measure of the innovative and creative processes of an organization, still flourishes today in many firms. Employees are rewarded for their suggestions if they are approved and implemented. Tracking the suggestion rates and comparing them with other organizations is an important benchmarking item for innovation and creative capability. Other measures, such as the number of new projects, products, processes, and strategies, can be monitored and measured in some way.

Some organizations actually measure the creative spirit of employees using inventories and instruments. Comparing scores of groups of employees over time reflects the degree to which employees are improving innovation and creativity in the workplace. Subjectivity often enters the measurement process with these issues, and having consistent and comparable measures is still a challenge. Because of the difficulty of converting data to monetary values, these measures are usually listed as intangibles.

Competencies

Organizations are interested in developing key competencies in particular areas such as in the mission and in key product lines and processes. Core competencies are often identified and implemented in critical job groups. Measuring competencies with self-assessments from the individual employee and assessments from their supervisors is possible. In some cases, other inputs may be desirable or necessary to measure. This approach goes beyond just learning new skills, processes, or knowledge to using a combination of skills, knowledge, and behavior on the job to develop an acceptable level of competence to meet competitive challenges. Because of the difficulty in converting competencies to monetary values, measures of improvement are often left as intangible.

Leadership

Perhaps the most challenging measure is leadership. Effective leadership can make the difference between the success and failure of an organization. Without appropriate leadership behaviors throughout the organization, resources can be misapplied or wasted.

Organizations can measure leadership with any of several instruments and inventories for assessing the leadership style, preference, or practice of managers. These inventories yield profiles that can be monitored over time and compared to expectations or desired level. The instruments can also assess the current leadership style and be related to expectations and targets.

One of the most common methods is known as 360-degree feedback. Here, a prescribed set of leadership behaviors desired in an organization is assessed by different sources to provide a composite of the overall leadership capability. The sources often include the immediate manager of the leader, a colleague in the same area, the employees under the direct influence of the leader, internal or external customers, and self-assessment. These assessments come from different directions, forming a 360-degree circle. The measure is basically an observation captured in a survey, often reported electronically. Although 360-degree feedback has grown rapidly in the United States, Europe, and Asia as a way to capture overall leadership behavior change, it is usually left as an intangible.

Ethics

In the wake of a variety of business scandals in recent years, the issue of ethics has gained a higher level of interest and priority in organizations. Several HR-driven programs focus on shaping the desired ethical behavior and conduct. The menu of available programs ranges from briefings and policies to role modeling and training. Also, these programs often provide an opportunity for employees to use hotlines or special contacts to expose unethical practices. While measures are available to show improvements in ethical behavior (or the perception of improvement), these measures are often not converted to monetary value but are left as intangibles.

Customer Satisfaction

Because of the need to build and improve customer service, several measures are often monitored and reported as a payoff of an HR program. HR-driven customer service programs have a direct influence on these measures. One of the most solid measures is survey data showing the degree to which customers are pleased with the products and services. These survey values, reported as absolute data or as an index, represent important data from which to compare the success of a customer service program.

As described earlier, customer satisfaction data are attracting much interest. The data's value is often linked to other measures such as revenue growth, market share, and profits. Several models are available to show what happens when customers are dissatisfied, along with the economic impact of those decisions. Even in the health care area, researchers are showing links between patient satisfaction and customer retention. Still others are demonstrating relationships between customer satisfaction and such measures as innovation, product development, and some tangibles. Techniques exist to convert survey data to monetary values, but in most situations the conversion is rarely attempted. Consequently, customer satisfaction improvements at the present time are usually reported as intangible benefits.

Customer Complaints

Most organizations monitor customer complaints. Each complaint is recorded along with the disposition and the time required to resolve the complaint, as well as specific costs associated with the complaint resolution. Organizations sometimes design HR programs to reduce the number of customer complaints. The total cost and impact of a complaint has three components:

- the time it takes to resolve the complaint
- the cost of making restitution to the customer
- the ultimate cost of ill will generated by the dissatisfaction (lost future business)

Because of the difficulty of assigning an accurate monetary value to a customer complaint, the measure usually becomes a very important intangible benefit.

Customer Loyalty

Customer retention is a critical measure that is sometimes linked to sales, marketing, and customer service programs. Long-term, efficient, and productive customer relationships are important to the success of an organization. Specific models can show the value of a customer and of keeping customers over a period of time. For example, the average tenure of a customer can translate directly into bottom-line profits. Although the benefits of customer retention are understood, the measure is not always converted to monetary value.

Tied closely to customer loyalty is the rate at which customers leave the organization. This churn rate can be expensive not only in lost business (profits from lost customers) but also in the cost necessary to generate a new customer. Because of the difficulty of converting directly to a specific monetary value, customer loyalty is usually listed as an intangible benefit.

Teamwork

You can monitor various measures that reflect how well teams are working. Although the output of teams and the quality of their work are often measured as hard data and converted to monetary values, you can monitor and report other interpersonal measures too. Sometimes organizations survey team members before and after an HR program to determine if the level of teamwork has increased. Using a variable scale, team members provide a perception of improvement. The monetary value of increased teamwork is rarely developed, and consequently, it is reported as an intangible benefit.

Cooperation

The success of a team often depends on the cooperative spirit of team members. Some instruments measure the level of cooperation before and after the implementation of an HR program using a perception scale. Because converting this measure to a monetary value is not easily accomplished, it is almost always reported as an intangible benefit.

Conflict

In team environments, the level of conflict is sometimes measured. A reduction in conflict may reflect the success of an HR initiative. Although conflict reduction can be measured by perception or by numbers of conflicts, the monetary value is an elusive figure. Thus, in most situations, a monetary value is not placed on conflict reduction, and it is reported as an intangible benefit.

Final Thoughts

Dozens of intangible measures are available to reflect the success of HR programs. Although they may not be perceived to be as useful as specific monetary measures, they are nevertheless a crucial part of an overall evaluation. Intangible measures should be identified, explored, examined, monitored, and analyzed for changes when they are linked to the program. Collectively, intangibles add a unique dimension to the overall program results because most, if not all, programs have intangible measures associated with them. Some of the most common intangible measures were covered in this chapter, but the coverage was not meant to be complete.

Chapter 9.
Communicating and
Using Evaluation Data

Okay, you have your data in hand, so what is next? Should the data be used to modify the program, change the process, show the contribution, justify new programs, gain additional support, or build goodwill? How should the data be presented? Who should present the data? Where and when should the data be communicated? This chapter delves into these and other questions, but most important, it tells you how evaluation data, properly communicated to the right audiences, can drive improvement in your organization.

Principles of Communicating Results

The skills required to communicate results effectively are almost as delicate and sophisticated as those needed to obtain results. Style is as pertinent as the substance. Regardless of the message, audience, or medium, a few general principles apply. Because they affect the overall success of the communication effort, these principles should serve as a checklist for the HR staff when disseminating program results.

Communication Must Be Timely

In general, you should communicate results as soon as they are known. From a practical standpoint, you may want to delay the communication until a convenient time, such as the next management meeting, quarterly sales meeting, or annual HR conference. Address issues of timing: Is the audience ready for the results, considering other things that may have happened? Is the audience expecting results? When is the best time for having the maximum effect on the audience? What circumstances may dictate a change in the timing of the communication?

Communication Should Be Targeted to Specific Audiences

Communication is more effective if it is designed for a particular group. The message should be specifically tailored to the interests, needs, and expectations of the target audience. The results described in this chapter reflect outcomes at all levels of evaluation. When results are communicated depends in part on when the data are developed. The data developed early in the project can be communicated during the project. Data collected after implementation can be communicated in a follow-up study. Therefore, the results, in their broadest sense, range from early feedback with qualitative data to ROI values in various quantitative terms.

Media Should Be Carefully Selected

For particular groups, some media are more effective than others. Face-to-face meetings may be better than special bulletins. A memo distributed exclusively to top management may be more impactful than the company's newsletter. Choosing the most appropriate method of communication can help improve the effectiveness of the process.

Communication Should Be Unbiased and Modest

Facts must be separated from fiction, and accurate statements must be separated from opinions. Some audiences are likely to be skeptical about accepting communication from the HR staff because they antici-pate receiving biased opinions. Boastful statements sometimes turn off recipients, resulting in the loss of most — if not all — of the content's significance. Observable, credible facts carry far more weight than extreme or sensational claims. Although such claims may get audience attention, they often detract from the value of the results.

Communication Must Be Consistent

The timing and content of the communication should be consistent with past practices. A special communication at an unusual time during the program may provoke suspicion. Also, if a particular group, such as top management, regularly receives communication on outcomes, it should continue receiving communication — even if the results are negative. If some results are omitted, employees may develop the impression that only positive results are reported.

Confidentiality and Privacy Are Paramount

The reputation of the HR staff is a substantial consideration. Negative comments or sensitive feedback may be detrimental to the source if not protected properly. Data should be treated confidentially to protect the privacy of individuals and be combined in such a way that an individual's responses cannot be identified. HR staff must strive to maintain a high level of credibility and respect when communicating results. Never jeopardize your credibility by compromising people's privacy.

Planning the Communication Is Critical

Communications must be planned carefully to produce the maximum results. Planning ensures that each audience receives the proper information at the right time and that appropriate actions are taken. Table 9.1 shows the areas that will need attention as you develop the communication plan.

Following these general principles will contribute to the overall success of the communication effort. They should serve as a checklist for the HR staff when disseminating program results.

Table 9.1 Communication Planning Questions

- Who are the target audiences?
- What will actually be communicated?
- When will the data be communicated?
- How will the information be communicated?
- Where will the communication take place?
- Who will communicate the information?
- What specific actions are required or desired?

Selecting the Audience for Communications

To the greatest extent possible, the HR staff should know and understand the target audience. The staff should find out what information is needed and why. Each group has its own needs relative to the information desired. Some seek detailed information, and others want brief information. You may need input from others to determine audience needs. HR practitioners should try to understand audience bias and differing views, and be empathetic. With this awareness, communications can be tailored to each group, thereby mitigating the potential for the audience to react negatively to the results. The questions presented in Table 9.2 should be addressed when selecting the audience.

Table 9.2 Key Questions for Selecting Audiences

- Are they interested in the program?
- Do they really want to receive the information?
- Has someone already made a commitment to them regarding communication?
- Is the timing right for this audience?
- Are they familiar with the program?
- How do they prefer to have results communicated?
- Do they know the team members?
- Are they likely to find the results threatening?
- Which medium will be most convincing to this group?

The potential target audiences who are to receive information about results have different job levels and responsibilities. One way to select your audiences is to analyze the reason behind the communication. Table 9.3 shows common target audiences and the basis for selecting the audience.

Perhaps the most important audience is the sponsor — the individual or team supporting the evaluation. This audience initiates the program, reviews the data, and weighs the final assessment of the effectiveness of the program. Another key target audience is the top management group, who is responsible for allocating resources for the HR program and needs information to help justify expenditures and gauge the effectiveness of the efforts.

Selected groups of managers (or all managers) are also target audiences. Management's support and involvement in the process and the HR department's credibility help ensure success. Effectively communicating program results to management can increase both support and credibility.

Communicating with the participants' team leaders (or immediate managers) is essential. In many cases, team leaders must encourage partic-

Table 9.3 Rationale for Specific Target Audiences

Reason for Communication	Primary Target Audiences
To secure approval for the program	Sponsor, Top Executives
To gain support for the program	Managers, Team Leaders
To secure agreement with the issues	Participants, Team Leaders
To build credibility for Human Resources	Top Executives, Managers
To enhance reinforcement of the processes	Immediate Managers
To drive action for improvement	Sponsor, HR Staff
To prepare participants for the program	Team Leaders, Participants
To enhance results and quality of future feedback	Participants
To show the complete results of the HR program	Sponsor, HR Staff
To underscore the importance of measuring results	Sponsor, HR Staff
To explain techniques used to results	Sponsor, HR Staff
To create desire for a participant to be involved	Team Leaders, Participants
To stimulate interest in Human Resources	Top Executives, Managers
To demonstrate accountability for expenditures	All Employees
To market future programs	Prospective Sponsors, Managers, Team Leaders

ipants to implement the program. Also, they often support and reinforce the objectives of the program. Positive results strengthen the commitment to human resources and improve the credibility of the HR staff.

Occasionally, you may communicate results to encourage participation in the program. This approach is especially effective for programs that employees attend on a voluntary basis. The potential participants are important targets for communicating results.

Participants (stakeholders) need feedback on the overall success of the effort. Some individuals may not have been as successful as others in achieving the desired results. Communicating the results adds additional pressure to implement the program proficiently and to improve results for the future. For those achieving excellent results, communication serves as a reinforcement of what is expected. Communicating results to participants is often overlooked because of the assumption that once the program is complete, participants do not need to be informed of its success.

The HR support staff also needs communication about program results. Those who designed, developed, and implemented the program should receive detailed information about the process so that they can make necessary adjustments and measure results.

All employees and stockholders are less likely targets. General-interest news stories may increase employee respect for human resources. Goodwill and positive attitudes toward the organization may also be by-products of communicating results. Stockholders, on the other hand, are more interested in the return on their investment.

Table 9.3 shows the most common target audiences, although organizations may have others. For example, management or employees could be divided into different departments, divisions, or even subsidiaries of the organization. The number of audiences can be large in a complex organization. At a minimum, you should communicate to four target audiences:

- a senior management group
- the participants' immediate manager or team leader
- the participants
- the HR staff

Developing the Information: The Impact Study

When an impact study is conducted, the data will be reported in detail in an impact and ROI study report. The impact study, which describes the program, methodology, and results achieved, is the beginning point for any communication. The formality and appearance of the report will depend on whether the report itself is actually distributed. It may only serve as a resource for other types of communication. However, early in the use of the ROI process, a complete evaluation study should be conducted and printed in a readable, descriptive manner. The case study presented in Chapter 11 is basically an impact study with added dialogue. When the dialogue and some detailed background are removed, it is essentially the impact study conducted for this particular project.

The impact study report contains the detailed information needed for the various target audiences. Brief summaries of results with appropriate charts may be sufficient for some communication efforts. In other situations, particularly with a significant program requiring extensive funding, a detailed evaluation report may be necessary. This report provides the base of information for specific audiences and various media. The report may contain the following sections:

The **executive summary** is a brief overview of the entire report, explaining the basis for the evaluation and the significant conclusions and recommendations. It is designed for individuals who are too busy to read a detailed report. It is usually written last but appears first in the report for easy access.

Background information provides a general description of the HR program. If applicable, the analysis that led to the implementation of the program is summarized, including the events that led to the evaluation. Integrate other items as necessary to provide a full description of the program.

The **objectives** for both the impact study and the HR program are outlined. The report details the particular objectives of the study itself so that the reader clearly understands the rationale for the study and how the data are to be used. In addition, this section highlights the HR program's specific objectives, from which the different types or levels of data will be collected.

The **evaluation strategy** outlines all the components that make up the total evaluation process. The specific purposes of evaluation are outlined, and the evaluation design and methodology are explained. Any unusual issues in the evaluation design are discussed. Finally, other useful information related to the design, timing, and execution of the evaluation is included.

The **data collection and analysis** section explains the methods used to collect data. Here, you describe the instruments used in data collection and present them as exhibits. The methods used to analyze data are presented, including methods to isolate the effects of the program and to convert data to monetary values.

The **reaction** section delineates the data you collected from key stakeholders (the participants involved in the process) to measure their reactions to the program and their levels of satisfaction with various issues and parts of the process. You may also include other input from the sponsor or managers to show the levels of satisfaction.

The **learning** section consists of a brief summary of the formal and informal methods for measuring learning. It explains how participants have learned new processes, skills, tasks, procedures, and practices.

The **application and implementation** section shows how the program was put into place and describes the success with the application of new skills and knowledge. This section also addresses implementation issues, including any major success or lack of success.

The section on **barriers and enablers** reveals the various problems and obstacles inhibiting the success of the HR program and presents them as barriers to implementation. Also, factors or influences that had a positive effect on the program are included as enablers. Together, they provide insight into what can hinder or enhance programs in the future.

Business impact (if applicable) shows the actual business impact measures reflecting the business needs that provided the basis for the program. This data summary shows the extent to which business performance has changed as a result of the program implementation.

Program costs are presented in this section, which includes a summary of the costs by category. Analysis, development, implementation, and evaluation costs are recommended categories for cost presentation. You should also briefly explain the assumptions made in developing and classifying costs.

Return on investment (if applicable) shows the ROI calculation along with the benefit/cost ratio (BCR). It compares the ROI value to what was expected and provides an interpretation of the ROI calculation.

The **intangible measures** section shows the various intangible measures directly linked to the program. Intangibles are those measures purposely not converted to monetary values.

Conclusions and recommendations are based on all the results. If appropriate, present a brief explanation of how each conclusion was reached. You may also provide a list of recommendations or changes in the program, if appropriate, along with a short explanation of each recommendation. These components make up the major parts of a complete evaluation report. Table 9.4 shows the table of contents from a typical impact study.

Table 9.4 Table of Contents for an Impact Study Report

• Executive Summary	• Results: Application and Implementation
• General Information	» Data Sources
» Background	» Data Summary
» Objectives of Study	» Key Issues
• Methodology for Impact Study	• Barriers and Enablers
» Levels of Evaluation	» Barriers
» Collecting Data	» Enablers
» Isolating the Effects of HR	• Results: Business Impact
» Converting Data to Monetary Values	» Linkage with Business Measures
» Assumptions	» Methods of Isolating
• Data Analysis Issues	» Converting Data to Money
• Results: General Information	• Results: ROI and Its Meaning
» Response Profile	» Costs
» Success with Objectives	» ROI
• Results: Reaction and Satisfaction	• Results: Intangible Measures
» Data Sources	• Conclusions and Recommendations
» Data Summary	» Conclusions
» Key Issues	» Recommendations
• Results: Reaction and Satisfaction	• Exhibits
» Data Sources	
» Data Summary	
» Key Issues	
• Results: Learning	
» Data Sources	
» Data Summary	

This report is an effective, professional way to present data. You should clearly explain the methodology along with assumptions made in the analysis. The reader should readily see how the data were developed and how the specific steps were followed to make the process more conservative, credible, and accurate. Place detailed statistical analyses in an appendix.

Because this document reports the success of groups of employees, complete credit for the success must go to the stakeholders involved. Their performance generated the success. Boasting about results should be avoided. Although the evaluation may be accurate and credible, it may still have some subjective issues.

Selecting Communication Media

Many options are available to communicate program results. In addition to the impact study report, the most frequently used media are meetings, reports, the organization's publications, e-mail, brochures, websites, and case studies. The following sections describe the use of these media for communicating evaluation results. Table 9.5 shows the variety of possibilities for reporting results.

Table 9.5 A Variety of Options for Communicating Results

Meetings	Detailed Reports	Brief Reports	Electronic Reporting	Mass Publications
Executive Briefings	Impact Study	Executive Summary	Website	Announcements
Manager Meetings	Case Study (Internal)	Slide Overview	E-mail	Bulletins
Project Team Meetings	Case Study (External)	One-Page Summary	Blogs	Newsletters
Stakeholder Meetings	Major Articles	Brochure	Video	Brief Articles

Meetings

In addition to meetings with the senior executives to discuss results, other meetings are fertile opportunities for communicating program results to individuals involved in the study. Attendees could include the managers of the participants involved, the project team that conducted the study, and various stakeholders who have a strong interest because of their involvement or support for the program. All organizations discuss HR results in meetings such as the following:

- staff meetings designed to review progress, discuss current problems, and distribute information
- manager meetings
- best-practices meetings
- business-update meetings to review progress and plans

You can integrate a few highlights of major program results into these meetings to build interest, commitment, and support for HR initiatives. Along with the selected results, you should mention operating issues, plans, and forecasts.

Interim and Progress Reports

Although usually limited to large evaluation projects, a highly visible way to communicate results is through interim and routine memos and reports. Published or disseminated via the intranet on a periodic basis, these reports inform management about the status of the program, communicate the interim results achieved in the program, and activate needed changes and improvements. A more subtle reason for the report is to gain additional support and commitment from the management group.

The Organization's Communication Tools

To reach a wide audience, HR staff can use in-house publications. Whether a newsletter, magazine, newspaper, or website file, these types of media usually reach all employees. The information can be quite effective if communicated appropriately. The scope should be limited to general interest articles, announcements, and interviews.

E-Mail and Websites

Internal and external internet sites, companywide intranets, and email are excellent vehicles for releasing results, promoting ideas, and informing employees and other target groups about HR results. E-mail, in particular, provides a virtually instantaneous means with which to communicate and solicit response from large numbers of people.

Brochures and Pamphlets

A brochure might be appropriate for voluntary HR programs conducted on a continuing basis. A brochure should be attractive, present a complete description of the program, and include a major section devoted to the results achieved. Measurable results and reactions from participants, or even direct quotes from individuals, could add spice to an otherwise dull brochure. Also, the results may provide convincing data that the HR program is successful.

Case Studies

Case studies are an effective way to communicate the results of an HR program. Develop case studies for major evaluation projects. A typical case study describes the situation, provides appropriate background information (including the events that led to the implementation of the program), presents the techniques and strategies used to develop the study, and highlights the key issues in the program. Case studies tell an interesting story of how the evaluation was developed and the problems and concerns identified along the way.

Case studies have value for both internal use and external use. As shown in Table 9.6, the internal use is to build understanding, capability, and support internally. Case studies are impressive to hand to a potential client and somewhat convincing for others who are seeking data about the success of HR programs. Externally, case studies can be used to bring exposure and recognition to the HR team and to help the organization brand its overall HR function and, in some cases, itself. A variety of publication outlets are available for case studies — not only in the HR print space but in general publications as well. Appendix B presents a few published ROI case studies for human resources.

Table 9.6 Internal and External Use of Case Studies

INTERNAL USE	EXTERNAL PUBLICATION
• Communicate results	• Provide recognition to participants
• Teach others	• Improve image of function
• Build a history	• Enhance brand of department
• Serve as a template	• Enhance image of organization
• Make an impression	

Communicating the Information

Perhaps the greatest challenge of communication is the actual delivery of the message. Delivery can be accomplished in a variety of ways and settings, based on the target audience and the media selected for the message.

Three particular approaches deserve additional coverage. Each approach is explored in more detail in the following sections.

Providing Feedback during Program Implementation

One of the most important reasons for collecting reaction, satisfaction, and learning data is to provide feedback quickly so that adjustments or changes can be made in the program. In most programs, data are routinely collected and quickly communicated to a variety of groups. Some of these feedback sessions result in identifying specific actions that need to be taken. This process becomes comprehensive and needs to be managed in a proactive way. Table 9.7 presents the steps for providing feedback and managing the feedback process.[1]

Following these steps will help move the project forward and provide critical feedback, often ensuring that adjustments are supported and made.

Table 9.7 Steps to Provide Feedback during Program Implementation

- Communicate quickly.
- Simplify the data.
- Explain the role of the HR staff and the program's sponsor in the feedback.
- Use negative data in a constructive way.
- Use positive data in a cautious way.
- Choose the language of the meeting and communication very carefully.
- Ask the sponsor for reactions to the data.
- Ask the sponsor for recommendations.
- Use support and confrontation carefully.
- React and act on the data.
- Secure agreement from all key stakeholders.
- Keep the feedback process short.

Presenting Impact Study Data to Senior Management

Perhaps one of the most stressful communications is presenting an impact study to the senior management team, which also serves as the client for the evaluation study. The challenges are (1) convincing this highly skeptical and critical group that outstanding results have been achieved (assuming they have) in a reasonable timeframe, (2) addressing the salient points, and (3) making sure the managers understand the process.

Two particular issues can create obstacles. First, if the results are impressive, HR leaders must assure the managers that the data are reliable. On the other extreme, if the data are negative, human resources must ensure that managers do not overreact to the negative results and look for someone to blame. Several guidelines can help make sure this process is planned and executed properly.

Plan a face-to-face meeting with senior team members for the first one or two major impact studies. If they are unfamiliar with the ROI Methodology, an in-person meeting is necessary to make sure they understand the process. The good news is that they will probably attend the meeting because they have not seen ROI data developed for this type of HR program. The bad news is that such meetings take a lot of time, usually one hour for the presentation. After a group has had a face-to-face meeting with a couple of presentations, an executive summary may suffice. At this point, the senior team understands the process, so a shortened version may be appropriate. After the target audience is familiar with the process, a brief version may be required, which will involve a one- to two-page summary with charts and graphs showing the six types of measures.

When making the initial presentation, the results should not be distributed beforehand or even during the session but saved until the end of the session. This strategy will allow you enough time to explain the process and audience members enough time to react to it before they see the ROI calculation. Present the ROI Methodology step-by-step, showing how the data were collected, when they were collected, who provided the data, how the effect of the program was isolated from other influences, and how data were converted to monetary values. The various assumptions, adjustments, and conservative approaches should be presented along with the total cost of the program so that the target audience will begin to buy into the process of developing the ROI.

When the data are actually presented, the results are given one level at a time, starting with Level 1, moving through Level 5, and ending with the intangibles. This approach allows the audience to see the reaction, learning, application and implementation, business impact, and ROI.

After some discussion on the meaning of the ROI, the intangible measures should be presented. Allocating time for each level as appropriate for the audience helps overcome the potentially emotional reactions to a very positive or negative ROI.

Show the consequences of additional accuracy if it is an issue. The tradeoff for more accuracy and validity often means more expense. Address this issue whenever necessary, agreeing to add more data if required. Also monitor concerns about, reactions to, and issues for the process and make adjustments accordingly for the next presentation.

Collectively, these steps will help you prepare for and present one of the most critical meetings in the ROI process with the management team. Improving communications with this group requires developing an overall strategy and a defined purpose. Figure 9.1 illustrates this approach.

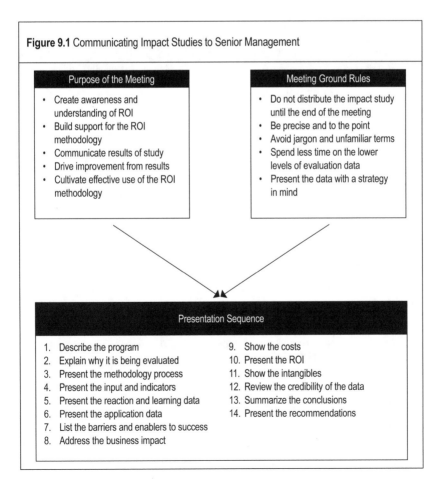

Figure 9.1 Communicating Impact Studies to Senior Management

Purpose of the Meeting

- Create awareness and understanding of ROI
- Build support for the ROI methodology
- Communicate results of study
- Drive improvement from results
- Cultivate effective use of the ROI methodology

Meeting Ground Rules

- Do not distribute the impact study until the end of the meeting
- Be precise and to the point
- Avoid jargon and unfamiliar terms
- Spend less time on the lower levels of evaluation data
- Present the data with a strategy in mind

Presentation Sequence

1. Describe the program
2. Explain why it is being evaluated
3. Present the methodology process
4. Present the input and indicators
5. Present the reaction and learning data
6. Present the application data
7. List the barriers and enablers to success
8. Address the business impact
9. Show the costs
10. Present the ROI
11. Show the intangibles
12. Review the credibility of the data
13. Summarize the conclusions
14. Present the recommendations

Table 9.8 is an example of a one-page summary that could be sent to the management team if its members understand the process.

Table 9.8 One-Page Summary of Impact Study	
ROI Impact Study	
Program Title: Values-Based/Culture-Based Selection	
Target Audience: New Candidates for Employment	
Description: New selection tool and peer interviews screen out candidates that do not fit the culture and values of this hotel chain.	
Technique to Isolate Effects of Program: Trend analysis	
Technique to Convert Data to Monetary Value: External studies for cost of early turnover, validated by the HR team	
Fully-loaded Program Costs: $47,000	
Results	
Level 1: Reaction	• 95% of HR team see this as necessary • 92% of peer group interviewers see this as important • No adverse reaction from candidates was experienced
Level 2: Learning	• 100% of HR employment team certified on use of selection tool • Successful skill practice demonstration on the discussion with candidates • Successful skill practice demonstration on behavioral interviewing techniques
Level 3: Application	• Selection instrument administered properly • Selection instrument administered each time • Peer group interviewers were consistent and thorough
Level 4: Impact	• Early turnover reduction: 32% to 12% • Cost per early turnover • Total improvement
Level 5: ROI	257%
Intangible Benefits	• Job satisfaction • Reduced absenteeism • Stress reduction • Improved recruiting image

Routine Communication with Executive Management and Sponsors

In the routine communication of HR results, no group is more important than top executives. In many situations, this group is also the sponsor. Improving communications with this group requires developing an overall strategy, which may include all or part of the following actions:

- *Strengthen the relationship with executives.* An informal and productive relationship should be established between the HR manager and the top executive at the location where the program is implemented. Each should feel comfortable discussing needs and results. One approach is to establish frequent, informal meetings with the executive to review problems with current projects and to discuss other performance problems or opportunities in the organization. Frank and open discussions can provide the executive with insight not possible from any other source.

- *Show how HR programs have helped solve major problems.* Although executives like to see hard results from recent programs, solutions to immediate problems may be more convincing. This presentation is an excellent opportunity to discuss future programs for impact analysis or ROI evaluation.

- *Distribute program results.* When a program has achieved significant results, make appropriate top executives aware of them by providing them with a one-page summary (Table 9.8) or a summary outlining what the program was supposed to accomplish, when it was implemented, who was involved, and what results were achieved. This summary should be presented in a for-your-information format that consists of facts rather than opinions. A full report or meeting may be presented later. All significant communications on evaluation projects, plans, activities, and results should include the executive group. Routine information on major evaluation projects, as long as it is not boastful, can reinforce credibility and accomplishments.

- *Ask executives to be involved in a review of human resources.* An effective way to sustain commitment from top executives is to ask them to serve on an HR review committee. A review committee provides input and advice to the HR staff on a variety of issues, including needs, problems with existing programs, and evaluation issues.

- *Use the CEO/CFO's preferred communication methods.* It is very important to speak the same language as the CEO/CFO, using the same channels and methods.

Analyzing Reactions to Communication

The best indicator of how effectively you have communicated the evaluation of an HR program is the level of commitment and support garnered from the management group. The allocation of requested resources and a strong commitment from top management are tangible evidence of management's perception of the results of programs. In addition to this top-level reaction, HR staff can use a few techniques to measure the effectiveness of their communication efforts.

Whenever results are communicated, the reaction of the target audiences can be monitored. These reactions may include nonverbal gestures, oral remarks, written comments, or indirect actions that reveal how the communication was received. Usually when you present results in a meeting, you have some indication of how the group is receiving the results. During the presentation, the audience may ask questions or challenge some of the information. If you tabulate these challenges and questions, you can use them to determine the type of information to include in future communications. You should also note and count positive comments about the results, whether they are offered formally or informally.

HR staff meetings are an excellent arena for discussing the reaction to the results communication. Comments may come from many sources depending on the particular target audiences. Input from different members of the staff can be summarized to help judge the overall effectiveness of the communication.

The purpose of analyzing reactions is to make adjustments in the communication process — if adjustments are necessary. Although the reactions may involve intuitive assessments, a more sophisticated analysis can provide more accurate information to make these adjustments. The net result should be a more effective communication process.

Using Evaluation Data to Drive Improvement

Evaluation is a process improvement tool. Evaluation data should drive changes to overcome lack of success or to enhance current success. In addition, evaluation data can provide useful information to elevate the image, credibility, and success of human resources, and to recognize all the stakeholders involved. This section explores the strategies for using evaluation data properly and describes how to monitor improvements generated from the evaluation data.

Adjust Program Design

Perhaps one of the most important reasons for evaluation is to make changes in the design of the HR program. This strategy is particularly appropriate in the early stages of the launch of a new HR solution. Reaction and learning data can indicate problems with content, design, and sequencing. This information can be quickly provided to designers to refine as needed. Even follow-up application and impact data may reveal design flaws or situations where design features need to be adjusted to achieve successful outcomes.

Influence Application and Impact

Sometimes a measurement is taken to reinforce to participants what they should accomplish during implementation. In effect, the measurement is a reminder of what they should be doing and the success they should be achieving. This use of data is particularly appropriate with follow-up questionnaires distributed before their due date, an action that makes participants aware of expectations that influence the success of the program. Some HR managers may argue that this use of data unfairly biases the evaluation and measurements that influence success. However, if the designers are convinced that this measurement adds value, then including it every time may help ensure success. It becomes built into the process.

Improve Management Support for Human Resources

Managers at the middle and top levels in the organization often do not support human resources for a variety of reasons. The value of HR efforts must be expressed in terms they understand and appreciate. Evaluation data, particularly showing the application, impact, and even ROI, can provide managers with valid evidence that will build support and commitment for future HR initiatives. Nevertheless, this approach works only if the data provided are understood and valued by managers. They are typically interested in application, impact, and ROI data.

Improve Satisfaction with Stakeholders

A variety of stakeholders are involved in implementing HR programs. Evaluation data gives stakeholders a sense of the success of the program. In essence, they become more satisfied with a program when they see the value that it is adding. Application and impact data in particular help these stakeholders see that their actions are really making a difference in the organization.

Recognize and Reward Stakeholders

The most critical stakeholder in human resources is the actual participant who must learn, apply, and achieve results if the HR program is to add value. When participants excel in terms of their application and desired impact of human resources on the job, they should be rewarded and recognized for their efforts. Evaluation data clarifies the role of the participant, giving the credit to the group that actually achieved the success — the participants involved in learning and development processes.

Justify or Enhance the HR Budget

In today's economic environment, one of the most important reasons for developing evaluation data is to show the value of human resources. In tough economic times, HR staff use evaluation to justify an existing budget or to augment the current budget. This use of data can only be accomplished if the evaluation is pushed to the levels of business impact and ROI. This way, executives approving budgets can clearly see the connection between human resources and value added to the organization. Conversely, many HR budgets are being cut because data are not available to prove the actual value of human resources.

Reduce Costs

Evaluation data can show efficiencies generated with adjustments in the design, development, and implementation of an HR program. For example, asking participants how the implementation could be successful with an alternative process often provides compelling insights into ways to save costs. Asking how the particular program could be improved or how success could be achieved reveals useful information for making cost-effective adjustments. In many situations evaluation data are used to drive changes that usually result in conserving budgets or in reducing expenditures.

Entice Perspective Participants to Be Involved in the HR Program

When participants have an option of attending a program, such as a wellness and fitness program, evaluation data can provide a convincing case for their involvement. Evaluation data can show how others have reacted to the HR program, used the knowledge and skills learned, and achieved success at the impact level. In essence, through evaluation data, the participants demonstrate the advantages of being involved in the HR program. You can include this information in brochures, documents, and other promotional materials to show others why they should be involved.

Marketing HR Programs

Closely tied with the previous use of the data is the development of marketing material designed to let others know about a particular program. Included in the marketing material should be evaluation data that show the success of the program. The data add an extra dimension to marketing by enticing individuals to become involved themselves or to send others to the program because of outcomes, not content. You can only develop this type of marketing message if data are collected to show application, impact, and even ROI. This added dimension provides a strategic marketing focus for human resources, moving it from the position of trying to sell itself to one of making it attractive based on its value proposition.

Expand Implementation to Other Areas

One of the most profitable ways to use evaluation data is to make a convincing case to implement an HR solution in other areas of the organization that have the same need. When a pilot program offered in one division shows substantial contribution and adds value to the organization, you can make a compelling case to implement it in other areas if a needs assessment or performance analysis has indicated the need. Previously, this decision has been made with qualitative data, often resulting from reaction to the program. Evaluation data showing application, impact, and ROI can provide a more persuasive case for program implementation and moves the HR department to results-based decision-making.

Using the Strategies

The uses of evaluation data are limitless, and the options for providing data to various target audiences are vast. Table 9.9 shows all the uses of data described in this chapter, linked to the various levels of evaluation. This matrix can help you understand how valuable evaluation data can be in terms of driving improvement in the organization.

Table 9.9 Matching Strategies to Levels

Strategies for Using Data	Appropriate Level of Data				
	1	2	3	4	5
Adjust Program Design	✓	✓			
Influence Application and Impact			✓	✓	
Improve Management Support for Human Resources			✓	✓	✓
Improve Satisfaction with Stakeholders			✓	✓	
Recognize and Reward Participants			✓	✓	
Justify or Enhance HR Budget				✓	✓
Reduce Costs		✓	✓	✓	✓
Entice Perspective Participants to Be Involved in HR Programs	✓	✓	✓	✓	
Marketing HR Programs			✓	✓	✓
Expand Implementation to Other Areas			✓	✓	✓

To ensure that data are applied as they were intended, drafting project plans or follow-up actions that can help track improvements made may be beneficial. For example, if evaluation indicated that a redesign of a program is necessary, having a plan of action to ensure that the redesign actually occurs is advisable. In some cases, this type of data should be provided to various stakeholders and sometimes even to participants themselves. They may need to understand that the evaluation is actually serving a purpose. The specific types of follow-up mechanisms may vary, and several options are available. This final step may be the most significant part of the process.

Final Thoughts

This chapter presented the final part in the evaluation process — communicating results and driving improvement. If this issue is not taken seriously, the organization will not be able to capitalize on the benefits of HR programs. A full array of possibilities exists to translate the communication into action. You have been equipped with the tools to communicate the results of program evaluation to a variety of audiences, which is the first step in helping the HR department prove its value on the organization's bottom line. Special emphasis was placed on communicating with senior executives. The next chapter focuses on implementing and sustaining the use of ROI.

Chapter 10.
Taking a Sensible
Approach to ROI

The best-designed model, technique, or process is worthless unless it is effectively integrated into the organization. Even a simple, methodical process fails in the best organizations if it is not fully supported by those who should make it work. As you begin to plan for and implement the ROI Methodology, you may encounter some resistance to ROI. Fundamentally, resistance to HR evaluation is much the same as resistance to any change process, but you can minimize resistance with careful implementation of a sensible approach to ROI.

The Basis for Resistance

HR staff members and others closely associated with HR programs usually resist ROI because they think the process will require a great deal of their time, which is already in short supply, or because they worry about the consequences of the final outcomes. These two concerns are not groundless. Implementing a comprehensive, high-level evaluation does take time, effort, and leadership. HR staff may already feel overwhelmed and fear having another task to do. The fear of poorly designed or implemented programs being "exposed" can cause resistance. Few people want the "world" to know that their program is not working. Also, discovering that a particular HR program really did cost too much can be unsettling.

The fundamental basis for resistance then is fear or uncertainty. The top 10 resistors to ROI, listed in the context of comments often made by stakeholders involved in evaluation implementation, are listed in the instrument presented as Figure 10.1. You can use the survey to assess the current level of resistance of the HR team and create a strategy to minimize it.

Figure 10.1 What Do You Think about ROI?

Rate the extent to which you agree with the following statements:
A rating of 1 = Strongly Agree
A rating of 5 = Strongly Disagree

	Strongly Disagree..Agree				
	1	2	3	4	5
1. I do not have time for ROI.	☐	☐	☐	☐	☐
2. An unsuccessful ROI evaluation will reflect on my performance.	☐	☐	☐	☐	☐
3. A negative ROI will kill my program.	☐	☐	☐	☐	☐
4. My budget will not allow for ROI.	☐	☐	☐	☐	☐
5. ROI evaluation is not part of my job.	☐	☐	☐	☐	☐
6. I did not have input on this process.	☐	☐	☐	☐	☐
7. I do not understand ROI.	☐	☐	☐	☐	☐
8. Our managers will not support ROI.	☐	☐	☐	☐	☐
9. Data will be misused.	☐	☐	☐	☐	☐
10. ROI is too subjective.	☐	☐	☐	☐	☐

If you scored:
10–25 = You like new challenges and are accepting of change.
21–30 = You go with the flow.
31–40 = You stress out and resist change.
41 and above = You are a strong resistor.

These issues can lead to opposition of any new evaluation process. The resistance is amplified when the term "ROI" is used. The remainder of this chapter focuses on specific actions that can be taken to reduce these fears, minimize the resistance to ROI, and use ROI in a sensible way.

Fearless Implementation

You can help people overcome their resistance to implementing an ROI evaluation by first recognizing that resistance is inevitable; it is a part of human nature. Regardless of the reason, any type of change causes a flurry of questions, doubts, and fears. At times the reasons behind resistance are legitimate; however, it often exists for the wrong reasons. An initial step in overcoming resistance to ROI is sorting out the reasons it exists by separating the myths from legitimate concerns. When legitimate barriers to implementation exist, minimizing or removing them altogether is the task.

As you conduct additional impact studies, consistency becomes a consideration. With consistency come accuracy and reliability. Consistency is achieved through clearly defined processes each time evaluation is pursued. Cost control and efficiency are also issues. Implementation tasks must be completed efficiently as well as effectively to keep costs to a minimum and to use time wisely.

The challenge is to implement evaluation systematically and consistently so that it becomes normal business behavior and a routine, standard process designed into programs. The implementation necessary to overcome resistance covers a variety of areas. Figure 10.2 shows actions outlined in this chapter, presented as building blocks to overcoming resistance. The actions are all necessary to establish the proper framework to dispel myths and to remove or reduce barriers. The remainder of this chapter presents specific strategies and techniques around each of the building blocks identified in Figure 10.2.

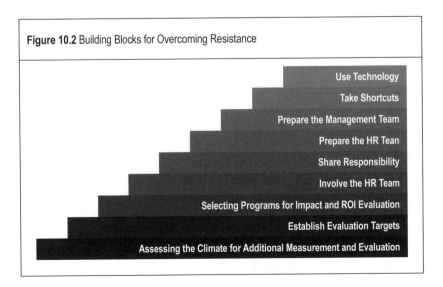

Figure 10.2 Building Blocks for Overcoming Resistance

Use Technology

Take Shortcuts

Prepare the Management Team

Prepare the HR Team

Share Responsibility

Involve the HR Team

Selecting Programs for Impact and ROI Evaluation

Establish Evaluation Targets

Assessing the Climate for Additional Measurement and Evaluation

Assessing the Climate

As a first step toward implementation, some organizations assess the current climate for achieving results. One way to assess is to use a survey to determine current perspectives of the management team and other stakeholders regarding HR program results. Appendix A shows an example of a survey designed for this purpose. Another assessment method is to conduct interviews with key stakeholders to determine their willingness to implement additional measurements and evaluation. With an awareness of the current status, the learning and development leaders can plan for significant changes and pinpoint particular issues that need support for more evaluation.

Establish Evaluation Targets

Specific targets for evaluation levels and projects are necessary to make progress with measurement and evaluation. Targets enable the HR staff to focus on the improvements needed within specific evaluation categories or levels. When establishing targets, determine the percentage of programs planned for each level of evaluation.

HR programs are varied; the list includes solutions (retention solution), benefits (health care cost containment), technology projects (HR website), special services (wellness/fitness center), administrative activities (tuition refund), learning (leadership development), and compensation processes (variable pay). Regardless of the type of HR program, the first step is to assess the present situation as shown in Table 10.1. The number of all programs is tabulated along with the corresponding level(s) of evaluation presently conducted for each program. Next, the percent of programs using reaction evaluation is calculated or estimated. The process is repeated for learning, application, impact, and ROI levels of evaluation.

After detailing the current situation, the next step is to determine a realistic target for each level within a specific time frame. Many organizations set annual targets for change. This process should involve the input of the HR staff to ensure that the targets are realistic and that the staff is committed to the evaluation process and targets. If the HR staff does not develop ownership for this process, targets will not be met.

Table 10.1 Establishing Evaluation Targets

	Current Situation	Target
Total Number of HR Programs		
Percentage of HR Programs Evaluated with Reaction Data		
Percentage of HR Programs Evaluated with Learning Data		
Percentage of HR Programs Evaluated with Application and Implementation		
Percentage of HR Programs Evaluated with Impact Data		
Percentage of Programs Evaluated with ROI data		

The improvement targets must be achievable, while at the same time challenging and motivating. Table 10.2 shows the targets established for Scripps Health, a health care chain with hundreds of HR programs.

Table 10.2 Evaluation Targets for Scripps Health

Level of Evaluation	Percentage of Programs Evaluated at This Level
Level 1—Reaction	100%
Level 2—Learning	80%
Level 3—Application and Implementation	30%
Level 4—Impact	10%
Level 5—ROI	5%

Using Scripps' example, 100 percent of the programs are measured at level 1 (reaction), consistent with practices at many other organizations. Eighty percent of the HR programs are measured at level 2, using a formal method of learning measurement. At this organization, informal learning measurement methods are counted as a learning measure. The level 2 measure may increase significantly in groups that conduct much formal testing or if informal measures (for example, self assessment) are included as a learning measure. Thirty percent of programs are measured at the level of application and implementation. This number means that almost one-third of the programs will have some type of follow-up method, at least for a small sample of participants in those programs. Ten percent of the programs are planned for business impact evaluation (level 4) and half of those for ROI (level 5). These percentages are typical and often recommended. Evaluating to more than 5 percent or 10 percent of programs at the level of ROI is rarely needed. Sometimes targets are established for gradually increasing evaluation processes — both in terms of numbers of evaluations and evaluation levels — over several years.

Target setting is a critical implementation issue. It should be completed early with the full support of the entire HR team. Also, when practical and feasible, the targets should have the approval of the key management staff, particularly the senior management team.

Select Programs for Impact and ROI Evaluation

Selecting a program for ROI evaluation requires consideration. Ideally, certain types of programs should be selected for comprehensive, detailed analyses. The typical approach for identifying programs for evaluation is to select those that are expensive, strategic, and highly visible. Figure 10.3 is a tool you can use to select programs for ROI evaluation. It is based on six criteria often used to select programs for this level of evaluation.

These are only the basic criteria; the list can be extended as necessary to bring the organization's particular issues into focus. Some large organizations with hundreds of programs use as many as 12 criteria. The HR staff rates programs using these criteria, using a rating scale of one through five. All programs are rated, and the program with the highest score is the best candidate for impact and ROI evaluation.

This process only identifies the best candidates. The actual number evaluated may depend on other factors such as resources and capability. The goal is to select HR programs designed to make a difference and to represent significant investments. Also, programs that command attention from management are ideal candidates for high-level evaluation. Almost any senior management group has a perception about the effectiveness of a particular HR program. Some want to know its impact, but others may not be very concerned. Therefore, management interest may drive the selection of many of the impact studies.

Figure 10.3 Selection Tool for ROI Impact Study

Selecting Program for ROI Evaluation		Programs				
		#1	#2	#3	#4	#5
Criteria						
1. Lifecycle of the Program						
2. Linked to Objectives						
3. Costs of Program						
4. Audience Size						
5. Visibility of Program						
6. Management Interest in the Evaluation						
Total						

Rating Scale	
1. Lifecycle of Program	5 = Long lifecycle 1 = Very short lifecycle
2. Linked to Objectives	5 = Closely related to organizational objectives 1 = Not directly related to organizational objectives
3. Costs of Program	5 = Very expensive 1 = Very inexpensive
4. Audience Size	5 = Very large audience 1 = Very small audience
5. Visibility	5 = High visibility 1 = Low visibility
6. Management Interest	5 = High level of interest in evaluation 1 = Low level of interest in evaluation

The next step is to determine how many impact ROI evaluation projects to undertake initially and in which particular areas. A good idea is to start with a small number of initial projects, perhaps two or three. The selected programs may represent the functional areas of human resources, such as recruiting and staffing, learning and development, compensations, reward systems, employee relations, compliance, and technology. Selecting a manageable number is advised, so the process will be implemented when considering the constraints.

Additional criteria should be weighed when selecting initial programs for impact evaluation. For example, the first program should be as simple as possible. Do not take on complex programs until skills have been mastered. Also, the initial program should be successful now; that is, all the current feedback data suggest that the program is adding significant value. This strategy helps avoid having a negative ROI on the first application of ROI analysis. Still another criterion is to select a program that is void of strong political issues or biases. Although such programs can be handled effectively with ROI study, they may present too many challenges for an early application.

Ultimately, the number of programs selected for ROI analysis depends on the resources available to conduct the studies, as well as the internal need for accountability. The percentage of programs evaluated in Table 10.2 can be accomplished for about 3 percent to 5 percent of the total HR budget. The costs of evaluation need not drain the organization's or department's resources.

Involve the HR Team

One group that often resists implementing a comprehensive measurement and evaluation process is the HR team who must design, develop, implement, and coordinate HR programs. These team members often see evaluation as an unnecessary intrusion into their responsibilities, absorbing precious time and stifling their freedom to be creative.

The HR team should be involved in key decisions in the process. Staff input is absolutely essential as policy statements are prepared and guidelines are developed. The team is unlikely to be critical of something they have been involved with from design to implementation. Using workshops, brainstorming sessions, planning sessions, and taskforces, the team should be involved in every phase of developing the framework and supporting documents.

As mentioned previously in the chapter, HR team members sometimes resist ROI evaluation because their programs will be fully exposed, placing their reputations on the line. They may have a fear of failure and are not interested in developing a tool that can be used to reveal their shortcomings and failures. To overcome this source of resistance, the ROI

Methodology should clearly be positioned as a tool for process improvement — not as a tool to evaluate HR staff performance, at least during its early years of implementation.

The HR team can often learn more from disappointment than from successes. If the program is not working, finding out quickly and understanding the issues firsthand rather than from others is preferable. If a program is ineffective and not producing the desired results, it will eventually be known to clients and to the management group, if they are not already aware of the situation.

A lack of results can cause managers to become less supportive of human resources. Dwindling support appears in many forms, ranging from budget reductions to refusing to be involved in programs. When the weaknesses of programs are identified and adjustments are made quickly, ineffective programs can be converted into effective programs, and the credibility and respect for the HR function and staff are enhanced.

Share Responsibility

An easy way to make evaluation routine is to have others do it. Some HR departments may choose to share the responsibility of various parts of ROI evaluation with a variety of other stakeholders. Part of that effort is to include evaluation responsibilities in stakeholder involvement. Include the stakeholders in collecting, analyzing, and communicating data and in reviewing and interpreting conclusions. They will take ownership in evaluation, and the burden will be lightened for staff directly responsible for the evaluation.

Prepare the HR Team

To make the transition to higher-level evaluation, enriching the HR staff's skills in the areas of measurement, evaluation, and ROI may be necessary so that they can support the methodology. Measurement and evaluation are not always a formal part of preparing to become an HR specialist or manager. Consequently, each member of the team may need to learn how the ROI Methodology is implemented, step-by-step.

In addition, HR team members must know how to develop plans to collect and analyze data and to interpret results from data analysis. A one-

or two-day workshop can help them attain adequate skills and knowledge to understand the process; it can also help them appreciate what ROI can accomplish for the organization, see its necessity, and participate in a successful implementation. A fundamental component in evaluation, staff expertise is required to develop the evaluation policy and to practice and implement it.

Prepare the Management Team

Perhaps no group is more critical to measurement, evaluation, and ROI efforts than the management team members who must allocate resources for human resources and support programs. In addition, they often provide input and assistance in the evaluation process. Carefully plan and execute specific actions to prepare the management team and to improve the relationship between HR staff and key managers. A productive partnership requires each party to understand the concerns, problems, and opportunities of the other. Developing this type of relationship is a long-term process that must be deliberately planned and initiated by selected HR staff members. Sometimes the decision to commit resources and support for HR solutions stems from the effectiveness of this relationship.

Take Shortcuts

One of the most significant barriers to the implementation of the ROI Methodology is the potential time and cost involved in implementing the process. Sometimes, the perception of excessive time and cost is only a myth; at other times it is a reality. As discussed earlier, the methodology can be implemented for about 3 to 5 percent of the HR budget. However, expenses and time requirements can be significant. Cost-saving approaches have commanded much attention recently and represent an essential part of the implementation strategy. The following sections offer some strategies that can help offset costs of ROI evaluation.

Take shortcuts at lower levels. When resources are a primary concern and shortcuts need to be taken, taking them at lower levels in the evaluation scheme is optimal. This is a resource allocation issue. For example, when an impact evaluation (level 4) is conducted, levels 1 through 3 do not have to be as comprehensive. This shift places most of the emphasis on the highest level of the evaluation so that it is credible and defendable.

Fund measurement and evaluation with savings from the use of ROI. Almost every impact study generates data from which to make improvements. Results at different levels often show how the program can be altered to make it more effective and efficient. Sometimes, the data suggest that the program can be modified, adjusted, or completely redesigned. All of those actions can results in cost savings. In a few cases, the program may have to be eliminated because it is not adding value, and adjustments will not necessarily improve it. In this case, a clear cost savings is realized when the program is eliminated. A logical argument can be made to shift a portion of these savings to fund additional measurement and evaluation. Some organizations gradually migrate to an HR budget target of 5 percent for expenditures for measurement and evaluation by using the savings generated from the use of evaluation. This transition provides a disciplined and conservative approach to additional funding.

Plan early and thoroughly. One of the most salient, cost-saving steps to evaluation is to develop program objectives and to plan early for the evaluation. Impact studies are successful because of proper planning. The best way to conserve time and resources is to know what must be done at what time. This knowledge prevents unnecessary analysis, data collection at an inappropriate time, and the necessity of reconstructing events and issues because they were not planned in advance.

Integrate evaluation into the HR program. To the extent possible, evaluation should be built into the HR program. Data collection tools should also be considered part of the HR program. If possible, these tools should be positioned as application tools and not necessarily as evaluation tools. This action enables the participants or others to capture data to understand clearly the success of the program on the job. Part of this issue is to build in expectations for stakeholders to provide the appropriate data.

Provide participants with a defined role. One of the most effective cost-saving approaches is to have participants conduct major steps of the process. Participants are the primary source for understanding the degree to which learning is applied and has driven success on the job. The responsibilities for the participants should be expanded from the traditional requirement of involvement in implementing the program. Now they must be asked to show the impact of those programs and to provide data about success. Consequently, the participant's role expands from learning and application to measuring the impact and communicating information.

Use quick methods. Each step of the ROI Methodology has shortcut methods that are quick but credible. For example, in data collection the simple questionnaire is a shortcut method that can be used to generate powerful and convincing data if administered properly. Other shortcut methods are available for isolating, converting, and reporting data.

Use sampling. Not all HR programs require a comprehensive evaluation, nor should all participants necessarily be evaluated in a planned follow-up. Sampling can be used in two ways. First, select only a few HR programs for ROI evaluation using the criteria in Figure 10.3. Next, when a particular HR program is to be evaluated, in most cases collecting data from a sample of participants is sufficient. This approach keeps costs and time to a minimum.

Use estimates. Estimates are the least expensive way to arrive at a number or value. Whether isolating the effects of human resources or converting data to monetary value, estimation can be a routine and reliable part of the process. Make sure that the estimate is valid and that it follows systematic, logical, consistent steps. Be sure to address estimation methods and assumptions when communicating results of your evaluation.

Use internal resources. An organization does not necessarily have to employ consultants to develop impact studies and address other ROI issues. Internal capability can be developed, eliminating a dependence on consultants. Several opportunities exist for HR staff to build skills and become certified in ROI evaluation. This approach is perhaps one of the most significant cost savers. By using internal resources instead of external consultants, you can save as much as 50 percent or 60 percent of the costs of a specific project.

Build on the work of HR practitioners who have implemented ROI in their organizations. You do not need to reinvent the wheel. Learn from others and build on their work. Listed below are three primary ways to accomplish this task:

- Use networking opportunities internally, locally, and globally.
- Read and dissect a published case study. More than 300 ROI cases have been published.
- Locate a similar case study in a database of completed case studies and contact the authors for more information.

These important shortcuts can help ensure that evaluation does not drain budgets and resources unnecessarily. Other shortcuts can be developed, but a word of caution is in order: Shortcuts often compromise the process. When a comprehensive, valid, and reliable study is needed, it will be time-consuming and expensive — there is no way around it. The good news is that many shortcuts can be taken to supply the data necessary for the audience and to manage the process in an efficient way.

Use Technology

A variety of software tools are available to help organizations develop consistent processes, use standard techniques, and produce consistent reports. Technology is essential for evaluation. Software not only reduces the time to conduct an impact study, but it also helps develop and report information, often in the form of a generated scorecard or report. Contact the authors for recommended software packages.

Final Thoughts

In summary, taking a sensible approach to ROI is necessary to make it successful in the organization. ROI will encounter some resistance, and the key to overcoming resistance is to develop a sensible implementation strategy. The actions identified in this chapter will help smooth fears and remove barriers, ensuring successful integration, and more important, sustaining ROI as a routine evaluation process.

This book clearly identifies how HR specialists, managers, and executives can show the value of the HR contribution. When considering the material covered and the progress made, perhaps it is beneficial to revisit the challenge facing human resources from two perspectives: reactive and proactive.

First is the reactive approach. Unless human resources shows its contribution, it will continue to struggle as a reliable and thriving part of the organization. Budgets will be cut; influence will diminish; and respect will deteriorate. Many executives now require this type of accountability. Sometimes justifying budgets or particular programs and projects is necessary. From a reactive posture, this validation is absolutely vital for the continued survival of the HR function.

On a more positive note, the proactive approach is very powerful. Some HR executives are showing the value of their contribution and are changing the mindset of the HR process and function. They are convincing top management that the HR function can add tremendous value to the organization. The reality is that many HR programs contribute significantly to the organization; the decision-makers often just need to see the data to be convinced. As expected, some programs do not add value, and we simply need sound data to identify those failing programs to make improvements. The proactive approach positions the HR function as an integral, respectable, and viable part of the organization.

Individuals are drawn to this methodology as a result of both proactive and reactive thinking. Whatever the rationale, the challenge is clear: Action is needed now, not later; steps need to be taken to show the contribution. We can no longer say that ROI is impossible, because literally hundreds of organizations are routinely accomplishing the evaluation. The next step is yours!

Chapter 11. Case Study:
Measuring ROI for a Work-at-Home Program Family Mutual Health and Life Insurance Company (FMI)

Authors' note: The following case study has been prepared in a teaching format. The case is presented as it developed and unfolded. We suggest that you read through the case study and try to respond to the questions at the end of each part before proceeding to the next part. This method is helpful to see how clearly the concepts are understood in a practical example. The next section provides the information about what actually occurred.

This case was prepared to serve as a basis for discussion rather than to illustrate either effective or ineffective administrative and management practices. Names, dates, places, and organizations have been disguised at the request of the organization.

FMI: Part A

Abstract
This case study shows the power of a work-at-home project designed to ease the environmental problems of traffic and congestion caused by the long daily work commute of more than 300 employees. This commute caused much stress, anxiety, and frustration for employees. From the company perspective, the project improved productivity, job engagement, job satisfaction, and image, while reducing office expenses and lowering turnover. From an environmental perspective, the study shows how an HR project can have significant impact on the environ-

247

ment by lowering carbon emissions. It represents a win-win project for participants, their initially reluctant managers, and the organization. Perhaps the greatest winner is the environment. Although this type of project may not be suitable for every organization, this case study is an excellent example of how an ROI project can be completed for many businesses and concerns.

Background

Family Mutual Health and Life Insurance Company (FMI) has enjoyed a rich history of serving families throughout North America for almost 80 years. The company's focus has been on health and life insurance products, and it is regarded as a very innovative and low-cost health insurance provider. The executives are proud of their cost-control efforts and of the low prices they can offer. Company advertisements regularly highlight their low-cost approach, quality of service, and ethical practices.

FMI has grown substantially in recent years because of increased health care concerns in North America, particularly in the United States. Rising health care costs have forced the company to raise premiums several times in recent years, while still maintaining a cost advantage over other suppliers.

The Challenge

Lars Rienhold, CEO, is very proud of the accomplishments of FMI and is perhaps its biggest fan. A man of considerable and contagious personality, he is continually trying to offer affordable health and life insurance policies, to provide excellent customer service, and to be a responsible citizen. As part of this effort, Lars wanted to ensure that FMI was doing all it could to help the environment. While FMI's carbon footprint is relatively low compared to manufacturing companies, its headquarters was located in a very congested area. Lars became concerned about helping the environment in as many ways as possible. During a recent trip to Calgary, Canada, he saw a television report about a local company that had implemented a work-at-home program. The report presented the actual amount of carbon emissions that this project had prevented. Lars thought that FMI should be able to implement a similar program, including the possibility of employees working from home. He brought this idea to Melissa Lufkin, Executive Vice President of Human Resources. The message was short. "I want us to make a difference. I think this is the way to do it." Although her team had already examined the issue, Melissa agreed to explore the possibility in a more formal way.

Exploring the Situation

Melissa began her investigation by discussing the issue with the operations chief. Although cautious, John Speegle, Executive Vice President of Operations, was interested in exploring the idea. John was concerned about the lack of productivity increase in the last three years within the largest segment of employees: the claims processors and the claims examiners. A total of 950 employees were involved in processing or examining claims submitted by customers or health care providers. Claims examiners reviewed claims that were disputed or that sparked an audit review. The number of claims processors and examiners had grown to the point where the office space they occupied in building two was overflowing; consequently, new building space or perhaps a new facility was needed to manage the growth.

John concluded, "I'm interested in the possibility of employees working from home if it can be controlled properly. Let's explore the arrangement if all parties are in agreement to pursue it." In summary, John was interested in lowering the real estate cost of new office space, which averaged about $17,000 per person per year, and in improving productivity, which was at a rate of 33.2 claims processed and 20.7 claims examined per day.

Melissa discussed the issue with Linda Green, the Vice President of Claims, to probe her concerns about processors and examiners working at home. Although this issue had been discussed in previous meetings, and many people had said that these jobs could be easily managed remotely, Melissa had never received direct communication on the topic. Linda was supportive but raised several concerns: "Some of our managers want to keep tabs on what is going on, and they feel like they have to be there to resolve issues and problems — and they want to see that everyone is working and busy. I am afraid it is a matter of control, which they may have a hard time giving up if people work remotely." Melissa realized that this initiative would take some extra effort with these managers, who would have to view it as necessary and feasible in their world to accept it. Linda added, "I realize that the right approach might make their jobs easier, but right now they may not be at that point."

Melissa next met with the IT department and discussed how it could equip work stations at home with the latest technology. She found a very supportive audience in Tim Holleman, Senior Vice President and Chief Information Officer, who thought that employees could be set up with adequate security and technology to work at home in the same manner as they were working onsite. Tim added, "They can have full access to all databases, and they could be using high-speed processes. It would cost FMI a substantial amount the first year but would not represent a very significant cost in the long run."

Next, Melissa discussed potential issues with the legal department. Margaret Metcalf, Chief Legal Officer, was cautious, as expected, and said several legal issues would have to be addressed from a liability perspective. She asked about other companies pursuing this route, and Melissa agreed to furnish examples and to make contacts with them to discover what problems they had encountered.

Melissa then contacted Anne Burson, Executive Vice President of Sales and Marketing, to uncover any customer service issues that may arise. Anne was in favor of the move as long as customer service would not suffer. She added, "The claims examiners are very much in contact with the customers, and I want to make sure that acceptable customer service is maintained. Also, many of the processors have to make routine direct contact with health care suppliers as well as [with] patients, and we want to maintain these contacts at an acceptable level. I can see that this would probably help morale and might even improve our service. Let's give it a try."

Finally, Melissa met with her Chief Financial Officer, Rodrick Harper, to discuss the project and the plan to measure its success. Melissa had held previous conversations with Rod about measuring success, and he had expressed some desire to show the value of major human resources initiatives. Melissa was eager to show the value of HR programs and had challenged her staff to measure success, even using ROI. Rod volunteered a member of his team to work with Melissa on these types of projects. When Melissa discussed the work-at-home idea with him, including the measurement plans and a financial ROI, Rod's interest really piqued. He said, "Let's make sure this is very credible analysis and that it is very conservative. Frankly, I think we want to be involved when you discuss ROI. I think it's proper that we use a standard approach to analysis, and we would like to be involved in this every step of the way, if you don't mind." Melissa was pleased with the support, but somewhat anxious about working with the finance and accounting team to evaluate a program that she would ultimately own. However, she felt the project was necessary and would be advanced by the very good relationship she and her team had with the finance and accounting group.

Melissa and her staff explored the attitudes of employees to determine how they would perceive a work-at-home program. She was not sure how many would take advantage of the opportunity, but she thought most would certainly be interested. The staff conservatively estimated that at least a third would opt to participate in the program. For many in this group, working at home would be a huge motivator and would probably make a difference in retaining them at FMI. From that perspective, the staff suggested that it be explored. Melissa cautioned, "They may have issues at home that they want to address, but we must be able to get eight hours of work out of them. They cannot discontinue daycare, trying to manage child care and work as well. If they have an elderly or disabled person at home, this cannot be a way for them to deal with both situations. We must have full productivity, and that is essential."

With this positive reaction (and a few concerns), Melissa and her team decided to undertake this substantial project. After much discussion, the group decided to engage a consulting group, Workforce Solutions (WSI), to manage the project. WSI had considerable experience in implementing alternative work systems, particularly work-at-home programs. The company knew what questions to ask and what situations were going to occur, and more important, it was able to anticipate the problems that could derail the project.

The Analysis and Initial Alignment

After some discussion, the group asked WSI for a proposal. Included in the request for proposal (RFP) to WSI was a forecasting component for the project. Essentially, WSI was asked to bid on analyzing the need for the project to determine its feasibility, forecast its value, design the appropriate program, and implement and monitor the success of the program. Success would be measured at the ROI level. Armed with this information, WSI was prepared to begin work on the proposal.

The Consultants

Deborah Rousseau was selected by Workforce Solutions as the lead consultant for this project. Deborah had previous experience with flexible work systems, had managed many successful projects, and was an outstanding consultant. Deborah believed in showing the value of her company's work and guided the proposal process toward an agreement to deliver the four components:

1. Clarifying that the solution is needed and connecting it to the appropriate business measures
2. Forecasting the impact and ROI of the project
3. Implementing the program with claims processors and examiners
4. Showing the value of the project using the ROI Methodology

With this focus on results, Deborah knew that she must skillfully present the best proposal and the most focused implementation possible. There was no room for error, and WSI was obligated to deliver the value desired by the clients.

To make the proposal meaningful, Deborah asked the client if WSI could forecast ROI after its consultants verified the solution, and FMI agreed. In essence, the proposal was developed in two parts. The first proposal validated the solution and provided a forecast ROI. The forecast would be developed and approved by the client before the program would be implemented. The second proposal focused on implementation and an impact study with ROI. This plan seemed reasonable because the analysis required to develop the forecast was part of the analysis that would verify the proper solution to drive the business measures. WSI proposed $31,000 for the first proposal ($21,000 for the initial analysis and assessment, and $10,000 for the forecasting ROI), which included a briefing to senior executives.

The Analysis

When the first contract was awarded, Deborah began meeting with appropriate individuals at FMI and the HR team, including employee relations, learning and development, recruiting, compensation, and HR planning. She examined records, facilitated employee focus groups, and conducted a survey of a small, select group of employees to understand their desire, need, and intentions to work at home if the option were available. In this survey, employees were asked about benefits from this type of arrangement. The focus groups and the survey revealed that this solution should drive business measures.

Part of this analysis involved the examination of other case studies of work-at-home projects to understand the payoffs of those projects and the barriers to success. This analysis focused on potential improvements in productivity and on reductions in absenteeism, health care costs, and real estate costs. The potential effect on health care costs was weak, so it was removed as a possible impact measure that could be influenced by this new arrangement. By using the employee feedback, analysis of other studies, and examination of internal records, Deborah and the HR team agreed that this solution could drive important business measures.

Alignment

Deborah's next task was to identify specific business measures. Her key input for this task was provided by the executive vice president (EVP) of operations, who thought that this program could reduce the real estate and productivity costs. The real estate costs could be improved, unless the cost of maintaining an at-home office proved to be excessive or if the same office space for each participant continued to be maintained at FMI. Deborah worked with the EVP to set clear objectives for office space and productivity. After some discussion, the EVP suggested that processors and examiners could both process an average of at least one more claim than they had been producing and that the office expense could be dramatically reduced by about 20 percent for the first year. When discussing the actual ROI of the study, the EVP was reluctant to set an objective. However, when Deborah suggested that the ROI should be more than an investment in a building, for example, the EVP agreed to set a goal. Given that FMI would average about 15 percent for capital expenditure investments, Deborah suggested that an ROI of about 25 percent would be appropriate, and the EVP agreed.

The vice president of claims confirmed the objectives regarding productivity and real estate costs with Deborah and then focused on turnover reduction. The annual turnover rate at the time was 22.3 percent, and both the VPC and Deborah felt that an improvement rate of at least a 5 percent — to 17.3 percent — should be achievable if the project was successful. They also reviewed the absenteeism rate and thought it could drastically improve from a current level of 7.3 percent to a new level of 4.0 percent. Deborah addressed the critical issues regarding implementation during this discussion.

Deborah met with Ginger Terry, Environmental Coordinator in the procurement function, to collect data about carbon emissions from automobiles and to set a goal to show the actual reduction in carbon emissions that could be realized by eliminating the office commute. Ginger had compiled data about the commute time of employees for these two groups, and the average time was estimated to be one hour and 44 minutes each day. In a work-at-home arrangement, this time could be reduced to about 15 minutes, assuming a visit to the office every seven days. Deborah realized that the benefit to the environment would not add to the ROI in monetary terms but would be a substantial intangible for the citizens of this city and of the country as a whole.

Finally, Deborah met with the chief financial officer, chief legal counsel, chief information officer, and the HR team. The principal focus of the meeting with this group was to review the tentative objectives for additional refinement and concurrence.

Deborah's meeting with the HR team generated some insights, in terms of what employees and managers must learn to make the process effective and successful. Several questions surfaced about working without distractions, such as child care issues, other people in the residence, elder parent care, and more. Also, associates would have to adjust their working habits from an office to the home environment. They would need to adopt the discipline and structure necessary to be effective, by following consistent rules, regulations, and working hours. The team also noted that managers must be able to effectively provide coaching and counseling along the way and to be there for associates to address particular issues.

Deborah also explored the issues of perception and desired reaction with the executives. The executives expressed their belief that the process was needed and that it would ultimately be motivational and rewarding for participants. With this data, Deborah began to develop the objectives that would lead to the ROI forecast.

Questions for Discussion

1. Critique the way in which the analysis has been conducted.
2. Are there additional questions or issues you would explore? If so, what are they?
3. Write the objectives for all five levels.
4. Complete the V-model showing the connection between the upfront assessment, objectives, and evaluation at five levels.

FMI: Part B

Objectives and Alignment

From the discussions, subsequent analyses, and potential solutions, Deborah, Melissa, and the HR team could develop all the objectives from the needs at different levels.

Objectives

Table 11.1 shows the objectives for the project by different levels, ranging from reaction to ROI. Deborah secured agreement on the objectives from those stakeholders involved. '

Alignment Model

The alignment model depicted in Figure 11.1 shows the connection between the upfront needs assessment, the objectives, and the evaluation. Deborah found constructing this model helpful in clearly determining if any pieces were missing. She worked through the analysis in order, beginning with level 5, and the project's value became obvious early in discussions. She then explored the business needs with different stakeholders. Job performance needs were revealed in concerns voiced by the senior vice president of claims. The learning needs evolved from that conversation, and the reaction needs were consequently developed from these discussions. Previous studies in which Deborah and her firm had been involved dictated some of the learning and reaction needs; that is, projects sometimes fail because people do not fully understand the rules or the work process or have an incorrect perception of the process. The objectives came directly from the needs assessment and were specifically developed based on each need. At this point, evaluation was tentative in terms of how the data would be collected. More detail on the evaluation side would be provided as the project unfolded, but the V-model provides the alignment necessary at the different levels of needs assessment, objectives, and evaluation.

Table 11.1 Detailed Objectives

After implementing this project:

Reaction
- Employees should see the work-at-home project as satisfying, important, rewarding, and motivational.
- Managers must see this project as necessary, appropriate, and important to FMI.

Learning
- Employees must know the realities of working at home, the conditions, roles, and regulations.
- Employees must have the discipline and tenacity to work at home.
- Managers must be able to explain company policy and regulations for working at home.
- Managers must be able manage remotely.

Application
- Managers should conduct a meeting with direct deports to discuss policy, expected behavior, and next steps.
- At least 30 percent of eligible employees should volunteer for at-home assignments within one month.
- At-home offices are built and properly equipped.
- Work-at-home employees should work effectively at home.
- The at-home workplace should be free from distractions and conflicting demands.
- Managers will properly administer the company's policy.
- Managers should manage the remote employees effectively.

Impact
For those involved in the program:
- Commute time should be reduced to an average of 15 minutes per day.
- Office expense per person should reduce by 20 percent in six months.
- Productivity should increase by 5 percent in six months.
- Employee turnover should reduce to 12 percent in six months.
- Unplanned absenteeism should be reduced.
- Stress should be reduced.
- Carbon emissions should be reduced.
- The company's image as a green company should be enhanced.
- Employee engagement should improve.

ROI
- Achieve a 25 percent return on investment.

Figure 11.1 Project Alignment

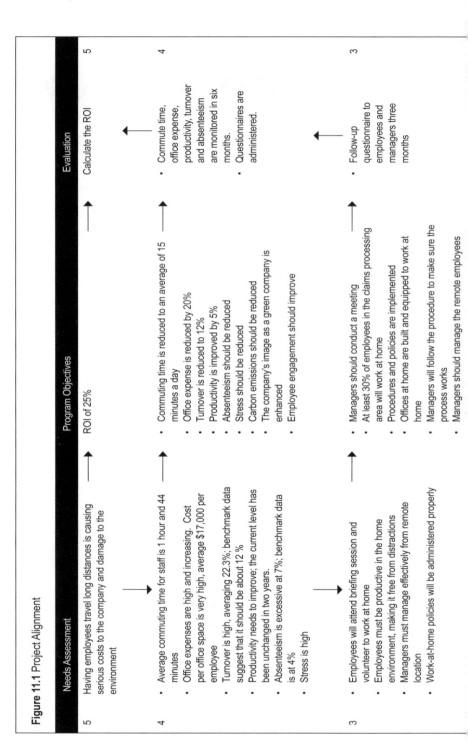

	Needs Assessment	Program Objectives	Evaluation	
5	Having employees travel long distances is causing serious costs to the company and damage to the environment	ROI of 25%	Calculate the ROI	5
4	• Average commuting time for staff is 1 hour and 44 minutes • Office expenses are high and increasing. Cost per office space is very high, average $17,000 per employee • Turnover is high, averaging 22.3%; benchmark data suggest that it should be about 12 % • Productivity needs to improve; the current level has been unchanged in two years. • Absenteeism is excessive at 7%; benchmark data is at 4% • Stress is high	• Commuting time is reduced to an average of 15 minutes a day • Office expense is reduced by 20% • Turnover is reduced to 12% • Productivity is improved by 5% • Absenteeism should be reduced • Stress should be reduced • Carbon emissions should be reduced • The company's image as a green company is enhanced • Employee engagement should improve	• Commute time, office expense, productivity, turnover and absenteeism are monitored in six months. • Questionnaires are administered.	4
3	• Employees will attend briefing session and volunteer to work at home • Employees must be productive in the home environment, making it free from distractions • Managers must manage effectively from remote location • Work-at-home policies will be administered properly	• Managers should conduct a meeting • At least 30% of employees in the claims processing area will work at home • Procedures and policies are implemented • Offices at home are built and equipped to work at home • Managers will follow the procedure to make sure the process works • Managers should manage the remote employees	• Follow-up questionnaire to employees and managers three months	3

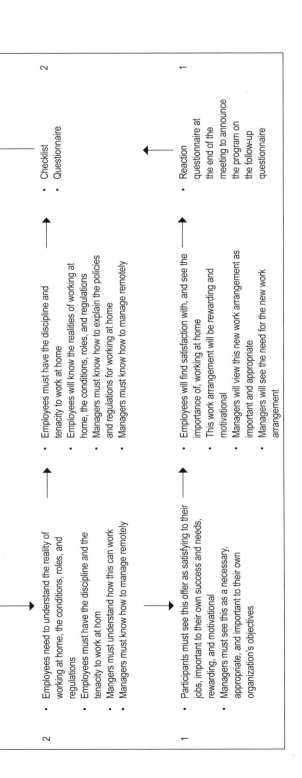

2

- Employees need to understand the reality of working at home, the conditions, roles, and regulations
- Employees must have the discipline and tenacity to work at hom
- Mangers must understand how this can work
- Managers must know how to manage remotely

2

- Employees must have the discipline and tenacity to work at home
- Employees will know the realities of working at home, the conditions, roles, and regulations
- Managers must know how to explain the policies and regulations for working at home
- Managers must know how to manage remotely

- Checklist
- Questionnaire

1

- Participants must see this offer as satisfying to their jobs, important to their own success and needs, rewarding, and motivational
- Managers must see this as a necessary, appropriate, and important to their own organization's objectives

1

- Employees will find satisfaction with, and see the importance of, working at home
- This work arrangement will be rewarding and motivational
- Managers will view this new work arrangement as important and appropriate
- Managers will see the need for the new work arrangement

- Reaction questionnaire at the end of the meeting to announce the program on the follow-up questionnaire

Questions for Discussion

1. What is the value of having objectives at all five levels? Please discuss.
2. Is developing a V-model on a program that is destined for implementation helpful or necessary? Please explain.

FMI: Part C

ROI Forecast Process

With a clear understanding of the solution and the connection to the business impacts, a forecast was now possible. Although Deborah could have forecast reaction, learning, and application, she limited her forecast to impact and ROI. This forecast was essentially what was requested in the RFP, with most of the emphasis on the ROI number itself. Deborah developed the forecast, following the assumptions from the various involved stakeholders.

Impact Forecast

The first significant input to the forecast was the expected number of employees who would participate. This program was voluntary, and both the advantages and disadvantages were clearly laid out for employees, along with conditions and regulations. Not everyone would be willing to work from home. As stated earlier, Deborah and the HR team thought that about one-third of employees would sign up for this program. One-third of 950 is 317, so the forecast was based on 317 participating employees. Based on the percentage makeup of the two groups, this number translated into 237 and 80, respectively, for processors and examiners.

What follows next in Figure 11.2 is the development of the monetary forecast, following the impact improvements. The estimated impacts were obtained directly from the chief of operations and the vice president of claims. Deborah also obtained from these stakeholders the estimated monetary value of a claim: $10 for processing a claim and $12 for reviewing a claim. The office expenses were estimated to be $17,000, and the cost of a turnover taken directly from a similar study (where the cost of turnover was pegged as a percent of annual pay) was provided at $24,500. With these values in mind, the calculations are presented in Figure 11.2.

Figure 11.2 Forecast of Monetary Benefits

Anticipated Participation

- Target Group: 950
- Predicted Enrollment: 1/3
- 950 x 33 1/3% = 317
- Allocation: 237 processors
  80 examiners

Estimated Impact

- Productivity: 1 additional claim processed
                   1 additional claim examined
- Office expenses: 20% reduction
                   $17,000 x 20% = $3,400
- Turnover reduction: 22.3% to 12% = 10.3% improvement

Converting Productivity to Money

- Value of one claim = $10.00
- Value of one disputed claim = $12.00
- Daily improvement = 1 claim per day
- Daily improvement = 1 disputed claim per day
- Annual value = 237 x 220 work days x 1 x 10.00 = $521,400
- Annual value = 80 x 220 days x 1 x 12.00 = $211,200

Office Expense Reduction

- Office expenses in company office: per person $17,000 annually
- Office expenses at home office: per person $13,600 first year
- Net improvement: $3,400, first year
- Total annual value = 317 x 3400 = 1,077,800

Converting Turnover Reduction to Money

- Value of one turnover statistic = $25,400
- Annual improvement related to program
- Turnover prevention: 317 x 10.3% = 33 turnovers prevented
- Annual value = $25,400 x 33 = $838,200

Estimated Costs and Forecast of the Project

The costs of the project were estimated to be about $1,000,000. This rounded-off estimate is the total cost, including both the cost of the initial analysis to determine the legitimacy of the solution and the development of the solution. The majority of the charges were in the IT support and maintenance, administrative, and coordination categories. When the monetary benefits were combined with the cost, the ROI forecast was developed, as shown in Figure 11.3.

Figure 11.3 Forecasted ROI

Total Forecasted Monetary Benefits	
Benefits =	$521,400 Processor Productivity
	211,200 Examiner Productivity
	1,077,800 Office Costs
	838,200 Turnover Reduction
	$2,648,600
Costs =	$1,000,000
BCR =	$\dfrac{\$2,648,600}{1,000,000} = 2.65$
ROI =	$\dfrac{\$2,648,600 - 1,000,000}{1,000,000} \times 100 = 165\%$

Presentation of Results

Although this number was quite impressive, Deborah cautioned the team not to make the decision solely on the ROI calculation. In her presentation to the senior executives, Deborah stressed that significant intangibles were present, first and foremost being the contribution to the environment, which is not included in this calculation. Other factors such as job satisfaction, job engagement, stress reduction, and image were huge intangibles that should also be considered. However, because these projects need to be founded on good business decisions, the ROI forecast was credible and conservative and based on only one year of value. Much more value will be realized after the first year because most of the office set-up expenses will occur in the first year.

Deborah also cautioned that for these results to materialize, the program would have to be implemented with a focus on results and the objectives set for the program. One by one, she presented each of the objectives and stressed that they would be communicated to all the stakeholders, including the employees. This process would ensure that all stakeholders would clearly grasp their responsibilities to make the program successful. While the program should deliver a significant ROI, most of the emphasis should be placed on the intangibles.

Questions for Discussion

1. What value does a forecast add to the situation? Is it needed in today's climate?

2. How helpful would including reaction, learning, application, and intangibles in the forecast be?

3. What prevents credible forecasts from being an option pursued by consultants and clients?

FMI: Part D

The Solution

The details of the solution were developed with proper input for this program to be successful. The design had to be acceptable and the execution flawless.

Design

The design of the program followed the traditional work-at-home model, in which employees work a full 40-hour week in a home office designated for this work. The office was equipped with the appropriate interconnectivity to the company, databases, and functions, much like an office in one of FMI's buildings. The pertinent ground rules for this arrangement included the following:

1. The office had to be free of distractions. For example, not locating a television in the room was recommended.

2. Employees had to work on a set schedule if they were required to have direct contact with customers, which most did. Employees had to log on at the time they began their work and log off when they had completed work for the day.

3. The workflow system contained mechanisms for monitoring the work being accomplished. Each activity could be easily tracked to provide a user performance profile. In essence, the system determined if a person was working and recorded the results.

4. The home office had to be designed for efficiency, good health, and safety.

5. Employees were urged to take short breaks, reenergize as necessary, and always take a lunch break. The total amount of expected actual work time was 40 hours per week.

6. Employees were required to negotiate expectations and agreements with the family and significant others.

7. When employees took time off for personal errands, visits to the doctor, or other breaks, this time was subtracted from their time worked. The employees were required to make up that time during the week.

8. Employees had to stay in touch with the office and to periodically make contact with the immediate manager.
9. Employees had to sign a work-at-home pledge and attend a session on "working at home."
10. Because there was an initial investment in equipment, computers, and connects, employees were required to sign a two-year commitment to continue to work for FMI, with certain conditions. If they were to leave the company before the end of two years, they would be required to pay back the set-up charges, estimated to be about $5,000.

The principal stakeholders agreed on the design. It was reviewed by a group of employees in focus groups and then modified to produce the final set of regulations.

Execution

With the design finalized, the program was launched via communications to the target group of 950 employees. Employees received memos explaining the program and were asked to attend briefing sessions during formal working hours to discuss the work-at-home arrangement. In all, 21 employee meetings were held for the 950 employees, and managers held meetings with their respective teams to discuss the advantages and disadvantages of the process. Employees were given three weeks to make a decision and to enroll in the program within that period of time.

Questions for Discussion

1. Critique the design of the work-at-home arrangement.
2. Discuss the implementation and execution.
3. What precautions must be taken in an experiment involving only one segment of the company?

FMI: Part E

ROI Planning

The next logical phase of the process was to plan for the ROI study. This step involved completing the data collection plan and the ROI analysis plan. This phase emerged from the objectives and the input that went into the V-model.

Data Collection Plan

The starting point for the data collection plan, shown as Figure 11.4, is the objectives listed in Table 11.1. The measures are further defined with those objectives. Methods of collection are identified, sources of data are pinpointed, and the timing for data collection is determined. The plan concludes with the responsibilities for collecting the data. The data collection is comprehensive and primarily focused on interviews, questionnaires, and monitoring the data in the system.

ROI Analysis Plan

Figure 11.5 shows the ROI analysis plan, which details the analysis for the impact study. This document begins with the impact measures planned for analysis. The first column of Figure 11.5 lists each of the data items, followed by the method of isolating the effects of the program on the data and the method of converting data to money. The intangibles anticipated from the project are listed after the particular cost categories. The individuals or groups targeted for the results are then identified, along with any influences that might make a difference in this evaluation.

When completed, the data collection plan and the ROI analysis plan provide a road map to conduct the study. These documents were approved by the various stakeholders, and the work began.

Data Collection and Integration

Data collection followed the data collection plan using interviews and questionnaires. The interviews were very few in number but did provide an opportunity to explore the issues that were included on detailed

Figure 11.4 Data Collection Plan

Data Collection Plan

Evaluation Purpose: Measure Success of Program

Program: FMI Work-at-Home Project

Level	Broad Program Objectives(s)
1	*Reaction* • Employees should see the work-at-home project as satisfying, important, rewarding, and motivational • Managers must see this project as necessary, appropriate, and important to FMI.
2	*Learning* • Employees must know the realities of working at home, the conditions, roles, and regulations • Employees must have the discipline and tenacity to work at home • Managers must be able to explain company policy and regulations for working at home • Managers must be able to manage remotely
3	*Application* • Managers should conduct a meeting with direct reports to discuss policy, expected behavior, and next steps • At least 30 percent of eligible employees should volunteer for at-home assignments within one month • At-home offices are built and properly equipped • The home workplace should be free from distractions and conflicting demands • Managers will properly administer the company's policy • Managers should effectively manage the remote employees
4	*Impact* • Commute time should be reduced to an average of 15 minutes per day • Office expense per person should reduce by 20 percent in six months • Productivity should increase by 5 percent in six months • Employee turnover should reduce to 12 percent in six months • Unplanned absences • Stress should be reduced • Carbon emissions should be reduced • The company's image as a green company should be enhanced • Employee engagement should improve
5	*ROI* • Achieve a 25 percent return on investment

Responsibility: HR/Consultants   **Date:** March 30

Measures	Data Collection Method/ Instruments	Data Sources	Timing
• Rating scale (4 out of 5)	• Questionnaires • Interviews	• Participants • Managers	• 30 days • 30 days
• Rating scale (4 out of 5)	• Questionnaires • Interviews	• Employees • Managers	• 30 days • 30 days
• Checklist • Sign Up • Rating Scale (4 out of 5)	• Data Monitoring • Data Monitoring • Questionnaires	• Company Records • Company Records • Participants • Managers	• 30 days • 30 days • 90 days • 90 days
• Direct Costs • Claims per day • Voluntary turnover • Rating scale (4 out of 5) • Rating scale (4 out of 5)	• Business Performance Monitoring • Survey	• Company Records • Participants • Managers	• 6 months • 6 months • 6 months • 90 days • 90 days
• Baseline Data:			

Figure 11.5 ROI Analysis Plan

Program:	FMI Work-at-Home Project	Responsibility: HR/Consultants				Date:
Data Items (Usually Level 4)	Methods for Isolating the Effects of the Program/Process	Methods of Converting Data to Monetary Values	Cost Categories	Intangible Benefits	Communication Targets for Final Report	Other Influential Issues during Application
• Office expenses • Productivity • Turnover	• Control group • Expert estimates • Control Group • Participant estimates • Control Group • Participant Estimates	• Standard value based on costs • Standard values • External studies	• Initial analysis and assessment • Forecasting Impact and ROI • Solution development • IT support and maintenance • Administration and coordination • Materials • Facilities and refreshments • Salaries plus benefits for employee and manager meetings • Evaluation and reporting	• Reduced commuting time • Reduced carbon emissions • Reduced fuel consumption • Reduced sick leave • Reduced absenteeism • Improved job engagement • Improved community image • Improved image as environmental friendly company • Enhanced corporate social responsibility • Improved job satisfaction • Reduced stress • Improved recruiting image	• Participants • Managers • HR team • Executive group • Consultants • External groups	• Must observe marketing and economic forces • Search for barriers/obstacles for progress

follow-up questionnaires. All participating employees and their managers received the questionnaires. In total, 342 questionnaires were distributed to employees and 45 of their managers. Figure 11.6 shows the data integration plan and how the data were collected and integrated to the results.

Figure 11.6 Data Collection Methods and Integration

Method	Level 1 Reaction	Level 2 Learning	Level 3 Application	Barriers/ Enablers	Level 4 Impact	Costs
Initial Participant Questionnaire	X	X	X		X	
Initial Manager Questionnaire	X	X	X		X	
Participant Interviews	X	X	X		X	
Follow-up Questionnaire: Participants	X		X	X	X	
Follow-up Questionnaire: Managers	X		X	X		
Company Records			X		X	X

Questions for Discussion

1. Critique the date collection plan.
2. Critique the ROI analysis plan.
3. How helpful is the data integration figure?
4. What improvements would you recommend for data collection and analysis?

FMI: Part F

Results: Reaction and Learning

The data were collected following the data collection plan. The results are presented by the levels of data, beginning with reaction and learning categories.

Reaction Data

Reaction data were collected early in the program and focused on reactions from both the employees involved in the project and their managers. Although open verbal and informal positive reactions were detected early in the process, four particular measures on the questionnaire were collected directly from the employees:

- the satisfaction with the new work arrangement
- the importance of this approach to their success
- the rewarding effect of this opportunity for them
- the motivation effect of this arrangement (the company anticipated this new work arrangement would result in more motivated employees who would produce more)

These four measures scored high numbers, and Table 11.2 shows the results. The reaction from the employee perspective averaged 4.4 on a 5.0-point scale.

Table 11.2 Reaction Data

From Participating Employees

- Rating of 4.6 out of 5 on satisfaction with new work arrangement
- Rating of 4.7 out of 5 on importance of new work arrangement to their success
- Rating of 4.2 out of 5 on the rewarding effect of the new work arrangement
- Rating of 4.1 out of 5 on motivational effect of new work arrangement

From Managers

- Rating of 4.2 out of 5 on importance of the work alternative
- Rating of 4.1 out of 5 on appropriateness of the work alternative
- Rating of 4.3 out of 5 on the need for the work alternative

From the managers' perspective, understanding how managers perceived this new work arrangement was important. Although this issue had many aspects, the objectives focused on three issues: how managers perceived this program to be necessary, appropriate, and critical to the company. Managers had to see the necessity of this program in today's work climate when considering the effect of commuting on the environment and the desire for the flexibility of working from home. Table 11.2 shows the managers' reactions, which exceeded expectations. The ratings averaged 4.2 out of 5.0 on the three items. In summary, the reaction exceeded the expectations of the implementation team.

Learning Data

Although this project is not a classic learning solution, in which a significant amount of skills and knowledge must be developed for the program to be successful, a learning component is still present. Employees must understand their roles and responsibilities, and managers must understand the policies of working at home. They must also have the ability to explain the policies and to successfully address any performance issues that can develop in the unique environment of a remote workforce. The managers and employees provided self-assessment input on their questionnaires, which typically showed the learning from the two groups. The managers were given an opportunity during meetings to practice the performance discussions so they would be able to address the issues effectively. The facilitator of the meeting was required to confirm that each manager involved in the program could successfully explain the policy and demonstrate four types of performance discussions. As Table 11.3 shows, the self-assessment ratings exceeded the expectations on five measures from employees, averaging 4.3 out of 5.0. Managers averaged 4.1 out of 5.0 on two measures. The confidence to explain the policy was 3.9 out of 5.0, just short of the goal of 4.0. Still, there was confidence that learning had occurred so that the program could be properly implemented. Also, each manager successfully demonstrated, through role playing, four types of performance discussions.

Table 11.3 Learning Data

From Employees
Rating of 4.0 of 5 on the discipline and tenacity to work
Rating of 4.1 of 5 on the tenacity to work at home
Rating of 4.3 of 5 on roles and responsibilities
Rating of 4.3 of 5 on conditions and regulations
Rating of 4.2 of 5 on the realities of working at home

From Managers
• Rating of 4.2 of 5 on key elements of the policy for working at home
• Rating of 3.9 of 5 on the confidence to explain policy
• Successful skill practice demonstration on performance discussions – all checked

Results: Application

Application Data

These types of programs can easily go astray if employees are not following the policies properly and the managers are not managing the process appropriately. Consequently, application and tracking the implementation of the process became a significant data set. Table 11.4 shows the key items monitored that are directly connected to objectives. In all, 93 percent of managers conducted meetings with employees to discuss the work-at-home arrangement. Although 100 percent would usually be expected, a few managers had either no direct employees or no employees who were interested in working at home. The possibility remained that some managers did not conduct the meetings when they

Table 11.4 Application Data

• Ninety-three percent of managers conducted meetings with employees to discuss working at home
• Thirty-six percent of eligible employees volunteered for at-home work assignments (342 participants)
• In total, 340 home offices were built and equipped properly (two employees changed their minds before establishing an office)
• Work-at-home employees rated 4.3 out of 5 on working effectively at home
• Ninety-five percent of employees reported that workplace was free of distractions and conflicting demands
• Managers rated 4.1 of 5 on administering policy properly
• Managers rated 3.8 of 5 on managing remote employees effectively

should have. Therefore, a complete briefing involving all employees covered most of the issues that the managers had explored in the meetings with staff. The meeting with the managers represented reinforcement and showed their connection to the project.

After all the briefings and information-sharing, 36 percent of the eligible employees volunteered for work-at-home assignments, representing 342 participants. This participation was better than expected and left the project team pleased. In the follow-up data, the participants rated 4.3 out of 5.0 on working effectively at home; in addition, 95 percent of the employees reported that the workplace was free of distractions and conflict. The managers rated themselves 4.1 out of 5.0 on properly administering policy. However, some managers rated themselves lower in the area of managing employees remotely, resulting in a rate of 3.8 out of 5.0.

Barriers and Enablers

With the recognition that many issues could derail the success of this program, the barriers and enablers were captured. Table 11.5 shows the barriers and enablers to success, and as expected some classic barriers to success were found; however, the barriers did not prove to be highly significant. The greatest barrier was lack of manager support, with 18 percent of participants indicating this as a concern. Following closely behind was lack of necessary support from staff who would normally support them in their office work. Additionally, 15 percent indicated communication breakdown, while 11 percent thought that this program would limit their career progression. A few felt that they would be left out of decision-making and that IT support would be inadequate, while some indicated that they were concerned about the loss of social interaction.

Regarding the enablers, the number one enabler on this list is the personal cost savings. Many employees signed up for this arrangement as a way to save costs by avoiding the commute. Followed closely behind was the flexibility of having some adjustments in their work schedule and of taking time for personal activities to be made up later. Next were the convenience of working in the home setting and improved work/life balance. Most employees said they had all the tools to make the

Table 11.5 Barriers and Enablers to Success	
Barriers	**Percent Indicated**
Managers support is lacking	18%
Lack of support staff	16%
Communication breakdowns	13%
Career progression is limited	11%
Left out of decisions	9%
IT support is lacking	7%
Lack of social interactions	5%
Enablers	**Percent Indicated**
Personal cost savings	89%
Flexibility to schedule	71%
Convenience of work	71%
Work life balance	64%
I have all the tools	54%
Support of manager	31%
Support of staff	14%

change work. Only 31 percent said the support of the managers helped to make it more successful. Finally, 14 percent said staff support helped them. These barriers and enablers provided an opportunity for process improvement.

Results: Impact

Isolating the Effects of the Program

As the impact data were collected, the key question was how much of this improvement was actually connected to this specific project. While several methods were considered, a classic method was used. The work-at-home group was considered an experimental group and compared to a matched group that would serve as a control group. This match group,

labeled the comparison group, was matched with the experimental group
on job category, length of service with the company, and gender, age,
marital, and family status. With so many variables, getting a perfect match
was difficult, but the team felt that the two groups compared favorably. As
a backup, expert estimates were used.

Impact

The impact data were monitored and included three measures:
productivity, office expense, and turnover. The team decided not to value
this program on absenteeism and instead left it as an intangible. Although
absenteeism is probably connected to the program, the HR team thought
not including absenteeism as a measurable objective would be best. If the
organization focused too much on this measure, some employees may
decide to work while sick. Table 11.6 shows the impact data of both the
experimental group and comparison group six months after the project
began. The differences are significant, representing distinct improvements
in the three measures and exceeding the objectives of the project. After
identifying the amount of data and isolating it to the project, the HR
team moved to the next step, converting data to money.

Table 11.6 Impact Data

Business Performance	Work-at-Home Group	Comparison Group	Change	Number of Participants
Daily Claims Processed	35.4	33.2	2.2	234
Daily Claims Examined	22.6	20.7	1.9	77
Office Expense Per Person	$12,500	$17,000	$4,500	311
Annualized Turnover (Processors and Examiners)	9.1%	22.3%	13.2%	311

Converting Data to Money

Table 11.7 shows how each of the data sets was converted to
monetary value. As the table explains, the method for converting the
productivity improvement to value used standard values. The value
was previously developed by a group of experts and analysts in finance

and accounting. The number was rounded to $10 for claim processing and $12 for claim examination. The calculation shows the annual cost savings.

Office expenses were rounded numbers taken directly from the procurement function. The first-year value of $12,500 was used with the at-home employees. This amount was compared to the annual cost to maintain the office for all employees, $17,000 per person. The first-year value included cost of a computer, desk, and other items that would certainly be present as long as that person works at home. The second-year value shows a very significant reduction. To be conservative, only the first-year value was used in the comparison.

For turnover reduction, several turnover cost studies were performed on jobs in the insurance industry, using the ERIC database. The cost ranged from 90 percent to 110 percent, which seemed consistent and credible to the project team. The 90 percent figure was used, and when multiplied by the average salary, yielded $25,400. In all, 41 turnovers were prevented in the first year based on six months' experience. The annual value is shown in the calculation, and the total is $3,959,692.

Table 11.7 Converting Data to Money

Productivity Improvement

- Cost (value) of processing one claim = $10.00
- Cost (value) of examining one disputed claim = $12.00
- Daily improvement = 2.2 claims per day
- Daily improvement = 1.9 disputed claims per day
- Annual value = 234 x 220 work days x 2.2 x 10.00 = $1,132,560
- Annual value = 77 x 220 days x 1.9 x 12.00 = $386,232

Office Expense Reduction

- Office expenses in company office: per person $17,000 annually
- Office expenses at home office: per person $12,500 first year; $3,600 second year
- Net improvement: $4,500, first year
- Total annual value = 311 x 4,500 = $1,399,500

Turnover Reduction

- Value of one turnover statistic = $25,400
- Annual improvement related to program = 41 turnovers (prevented), first year
- Annual value = $25,400 x 41 = $1,041,400

Costs

The costs of the entire project as developed and monitored were estimated and are shown in Table 11.8. These costs include the initial analysis to determine the suitability of the solution, the ROI forecast, and the actual development of the solution. Most of the charges are for IT support and maintenance, administration, and coordination categories.

Table 11.8 Project Costs	
Initial Analysis and Assessment	$21,000
Forecasting Impact and ROI	$10,000
Solution Development	$35,800
IT Support and Maintenance	$238,000
Administration and Coordination	$213,000
Materials (400 @ $50)	$20,000
Facilities and Refreshments – 21 meetings	$12,600
Salaries Plus Benefits for Employee and Manager Meetings	$418,280
Evaluation, Monitoring, and Reporting	$23,000
Total First Year Costs	**$991,680**

Questions for Discussion

1. Calculate the benefit cost ratio and ROI for this project.
2. Interpret these two calculations and what they mean.
3. Are the results of this study credible? Explain.

FMI: Part G

Results: ROI and Intangibles

ROI Calculations

The ROI is calculated when the costs are totaled, and the monetary benefits are tallied. Table 11.9 shows the calculation of the benefit cost ratio and the ROI. The ROI calculation at 299 percent greatly exceeded the initial objective of 25 percent. However, important results were not included in the calculation. The intangibles were very critical to this study.

Table 11.9 ROI Calculations

$$BCR = \frac{\text{Consulting Monetary Benefits}}{\text{Consulting Costs}} = \frac{\$3,959,692}{\$991,680} = 3.99$$

$$ROI = \frac{\text{Net Consulting Benefits}}{\text{Consulting Costs}} = \frac{\$3,959,692 - \$991,680}{\$991,680} \times 299\%$$

Intangible Benefits

Table 11.10 shows a list of the intangible benefits connected to the project. To compile this list, an individual had to indicate a 3, 4, or 5 on a 5-point scale where 3 is moderate influence, 4 is significant influence, and 5 is very significant influence. A list of expected intangibles was included on the participants' and managers' questionnaires. In addition, at least 10 percent had to check 3, 4, or 5 to make the table. These were impactful intangibles, including those connected to the environment. Participants and managers could clearly see the environmental connection. Executives in particular may have viewed this data set as exceptional, because the intangible image of helping the environment often drives these types of projects. When these data sets were combined with the very high ROI, seeing the program's payoff was easy.

Table 11.10 Intangible Benefits

- Reduced commuting time
- Reduced carbon emissions
- Reduced fuel consumption
- Reduced sick leave
- Reduced absenteeism
- Improved job engagement
- Improved community image
- Improved image as an environmental-friendly company
- Enhanced corporate social responsibility
- Improved job satisfaction
- Reduced stress
- Improved recruiting image

Fuel Savings

Because the individuals involved in this program eliminated their commute time (with the exception of an occasional required visit to the office), the fuel savings were significant. The average daily commute time reduced from 104 minutes to 15 minutes. When considering the average speed (30 mph), the average miles per gallon of gasoline (20 mpg), and the cost of fuel ($3.00 per gallon), a savings of $1,470 per year was realized in fuel costs alone.

Carbon Emissions

From the perspective of the top executive, the principal motivating factor of this program was to reduce carbon emissions. With reduced fuel consumption, carbon emissions were consequently reduced. A total of 490 gallons of fuel per person was saved, for a total of 152,390 gallons each year. This value translates into 1,478 tons of carbon emissions.

What Makes the Results Credible

Understanding what makes this data credible is necessary. The numbers are impressive, but some specific attributes make the data especially credible.

- The impact data improvements were taken directly from the records and were not estimated.

- The effects of the program were isolated from other factors using a comparison group.
- Several impact measures were not converted to money, although they had significant value.
- All the costs were included, including the very heavy start-up cost.
- Only the first-year values were used in the analysis. This program will have a lasting effect as long as each individual is employed with FMI.
- When estimates were used, they were taken from the most credible sources.
- All the data sets and methods had buy-in from the appropriate operating executives and key managers.
- There is no reason to dispute the results presented in this process.

Questions for Discussion

1. Which audiences should receive the results of this study?
2. What specific methods should be used to communicate results?
3. What specific improvements could be made to this program going forward?

Epilogue

As we finish writing this second edition, the United States and other countries around the world are coming out of a deep recession. Unfortunately, we have seen its effects on the HR community. Unique situations have occurred, with some companies eliminating much of human resources early in the recession. Most were trimming their HR expenses and eliminating "other unnecessary expenses." In many, if not most, of these situations, these firms were not losing money but were trimming their expenses so that they could be lean and efficient. Human resources was one of the first areas cut, and proportionately was cut the most. When you consider the budgets of all functions, in particular the support functions such as marketing, human resources, IT, and quality, human resources received the greatest cuts.

At the same time, *Economist* magazine labeled human resources the "loser" executive during this recession, while the chief financial officer (CFO) is the winner during this recession. The CFO is the winner because this is the most important executive, according to the magazine. This is the executive who will continue to guide firms out of this recession and try to keep them from having problems in the next recession. Human resources, on the other hand, was cut more dramatically than the other functions and at the same time must work with the aftermath of the recession — layoffs, integrations, consolidations, and bankruptcies. We have also seen some HR functions in other companies go untouched during this recession. This action is encouraging. While they trimmed other expenses, they have not cut back on the investment in employees.

In an ideal world, top executives of every company would view investments in human resources as essential during tough economic times, and in most situations, they would demand additional investment, instead of less. In a smaller company, the combination of having only a few employees and the pressure to bring more business in this economy can be challenging. An additional HR investment can make employees tougher in their approach and more skilled in their execution and make the organization more effective and efficient. Fewer employees may also mean that the remaining employees have to take up the slack, so additional capability is needed for them as well.

Regrettably, however, most executives do not see it this way. For the most part, they view human resources as something that is necessary but not a process yielding a return on investment. They have a desire to see more data, more value, and more connection to the business, but the majority of those responsible for the HR function have not stepped up to this challenge. It is vital that HR leaders set the right priorities, have the discipline to follow through on them, and tenaciously make them sustainable — and this book provides the "how to" for doing this. The challenge is left up to the leaders of the HR community to position their function as a crucial, business-contributing process that helps drive the organization in good times and bad.

We encourage readers of this book to meet this challenge, because we have seen it pay handsome rewards in the future. If you need more dialogue on this issue, please contact us and join our network.

Jack J. Phillips
jack@roiinstitute.net
Patti Pulliam Phillips
patti@roiinstitute.net

Fall 2011

Appendix A. Self-Test: How Results-Based Are Your Human Resources Programs?*

Select the response that best describes the situation in your organization and circle the letter preceding the response.

1. Measurements have been developed and are used to determine the effectiveness of:
   a. All human resources (HR) functions
   b. Approximately half of the HR functions
   c. At least one HR function

2. Major organizational decisions:
   a. Are usually made with input from the HR function
   b. Are usually made without input from the HR function
   c. Are always made with input from the HR function

3. The return on investment in human resources is measured primarily by:
   a. Intuition and perception by senior executives
   b. Observations by management and reactions from participants and users
   c. Improvements in productivity, costs, time, quality, etc.

4. The concern for the method of evaluation for a new HR program occurs:
   a. Before the program is developed
   b. After the program is implemented
   c. After the program is developed but before it is implemented

---

This survey is adopted from previous versions developed by the author and published in several publications.

5. Without some formal method of measurement and evaluation, new HR programs are:
   a. Never implemented
   b. Regularly implemented
   c. Occasionally implemented

6. The costs of specific HR programs are:
   a. Estimated when the programs are implemented
   b. Never calculated
   c. Continuously monitored

7. The costs of absenteeism and turnover:
   a. Are routinely calculated and monitored
   b. Have been occasionally calculated to identify problem areas
   c. Have not been determined

8. Benefit/cost comparisons of HR programs are:
   a. Never developed
   b. Occasionally developed
   c. Frequently developed

9. In an economic downturn, the HR function will:
   a. Be retained at the same staffing level, unless the downturn is lengthy
   b. Be the first to have its staff reduced
   c. Go untouched in staff reductions and possibly be increased

10. The cost of current or proposed employee benefits are:
    a. Regularly calculated and compared with national, industry, and local data
    b. Occasionally estimated when there is concern about operating expenses
    c. Not calculated, except for required reporting

11. The chief executive officer (CEO) interfaces with the senior HR officer:
    a. Infrequently
    b. Occasionally, when there is a pressing need
    c. Frequently, to know what is going on and to provide support

12. On the organizational chart, the top HR executive:
    a. Reports directly to the CEO (one level below the CEO)
    b. Is more than two levels removed from the CEO
    c. Is two levels below the CEO
13. Management involvement in implementing HR programs is:
    a. Limited to a few programs in its area of expertise
    b. Not planned; only HR specialists are involved in implementing programs
    c. Significant; most of the programs are implemented through management
14. The HR staff involvement in measurement and evaluation consists of:
    a. No specific responsibilities in measurement and evaluation with no formal training in evaluation methods
    b. Partial responsibilities for measurement and evaluation, with some formal training in evaluation methods
    c. Complete responsibilities for measurement and evaluation; even when some are devoted full time to the efforts, all staff members have been trained in evaluation methods
15. Human resources development (HRD) efforts consist of:
    a. A full array of courses designed to meet individuals' needs
    b. Usually one-shot, seminar-type approaches
    c. A variety of leadership and development (L&D) programs implemented to improve/change the organization
16. When an employee participates in an HR program, his or her immediate manager usually:
    a. Asks questions about the program and encourages program implementation
    b. Requires implementation and uses positive rewards when the employee meets program objectives
    c. Makes no reference to the program

17. Variable pay (such as bonuses or incentive plans):
    a. Exists for a few key employees
    b. Is developed for all frontline employees
    c. Is developed for most employees, both operating and support staff
18. Productivity improvement, cost reduction, or quality improvement programs:
    a. Have not been seriously considered in the organization
    b. Are under consideration at the present time
    c. Have been implemented with good results
19. The results of HR programs are communicated:
    a. Occasionally, to members of management only
    b. Routinely, to a variety of selected target audiences
    c. As requested, to those who have a need to know
20. With the present HR organization and status, the HR function's impact on the organization's concerns:
    a. Can be estimated, but probably at a significant cost
    b. Can be estimated (or is being estimated) with little additional cost
    c. Can never be assessed

Scoring and Interpretation

Scoring: Assign a numeric value to each of your responses to the questions as indicated below. Total your score and compare it with the analysis that follows.

POINTS	POINTS	POINTS	POINTS
1. a - 5	6. a - 3	11. a - 1	16. a - 3
b - 3	b - 1	b - 3	b - 5
c - 1	c - 5	c - 5	c - 1
2. a - 3	7. a - 5	12. a - 5	17. a - 1
b - 1	b - 3	b - 1	b - 3
c - 5	c - 1	c - 3	c - 5
3 a - 1	8. a - 1	13. a - 3	18. a - 1
b - 3	b - 3	b - 1	b - 3
c - 5	c - 5	c - 5	c - 5
4. a - 5	9. a - 3	14. a - 1	19. a - 3
b - 1	b - 1	b - 3	b - 5
c - 3	c - 5	c - 5	c - 1
5. a - 5	10. a - 5	15. a - 3	20. a - 3
b - 1	b - 3	b - 1	b - 5
c - 3	c - 1	c - 5	c - 1

Interpretation: Explanations for responses are provided below.

1. Measurements should be developed for all HR functions. When performance measures are not feasible, at least a few lower level measures should be in place for each function or new project. Otherwise, human resources may be perceived to be not important or not contributive.

2. Major organizational decisions should always involve input from human resources. HR policy-makers should provide comments, advice, or approval when human resources issues are involved.

3. Whenever possible, the return on investment in human resources should be measured by improvements in productivity, costs, time, and quality. Although other types of evaluation are important and acceptable, these measures are the ultimate proof of results.

4. The concern for the method of evaluation should occur before the program is developed. At program conception, some consideration should be given to how the data will be collected and to how the program will be evaluated. This approach ensures that the proper emphasis is placed on accountability.

5. HR programs should never be implemented without a provision for at least some type of formal method of measurement and evaluation. Otherwise, the effectiveness or efficiency of the program may never be known.

6. The costs of all individual HR programs should be continuously monitored to provide management with an assessment of the financial impact of these programs at all times — not just when the program is implemented.

7. Because these important variables represent a tremendous cost for the organization, the cost of absenteeism and turnover should be routinely calculated and monitored.

8. Benefit/cost comparisons of HR programs should be conducted frequently, particularly when a significant investment is involved. Even rough estimates of payoffs versus estimated costs can be helpful in the evaluation of a program.

9. In an economic downturn, the HR function should be untouched in staff reductions or possibly increased. Ideally, the function should enhance performance by improving productivity, raising profits,

increasing quality, and/or reducing costs. These actions can keep the organization competitive in the downturn.

10. Because employee benefits represent a significant portion of operating expenses, they should be routinely monitored and compared with national data, industry norms, and localized data. Projected future costs of benefits should also be periodically reviewed.

11. The CEO should frequently interface with the executive responsible for human resources. The CEO needs to know the status of human capital and receive input on employee satisfaction, commitment, or engagement. Such interaction provides an opportunity for the CEO to communicate concerns, desires, and expectations to the HR executive. Frequent meetings are important.

12. The chief HR executive should report directly to the CEO. A direct link to the top will help ensure that human resources receives proper attention and that it commands the influence necessary to achieve results.

13. Management involvement in the implementation of HR programs should be significant. Management participation in the design, development, and implementation of HR programs will help ensure its success. Managers should be partners with the HR staff.

14. The entire HR staff should have some responsibility for measurement and evaluation. Even when some individuals are devoted full time to the effort, all staff members should have a partial responsibility for measurement and evaluation. Staff members should also have training/briefings in measurement and evaluation methods. This comprehensive focus on evaluation is necessary for successful implementation.

15. Human resources development (HRD) efforts should consist of a variety of learning and development programs implemented to increase the effectiveness of the organization. HRD involves more than just courses or short seminars. It should include a variety of delivery methods aimed at improving organizational effectiveness.

16. When an employee completes an HR program, his or her immediate manager should require use of the knowledge/skills learned and reward the employee for meeting or exceeding program objectives. This positive reinforcement will help ensure that the appropriate results are achieved.

17. Variable pay programs should be considered for most employees, both operating and support staff. Although usually limited to a few key line employees, variable pay is appropriate for most employees. Through gain-sharing plans, bonuses, incentives, and stock options, employees can see the results of their efforts and are rewarded for their achievement. This practice should be fundamental to a results-based philosophy for the HR function.

18. Productivity improvement, cost reduction, or quality improvement programs should be implemented in many locations and should achieve positive results. These programs are at the very heart of the HR contribution and have been proven successful in all types of settings. The HR function should ensure that these programs are administered efficiently and that they are successful.

19. The results of HR programs should be routinely communicated to a variety of selected target audiences. Different audiences have different interests and needs, but several key audiences should always receive information on the success of HR programs. While some may need only limited general information, other audiences need detailed, bottom-line results.

20. The impact of the HR function can be estimated with little additional costs. If measurement and evaluation are integral parts of the organization's philosophy, data collection can be built into the human capital management system. It adds a little cost but should generate data necessary to calculate HR results.

Analysis of Scores

Total score should range from 20 to 100. The higher the score, the greater your organization's emphasis on achieving results with the HR function.

Score

Range Analysis

81-100. This organization is truly committed to achieving results with human resources. Additional efforts to improve measurement and evaluation for the HR function are not needed as there is little room for improvement. All HR functions and programs appear to be contributing to organizational effectiveness. Management support is excellent. Top management commitment is strong. This HR department is taking the lead in measurement and evaluation by showing the contribution it can make to the organization's success. Chances are it is a vital part of an effective and successful organization.

61-80. This HR function is effective and contributing to organizational success. The organization is usually better than average regarding measurement and evaluation. Although the attitude toward achieving results is good, and some of the approaches to evaluation appear to be working, there is still some room for improvement. Additional emphasis is needed to make this department more successful.

41-60. Improvement is needed in this organization. It ranks below average in accountability with other HR functions. The attitude about results and the approach used in implementing HR programs are less than desirable. Evaluation methods appear to be ineffective, and action is needed to improve management support and to change the culture of the organization. Over the long term, this HR function falls far short of making the desired contribution to the organization.

20-40. This organization shows little or no concern for achieving results from the HR function. Human resources appears to be ineffective, and improvement is needed if the function is to survive in its current form and with its current leadership. Urgent attention is needed to make this department more effective and able to contribute to the success of the organization.

This instrument has been administered to HR managers and specialists attending local, regional, national, and international HR conferences. The typical respondent has been the individual responsible for the HR function. The instrument was administered anonymously, and the respondents were provided ample time at the beginning of the meeting to complete it. Questions and answers were allowed during the administration of the instrument. To date, there have been more than 1,500 usable responses representing an average score of 62.9 with a standard deviation of 5.4.

The score can reveal much about the status of human resources in an organization and about the attitude toward measurement and evaluation. A perfect score of 100 is probably unachievable and represents utopia; however, it is the ultimate goal of many HR leaders and other executives. On the other extreme, a score of 20 reveals an ineffective organization, at least in terms of the contribution of the HR function. The organization will probably not exist for long in its current form or with the current staff.

Although the analysis of these scores is simplistic, the message from the exercise should be obvious. Achieving results from human resources is more than just evaluating a single program or service. It represents a comprehensive philosophy that must be integrated into the routine activities of the HR staff and supported and encouraged by top executives.

Appendix B.
ROI Case Studies

This appendix contains a brief listing of a few published case studies on the use of the ROI Methodology for a variety of HR issues, including compensation, compliance, health and safety, diversity, retention improvement, leadership, learning and development, and more. These ROI case studies are offered to illustrate the range of applications that have been addressed with this methodology. Additional information and complete copies of the studies are available from the ROI Institute (www.roiinstitute.net). Table B.1 contains 15 human resources case studies and is available at a reader discount of $20 plus shipping.

From the beginning of the implementation of ROI Methodology, case studies have been a valuable tool to understand the issues involved in making ROI work in an organization. Although the number of impact studies conducted annually is hard to pinpoint, our best estimate is that approximately 3,000 to 5,000 studies are conducted each year. This estimate is derived from the number of people who have participated in an in-depth certification process to develop skills to implement the ROI Methodology (see www.roiinstitute.net for more details). In those organizations, the number of case studies annually range from one to as many as 40.

Table B.1

HR Program and Organization Type	Key Impact Measures	ROI
Leadership Development for First Level Managers (Car Rental)	A variety of measures, such as productivity, quality, time, costs, turnover, and absenteeism	105%
Performance Management (Restaurant Chain)	A variety of measures, such as productivity, quality, time, costs, turnover, and absenteeism	298%
Process Improvement Team (Apple Computer)	Productivity and labor efficiency	182%
Skill-Based Pay (Construction Materials Firm)	Labor costs, turnover, and absenteeism	805%
Sexual Harassment Prevention (Healthcare Chain)	Complaints, turnover, absenteeism, and job satisfaction	1,052%
Safety Incentive Plan (Steel Company)	Accident frequency rate, accident severity rates	379%
Diversity (Nextel Communications)	Retention, employee satisfaction	163%
Retention Improvement (Financial Services)	Turnover, staffing levels, and employee satisfaction	258%
Absenteeism Control/Reduction Program (Major City)	Absenteeism, customer satisfaction	882%
Stress Management Program (Electric Utility)	Medical costs, turnover, and absenteeism	320%
Executive Leadership Development (Financial)	Team projects, individual projects, and retention	62%
E-Learning (Energy)	Sales	206%
Internal Graduate Degree Program (Federal Agency)	Retention, individual graduate projects	153%
Executive Coaching (Hotel Chain)	Several measures, including sales growth, productivity, operation efficiency, cost control, talent retention, and customer satisfaction	221%
Competency Development (Veterans Health Administration)	Time savings, improve work quality, and faster response	159%
Machine Operator Training: ROI Forecasting (Valve Company)	Training time, machining scrap, turnover, accidents, and maintenance expense	132%
Sales Training (Retail Store Chain)	Weekly Sales Data	118%

Appendix C.
Resources

To continue to build your expertise in ROI, additional resources may be desired. Here is a list of most of the recent books on the ROI Methodology.

Phillips, Jack, and Phillips, Patricia Pulliam. *The Consultant's Scorecard: Tracking ROI and Bottom-Line Impact of Consulting Projects*, 2nd ed. New York: McGraw-Hill, 2011.

Phillips, Patricia Pulliam. *The Bottomline on ROI*, 2nd ed. King of Prussia, PA: HRDQ Press, 2012.

Phillips, Patricia Pulliam, and Phillips, Jack J. *The Green Scorecard: Measuring the Return on Investment in Sustainability Projects*. Boston: Nicholas Brealey, 2011.

Phillips, Patricia Pulliam, and Phillips, Jack J. *Proving the Value of HR: ROI Case Studies*, 2nd ed. Birmingham, AL: ROI Institute, 2010.

Patricia Pulliam Phillips, ed. *ASTD Handbook of Measuring and Evaluating Training*. Alexandria, VA: ASTD Press, 2010.

Phillips, Jack J., and Phillips, Patricia Pulliam. *Measuring for Success: What CEOs Really Think About Learning Investments*. Alexandria, VA: ASTD Press, 2010.

Phillips, Jack J., and Phillips, Patricia Pulliam. *The Consultant's Guide to Results-Driven Business Proposals: How to Write Proposals that Forecast Impact and ROI*. New York: McGraw-Hill, 2010.

Phillips, Jack J., and Edwards, Lisa. *Managing Talent Retention: An ROI Approach*. San Francisco: Pfeiffer, 2009.

Phillips, Jack J., and Phillips, Patricia Pulliam. *Beyond Learning Objectives: Develop Measurable Objectives That Link To The Bottom Line.* Alexandria, VA: ASTD, 2008.

Phillips, Patricia Pulliam, and Phillips, Jack J. *The Measurement and Evaluation Series (ROI Fundamentals: Why and When to Measure Return on Investment; Data Collection: Planning For and Collecting All Types of Data; Isolation of Results: Defining the Impact of the Program; Data Conversion: Calculating the Monetary Benefits; Costs and ROI: Evaluating at the Ultimate Level; Communication and Implementation: Sustaining the Practice).* San Francisco: Pfeiffer, 2008.

Phillips, Patricia Pulliam, and Phillips, Jack J. *The Value of Learning: How Organizations Capture Value and ROI and Translate It into Support, Improvement, and Funds.* San Francisco: Pfeiffer, 2007.

Phillips, Patricia Pulliam, and Phillips, Jack J., eds., *ROI in Action Casebook.* San Francisco: Pfeiffer, 2008.

Phillips, Jack J., and Phillips, Patricia Pulliam. *Show Me the Money: How to Determine ROI in People, Projects, and Programs.* San Francisco: Berrett-Koehler, 2007.

Endnotes

Preface

[1] Archibald Bowman, "Reporting on the Corporate Investment," *Journal of Accountancy*, May 1938, 399.

Chapter 6

[1] Paul W. Farris, Neil T. Bendle, Phillip E. Pfeifer, and David J. Ribstein, *Marketing Metrics: 50+ Metrics Every Executive Should Master* (Upper Saddle River, NJ: Wharton School Publishing, 2006).

[2] Nancy S. Ahlrichs, *Competing for Talent: Key Recruitment and Retention Strategies for Becoming an Employer of Choice* (Palo Alto, CA: Davies-Black, 2000).

[3] David Ulrich, ed., *Delivering Results: A New Mandate for Human Resource Professionals* (Boston: Harvard Business School Press, 1998).

Chapter 7

[1] Horngren, Charles T., Harris, John K., *Professional Examination Questions and Answers, a Self Study Approach: [to Accompany] Cost Accounting, a Managerial Emphasis, 5th Ed.*, Upper Saddle River, New Jersey: Prentice-Hall, 1982.

Chapter 8

[1] Hubert Saint-Onge, "Shaping Human Resource Management within the Knowledge-Driven Enterprise," in *Leading Knowledge Management and Learning*, ed. Dede Bonner (Alexandria, VA: American Society for Training and Development, 2002), 275-300.

Chapter 9

[1] Peter Block, *Flawless Consulting: A Guide to Getting Your Expertise Used* (San Francisco: Jossey-Bass/Pfeiffer, 2000).

Index

About the Authors

Dr. Jack J. Phillips, a world-renowned expert on accountability, measurement, and evaluation, provides consulting services for *Fortune* 500 companies and major global organizations. As the author and editor of more than 50 books, he conducts workshops and presents conferences throughout the world. Dr. Phillips also regularly consults with clients in manufacturing, service, and government organizations in 60 countries in North and South America, Europe, Africa, Australia, and Asia.

Phillips has received several awards for his books and work, including being named one of the 25 Most Powerful People in the Meetings and Events Industry three times by *Meeting News*, based on his work on ROI. The Society for Human Resource Management honored him with an award for one of his books, as well as its most prestigious award for creativity for a Phillips ROI study. The American Society for Training and Development also gave him its highest award for his work on ROI, the Distinguished Contribution to Workplace Learning and Development award. His work has been featured in the *Wall Street Journal, Businessweek, Fortune* magazine, and on CNN and a dozen other television programs. Over 4,000 organizations, including the United Nations, use his methodology.

His expertise in measurement and evaluation is based on more than twenty-seven years of corporate experience in the aerospace, textile, metals, construction materials, and banking industries. Dr. Phillips has served as training and development manager at two *Fortune* 500 firms, as senior human resource officer at two firms, as president of a regional bank, and as management professor at a major state university.

Phillips and his wife, Dr. Patti P. Phillips, serve as authors and series editors for the *Measurement and Evaluation Series,* published by Pfeiffer. Other books recently authored or co-authored by Phillips include *The Green Scorecard: Measuring Return on Investment in Sustainability Initiatives* (Nicholas Brealey, 2011); *Managing Talent Retention: An ROI Approach* (Jossey-Bass, 2009); *ROI for Technology Projects: Measuring and Delivering Value* (Butterworth-Heinemann, 2008); *Return on Investment in Meetings and Events: Tools and Techniques to Measure the Success of all Types of Meetings and Events* (Butterworth-Heinemann, 2008); *ROI in Action: Case Studies* (Pfeiffer, 2009); *Show Me the Money: How to Determine ROI in People, Projects, and Programs* (Berrett-Koehler, 2007); *The Value of Learning* (Pfeiffer, 2007); *How to Build a Successful Consulting Practice* (McGraw-Hill, 2006); and *Investing in Your Company's Human Capital: Strategies to Avoid Spending Too Much or Too Little* (Amacom, 2005). Phillips served as series editor for ASTD's In Action casebook series, an ambitious publishing project featuring thirty titles. He currently serves as series editor for Elsevier Butterworth-Heinemann's *Improving Human Performance* series.

Patti P. Phillips, Ph.D., is President and CEO of the ROI Institute, Inc., the leading source of ROI competency building, implementation support, networking, and research. She assists organizations with the implementation of the ROI Methodology in countries around the world.

Phillips' academic accomplishments include a Ph.D. in international development and a master of arts degree in public and private management. She is certified in ROI evaluation, has been awarded the Certified Professional in Learning and Performance designation by ASTD, and the Certified Performance Technologist designation by the International Society for Performance Improvement (ISPI). Phillips' publications include *The Bottomline on ROI,* 2nd edition, which won the ISPI Award of Excellence; *The Green Scorecard: Measuring the Return on Investment in Sustainability Initiatives; The Value of Learning; and Return on Investment in Meetings & Events.* She is published in a variety of journals, and serves as Professor of Practice at The University of Southern Mississippi's Ph.D. in Human Capital Development Program. She speaks on the subject of measurement and evaluation, and ROI at a variety of conferences. Phillips can be reached at patti@roiinstitute.net.

Additional SHRM-Published Books

Business Literacy Survival Guide for HR Professionals
by Regan W. Garey

Business-Focused HR: 11 Processes to Drive Results
by Scott P. Mondore, Shane S. Douthitt, and Marisa A. Carson

The Chief HR Officer: Defining the New Role of Human Resource Leaders
edited by Patrick M. Wright, John W. Boudreau, David A. Pace, Elizabeth "Libby" Sartain, Paul McKinnon, and Richard L. Antoine

Cultural Fit Factor: Creating an Employment Brand that Attracts, Retains, and Repels the Right Employees
by Lizz Pellet

From Hello to Goodbye: Proactive Tips for Maintaining Positive Employee Relations
by Christine V. Walters

Got a Minute? The 9 Lessons Every HR Professional Must Learn to Be Successful
by Dale J. Dwyer and Sheri A. Caldwell

HR Competencies: Mastery at the Intersection of People and Business
> by Dave Ulrich, Wayne Brockbank, Dani Johnson, Kurt Sandholtz, and Jon Younger

Human Resource Essentials: Your Guide to Starting and Running the HR Function
> by Lin Grensing-Pophal

Managing Diversity: A Complete Desk Reference & Planning Guide
> by Lee Gardenswartz and Anita Rowe

The Manager's Guide to HR: Hiring, Firing, Performance Evaluations, Documentation, Benefits, and Everything Else You Need to Know
> by Max Muller

Staffing Forecasting and Planning
> by Jean M. Phillips, Stanley M. Gully

Special Offer

Send for your own ROI Process Model, an indispensable tool for implementing and presenting ROI in your organization.

Jack and Patti Phillips are offering an exclusive gift to readers of this collection of case studies. The 11" x 25" multicolor foldout shows the ROI Methodology flow model and key issues surrounding the implementation of the ROI Methodology. This easy-to-understand overview has proven invaluable to countless trainers, HR executives and specialists when implementing the ROI Methodology. Please return this page or e-mail your information to the address below to receive your free foldout (a $6.00 value). Please check your area(s) of interest in ROI

Please send me the ROI Process Model described in the book. I am interested in learning more about the following ROI materials and services:

☐ Workshops and briefings on ROI	☐ Books and support materials on ROI
☐ Certification in the ROI Methodology	☐ ROI software
☐ ROI consulting services	☐ ROI network information
☐ ROI benchmarking	☐ ROI research

Name:

Title:

Organization:

Address:

Phone:	E-mail Address:

Functional area of interest:

☐ Human Resources/ Human Capital	☐ Compliance
☐ Learning and Development	☐ Performance Improvement
☐ Health and Safety	☐ Compensation and Benefits
☐ Organizational Development	☐ Other (Please Specify)
☐ Recruiting and Selection	

Organizational Level

☐ executive	☐ student
☐ management	☐ evaluator
☐ consultant	☐ researcher
☐ specialist	

Return this form or contact
The ROI Institute   or e-mail information to jack@roiinstitute.net
P.O. Box 380637
Birmingham, AL 35238-0637

Please allow four to six weeks for delivery